HOW TO MAKE BUILT-IN FURNITURE

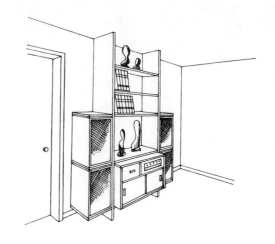

HOW TO MAKE

Mario Dal Fabbro

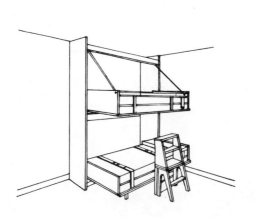

BUILT-IN FURNITURE

Second edition

McGRAW-HILL BOOK COMPANY

New York   St. Louis   San Francisco   Düsseldorf

Johannesburg   Kuala Lumpur   London   Mexico   Montreal

New Delhi   Panama   Paris   São Paulo   Singapore

Sydney   Tokyo   Toronto

Library of Congress Cataloging in Publication Data

Dal Fabbro, Mario, date.
  How to make built-in furniture.

  1. Built-in furniture. I. Title.
TT197.5.B8D34   1974   684.1'6   74-6265
ISBN 0-07-015181-4

1234567890   VHVH   7987654

CONTENTS

PREFACE

Built-in furniture is becoming more and more a mark of the modern interior. The old method of dividing the living area by wall partitions is gradually giving way to the practice of leaving the area open and permitting the occupants to adapt the space to their own needs in accordance with their taste. Thanks to built-ins, a room can have its own individual design, free of the monotonous uniformity of mass-produced furniture. In addition to these esthetic considerations, with built-ins real space economies can be achieved either by utilizing wall recesses, attics, and space beneath a sloping ceiling or by making full use of a wall area, from floor to ceiling and side to side.

The designs for built-in furniture which this book contains have been planned to help the home-owner and craftsman make the most of these possibilities, but they should also be of interest to such specialists as architects, interior decorators, builders, and lumber dealers.

This second edition of *How to Make Built-in Furniture* reflects the many changes in new techniques, materials, and methods of construction that have taken place since the first edition was published. The first part of the book contains general instructions for measurement, woodworking, hardware selection, and furniture installation, as well as for the construction of a number of standard furniture details. By far the largest number of pages, however, is devoted to designs for 102 pieces of modern built-in furniture. Among these, home craftsmen should be able to find many to suit both their needs and their skills. Each piece is illustrated in full detail, and a simple method is presented for calculating dimensions that may vary with the size and shape of the room. A list of materials accompanies each design. These projects may be attempted with complete confidence, for they have been planned to be practical in construction as well as in use.

The simple construction and detailed directions combine to make possible a substantial do-it-yourself saving. But it is also the author's hope that this book may make some real contribution to better living in the home not only through its practicality but also through the usefulness and esthetic merit of the designs themselves.

Mario Dal Fabbro

SECTION 1: General instructions

MEASUREMENT OF THE ROOM

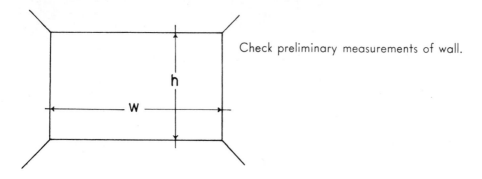

Check preliminary measurements of wall.

Measurements of the space where the furniture is to be installed must be made accurately if later difficulties are to be avoided.

Settling or irregular house construction will cause distances from floor to ceiling or from wall to wall to vary in different parts of the room. It is safest, therefore, to take a series of measurements for each dimension and to use the short ones. Most rooms can be measured with a rule, but if they are irregular or complicated, it is wise to assure true vertical and horizontal measurements with the aid of plumb bob, square, and carpenter's level.

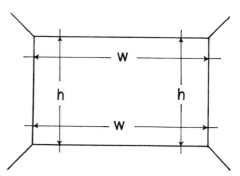

Obtain the construction measurements as shown.

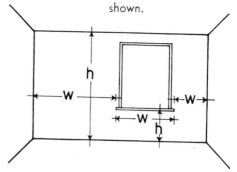

These measurements are necessary for a wall with window or door.

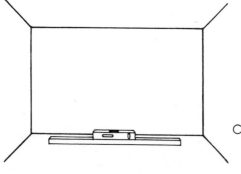

Check the levelness of floor with carpenter's level.

Key to Symbols

(h) Height from floor to ceiling.

(w) Width from wall to wall.

(d) Depth of recess, or wall thickness.

(h_1) Height of component unit obtained by subtracting a given dimension from floor-to-ceiling height *(h)*.

(w_1) Width of component unit obtained by subtracting a given dimension from wall-to-wall width *(w)*.

(w_2) Width of second component unit; determined jointly with *(w_1)*, above.

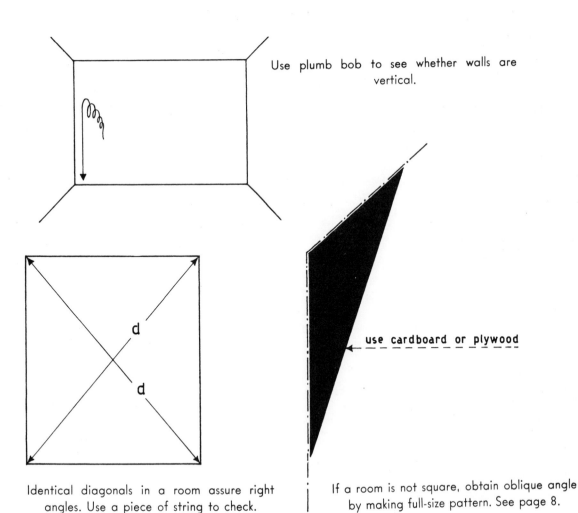

Check right angles with the try square.

Use plumb bob to see whether walls are vertical.

use cardboard or plywood

Identical diagonals in a room assure right angles. Use a piece of string to check.

If a room is not square, obtain oblique angle by making full-size pattern. See page 8.

Measurement of the Room

3

INSTRUCTIONS FOR READING DRAWINGS

The drawings used in this book have been especially planned to help the home craftsman visualize the finished piece, its parts, and the way they are fitted together. Each design includes (a) a complete view of the finished piece, (b) front, side, and sectional views as they would appear in a professional cabinet maker's drawings, and (c) an exploded drawing, with parts shown in detail for ordering and cutting. Accompanying instructions give step-by-step procedure for assembly.

Most of the construction details are standard, and are repeated in many different designs. Cross references clearly indicate the details to be used. Note, however, that letters identifying individual cut pieces refer only to the design in question.

Each set of drawings is accompanied by a list of materials (complete except for minor items of hardware) and a few words suggesting possible applications.

Variations

The designs can be easily varied to fit individual needs by adding or omitting doors, shelves, or units. Decorative moldings may also be added, but it is not advisable for beginners in woodworking to make changes in basic construction.

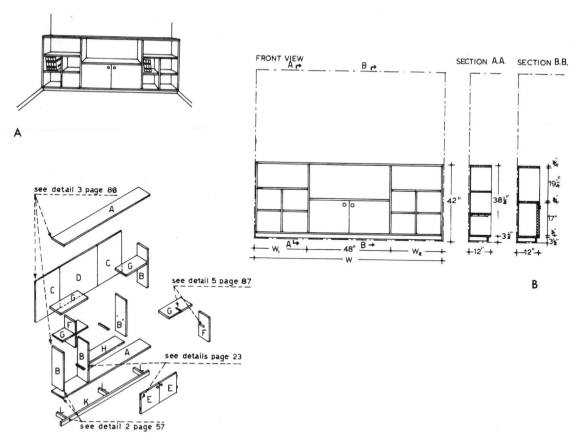

Fitting Furniture to Wall

Usually 1 in. of space should be allowed between built-in furniture and the walls or ceiling. This space is filled with strips of wood or metal ½ in. to 1 in. wide on both sides of the piece and 1 in. around the top.

Boards which extend from wall to wall or floor to ceiling must be measured to fit exactly, following any irregularities.

FRONT VIEW   furniture wall to wall
space closed with strip

$\frac{1}{2}$"

exterior furniture line

each side

wall line

FRONT VIEW   board wall to wall

wall line

board to fit with wall

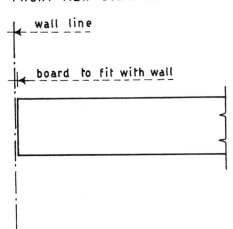

SIDE SECTION furniture floor to ceiling
space closed with strip

1"

ceiling line

furniture line

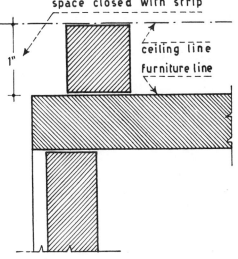

VARIABLE DIMENSIONS

The furniture shown in this book has been planned to fit into a wide variety of rooms and spaces. Naturally some of the dimensions will be determined by the space the piece will occupy. The calculation of such dimensions for: (1) straight boards, (2) furniture parts, and (3) furniture under sloping ceilings is fully explained on this and the two following pages.

Boards

Boards that run from wall to wall or from floor to ceiling must be cut according to precise wall-to-wall or floor-to-ceiling measurements. Where a piece or pieces of known dimension fill a part of such a span, the length of the remaining board or boards is naturally the floor-to-ceiling (h_1, h_2) or wall-to-wall (w_1, w_2) measurement minus the known dimensions.

EXAMPLE—FRONT VIEW

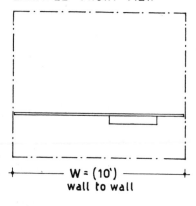

W = (10')
wall to wall

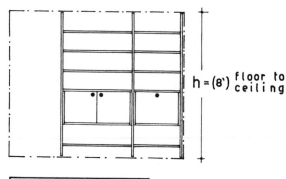

h = (8') floor to ceiling

| h = HEIGHT OF THE ROOM |
| W = WIDTH OF THE ROOM |

EXAMPLE—FRONT VIEW

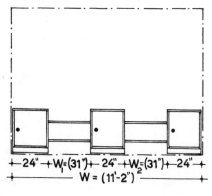

24" + W_1=(31") + 24" + W_2=(31") + 24"
W = (11'-2")

| W = WIDTH OF THE ROOM |
| W_1 + W_2 = WIDTH OF ROOM LESS 72" |

Relations of Part Sizes

Variable dimensions of cabinets and bookcases that run from wall to wall or floor to ceiling can be determined in the following manner:

1. Subtract the fixed lengths or heights from precise wall-to-wall or floor-to-ceiling measurement (see diagrams) to obtain the longest dimension of the variable section.
2. Using the longest dimension, make a scale drawing of the variable section.
3. Calculate related dimensions of bottom,

EXAMPLES — FRONT VIEW

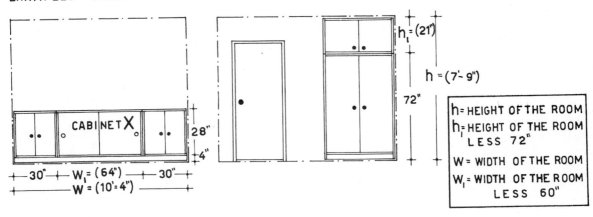

h = HEIGHT OF THE ROOM
h_1 = HEIGHT OF THE ROOM LESS 72"
W = WIDTH OF THE ROOM
W_1 = WIDTH OF THE ROOM LESS 60"

shelves, doors, and back panel. (Note in the drawing below that the longest dimension is that of the top. The length of the bottom piece is found by subtracting the thickness of the two side pieces from the length of the top. The back panel, however, in effect overlaps the sides, as ½ in. on each side is to be inserted in a rabbet joint, so that the back will measure 1 in. longer than the bottom. A simpler method of attaching the back is shown on page 248, detail 3. This construction uses the same size panel for the back, but as it is not recessed the front-to-back dimension of the piece will be increased by the thickness of the back—usually ¼ in.)

REPRODUCTION OF CABINET X FROM EXAMPLE ABOVE
scale $\frac{3}{4}$" = 1'-0" with relation to room measurements shown

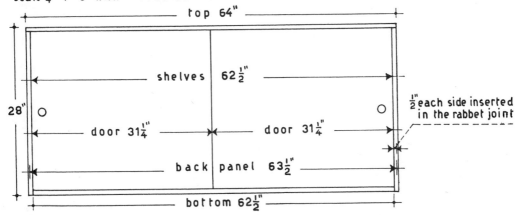

Sloping Ceilings

If a piece of furniture is to be built against a sloping attic ceiling or odd-angle corner, a pattern must be made in order to reproduce the angle exactly. A simple method is to run one leg of a pair of dividers along the walls or ceiling and the other leg on a sheet of paper to trace a pair of intersecting lines parallel to the lines of the room. A full scale drawing can then be constructed, following the instructions for the piece to be built and incorporating the angle that has been traced. Parts can be cut according to dimensions taken from this drawing.

SCALE DRAWING OF CLOSET SECTION scale $\frac{3}{4}$ = 1'- 0"

with the dimension in relation to the room measurements

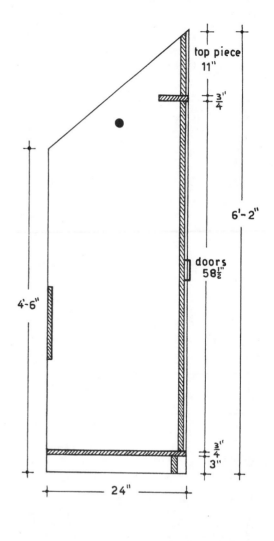

top piece 11"

$\frac{3}{4}$

6'- 2"

doors 58$\frac{1}{2}$"

4'-6"

$\frac{3}{4}$

3"

24"

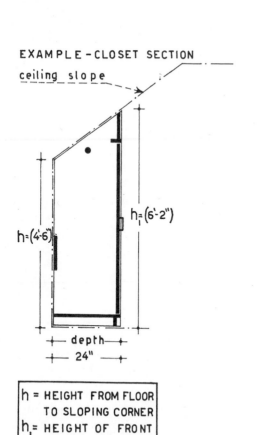

EXAMPLE - CLOSET SECTION

ceiling slope

h_1=(6'-2")

h=(4'-6")

depth

24"

h = HEIGHT FROM FLOOR
    TO SLOPING CORNER
h_1= HEIGHT OF FRONT
    OF THE FURNITURE

Variable Dimensions

BUYING MATERIALS: WOOD, PLASTIC, METAL, ETC.

After the design has been selected and studied, the next step is the ordering of material. Wood and plywood are generally indicated in all the projects included here, but many other materials can also be used, and they can be easily purchased from lumber dealers. Such materials include flakeboard and hardboard already covered with laminated plastic or vinyl overlays of various colors; other materials available are factory-finished hardwood plywood paneling, plexiglas, and aluminum sheets in a wide variety of patterns. An extensive variety of molding strips and carved panels from which you can choose to satisfy your taste and requirements is also on the market.

When choosing wood, the usual procedure is to buy the lumber in standard lengths and cut the required pieces as listed. Another method is to ask the lumber dealer to cut the material into the sizes you need. There will be a minimum of waste whichever method is used, because standard lumber sizes have been considered in the planning of the designs.

Avoid using solid wood and plywood together in the same piece of furniture, particularly if a flush board is to be visible. If such a combination of materials is unavoidable, glue should never be used for bonding the parts. Plywood and solid wood react differently to drying glue or atmospheric conditions, but screws or loose joints will permit shrinkage or expansion.

Another point to keep in mind is that both soft and hard wood shrink in the process of seasoning. Thus the wood is usually 1/16 in. narrower than the nominal thickness. This difference is of consequence only in fitting such parts as doors, shelves, or drawers. If the wood is of a different thickness from that specified in the design, an adjustment must be made in the measurements of the part to be applied. Therefore, it is best to secure lumber of a thickness as close as possible to that specified in the list of materials.

MAKING THE FURNITURE

Accurate cutting, whether done by hand or by machine, is essential to good furniture construction. The wood should be carefully chosen, and the parts laid out in such a way that the handsomest surfaces will be seen in the finished piece. The parts must be accurately marked with identifying letters, copied from the exploded drawings, to facilitate joining.

To avoid any inconvenience in construction the lumber must be cut at the correct angle. The saw cut should fall *outside* the pencil line, so that the board can be planed or filed to correct dimensions. (A plane is used on flat surfaces, and a file on curved edges.)

When the parts have been cut and finished to the right sizes, the joints may be marked and executed as indicated in the details. Sometimes it is possible to save time by eliminating the joint and substituting nails. Before any parts are joined, all should be checked to make sure they will fit correctly. Instructions for assembly are provided with each design. The glue must be spread on both surfaces to be joined, and the pieces clamped together for several hours. Simple clamps or screws and nails may be used to apply pressure. Wood clamps may be made by nailing blocks of wood to the ends of a rail slightly longer than the piece being glued and applying pressure by inserting wedges between the wood and the blocks.

Large Assemblies
Before assembling a large built-in unit, it is wise to measure passageways to make sure it can be moved from the shop to the site that has been picked for it. It may be necessary to assemble the piece in two or three units in the shop, and complete the assembly in the room where the piece is to be installed.

VARIATIONS OF ORIGINAL FURNITURE DESIGNS

Several variations can be obtained by the simple addition of molding strips and carved panels to a plain plywood door or by completely changing the door to a framed door. All this can be achieved without changing the basic construction of the built-in furniture, and it affords the opportunity of giving each furniture piece a personal touch. Variations involving changes in basic construction, however, are best left to expert carpenters or cabinet makers.

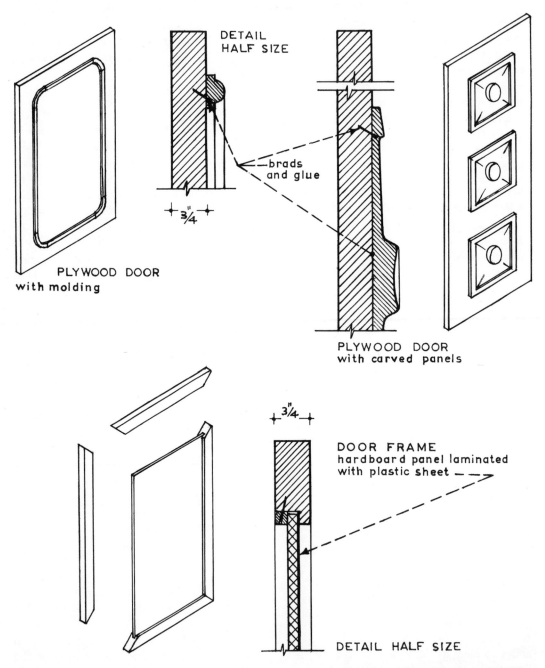

DETAIL HALF SIZE

brads and glue

3/4"

PLYWOOD DOOR
with molding

PLYWOOD DOOR
with carved panels

3/4"

DOOR FRAME
hardboard panel laminated
with plastic sheet

DETAIL HALF SIZE

FINISHING

The kind of finish a built-in should receive will depend upon the quality and appearance of the wood, the use it will receive, decorating tastes and so on. Nothing shows off the beauty of the wood—and the builders' achievement!—quite so well as a "natural" finish. Or it may seem advisable to integrate the piece into the room by painting it the same color as the walls. On the other hand, striking color effects can be obtained by use of harmonizing or matching shades. One word of caution: room furnishings may come and go, but the built-in is relatively permanent. Keep in mind the adaptability of a color or tone scheme to possible future changes.

The subject of wood finishing is too extensive to receive adequate treatment here, but a few general pointers are worth giving:

Carefully sand smooth all surfaces, both before and between coats of finish. Grade 100 to 150 sandpaper is recommended for finishing rough wood. Finer grades of sandpaper —from 220 to 280, wet or dry—are suitable between finish coats. Before the final coat is applied, the surface should be lightly rubbed with sandpaper of grades 320 to 400. The sandpaper may be dipped in water to prevent clogging and minimize dust. Other methods of smoothing the surfaces, such as rubbing with fine steel wool, pumice, or other fine abrasives, may also be used. Dust should be allowed to settle before liquid finishes are applied, and the air in the workroom should

be clear and still. Be sure that a coat of finish is thoroughly dry before sanding and proceeding with the next coat, and never rub or sand the final coat of paint or enamel. Various rubbing compounds or sandpaper of grades 320 to 400 may be sparingly used after the final coat of shellac or varnish.

Preparation of Surface

Most raw woods need careful preparation before they can be painted or finished. Neglect of this essential preliminary will not only increase the number of coats necessary to obtain the proper coverage—with consequent waste of materials and labor—but will produce less satisfactory results. Fillers, primers, and undercoats are not cheaper types of finishing material to be used where they won't "show"—they are indispensable components of a proper finish.

In applying finishes, use good brushes and keep them in good condition. It is best to keep special brushes for special uses: one brush for shellac, another for varnish, a third for lacquer. A nylon brush should not be used with shellac, as the alcohol solvent will attack the bristles.

Open-grained hardwoods—such as oak, birch, walnut, mahogany, cherry, elm, hickory, chestnut, or butternut—must be filled. If the wood is to be stained, this operation should precede filling or be combined with it —filler-stain preparations are available in a number of shades. If wood filler is applied separately, it should be brushed or wiped on and the excess rubbed off with a clean rag. It is important to follow the manufacturers' instructions faithfully with all finish materials.

Close-grained woods—such as maple, pine, fir, gum, cedar, poplar, beech, basswood, or cottonwood—do not need to be filled, but a coat of thin shellac is recommended to seal fir before varnishing, because of the absorbency of the soft grain. If there are any knots or resin pockets in the wood, they should be sealed with shellac or knot-sealer.

Plastic wood or crack filler (in shades to match the wood, if a natural finish is selected) should be used to fill nail holes or crevices after they have been primed, either by the first finish coat or by swabbing with linseed oil or varnish.

Natural Finishes

Among natural finishes, the least discoloration of the raw wood is obtained with wax, but this method also offers least protection against hard usage. A single coat of white shellac or clear varnish should precede the wax. Combined varnish-wax preparations are also available.

Clear lacquer can yield striking results, and there are now preparations available which make it possible to apply this traditionally difficult material with a brush instead of a spray-gun.

A "white" shellac finish will discolor wood less than varnish, but is not waterproof. A "5-lb. cut" shellac contains 5 lb. of shellac gum to the gallon of alcohol; "4-lb. cut" contains only 4 lb. Either of these concentrations will give good results, but the "3-lb. cut" which is frequently found in stores is not recommended, except for preliminary coats, which should be thin.

Varnish finish combines durability with the attractiveness of a natural finish, and spar varnish is suitable for pieces like kitchen cabinets, that are exposed to moisture. Other types of varnish are suitable for high-gloss effects, and some types are combined with pigment to combine the coloring effect of paint with the natural grain of the wood.

Oil finish is another type of wood finish, and, although it is not waterproof, its beauty can be restored easily and quickly. For other finishes on the market which may satisfy your requirements and preferences, it is advisable to consult the dealer. In addition, manufacturers usually supply very detailed information as to the use of their products. Some products you may find very useful and time-saving are, for instance, a type of one-step filler and sealer and several types of spray varnish and lacca.

Paint or Enamel Finish

If the wood is to be painted, it must first be primed, although some special formulations and most rubber-base paints are self-priming. If it is to be enameled, best results will be obtained by using an enamel undercoat preparation. It is generally advisable to mix a little of the finish coat into the white primer or enamel undercoat, in order to tint it, and provide a better base for the final pigment. This measure is especially advisable if the final color is very deep.

For extensive information on wood finishes, consult Robert Scharff, *Complete Book of Wood Finishing,* 2nd edition, McGraw-Hill Book Company, 1974.

HARDWARE

The hardware illustrated in this book is standard and can be purchased in most hardware stores. Items frequently used are shown here to facilitate identification.

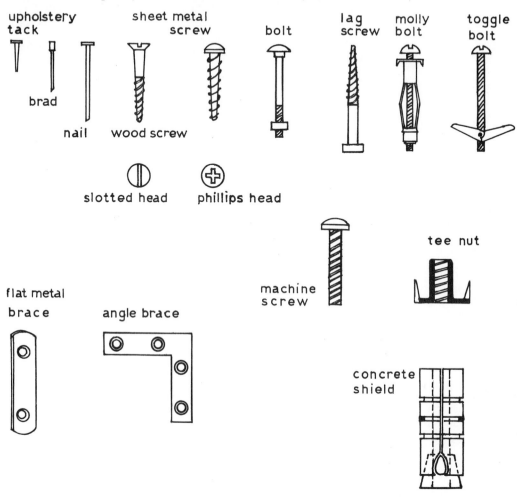

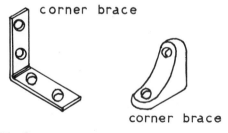

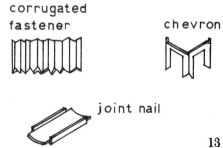

hinge

screen
hinge

pivot hinge

angle pivot hinge

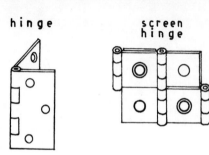

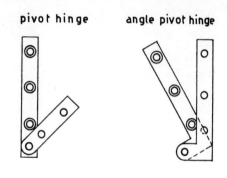

lid support

quadrant

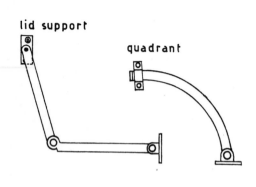

shelf support

bracket and standard

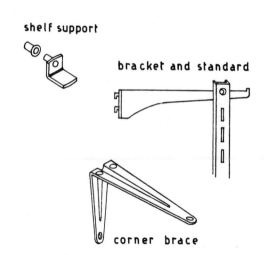

corner brace

knob

pull

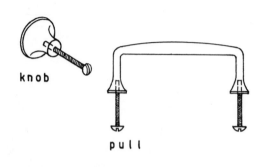

sliding door sheave

metal track

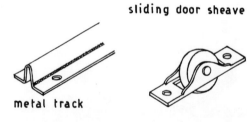

Hardware

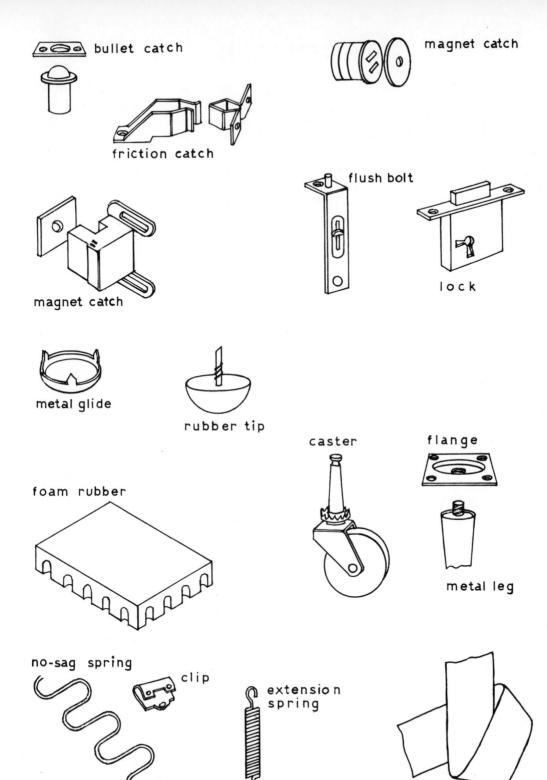

bullet catch

magnet catch

friction catch

magnet catch

flush bolt

lock

metal glide

rubber tip

caster

flange

foam rubber

metal leg

no-sag spring

clip

extension spring

rubber strap

found in upholstery repair shop

Hardware

INSTALLATION

The final step in making built-in furniture is to install the piece in the place where it is to be used. If instructions have been followed, installing the sections in order will be a simple matter. The drawings that follow illustrate methods of fixing furniture to floor, wall, or ceiling. The right size and type of hardware must be selected for the room in which you are working and for the size and weight of the furniture being installed.

Anchoring to Floors

Furniture can be easily attached to wood floors (or to wood covered with rubber, plastic, or linoleum flooring) by screws and hardware. The drawings illustrate several methods.

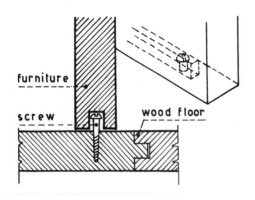

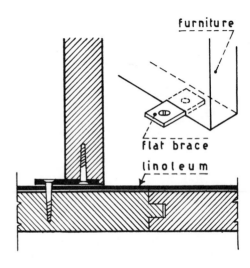

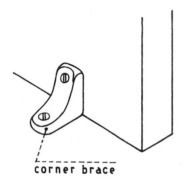

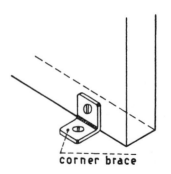

Furniture should be attached to concrete, tile, and marble floors (or to linoleum, rubber, or plastic floor coverings which are used over these materials) only if absolutely necessary. Such materials are easily marred and difficult to repair. If the work must be done, the first step is to make a hole in the floor with a stone chisel or a star drill. Next insert the metal brace and fill the hole with cement. To apply a molly bolt, make a hole of the right size, insert the anchor of the bolt, and tighten the screw.

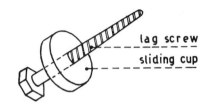

Floor-to-Ceiling Installation
Usually it is practicable to wedge floor-to-ceiling furniture in place by means of pressure. The upper drawing at the right shows what can be done with such common hardware as a lag screw covered by a cup, but a better decorative effect can be obtained with a custom-built brass piece which can be ordered from any metal shop. The lower drawing shows a simple and practical method of making a piece fit tightly to the ceiling, particularly if flooring is irregular.

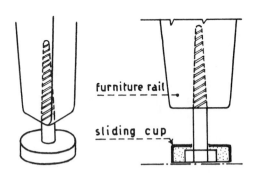

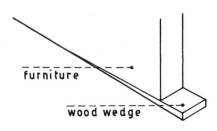

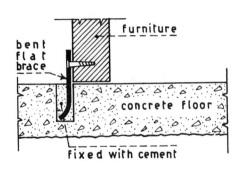

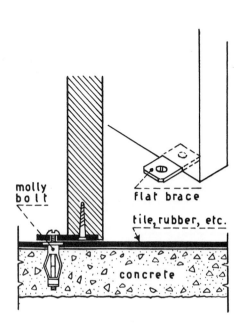

Wall Mounting

Furniture can be fixed to a frame wall (the standard type in American houses today) either with toggle bolts between the studs or —a preferable method for heavy loads— with screws or nails driven directly into the studs.

To use toggle bolts, mark the position, make matching holes in furniture and plaster, then insert the bolt and close tight.

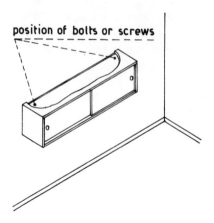

position of bolts or screws

SIDE SECTION – DETAIL

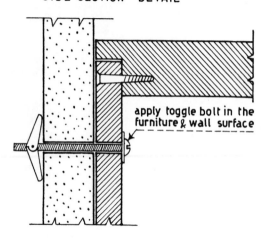

apply toggle bolt in the furniture & wall surface

toggle bolt closed

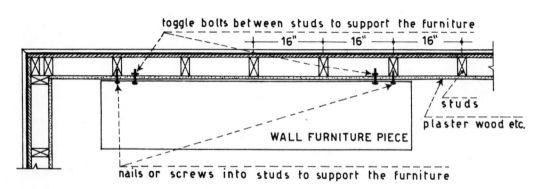

toggle bolts between studs to support the furniture

16"   16"   16"

studs

plaster wood etc.

WALL FURNITURE PIECE

nails or screws into studs to support the furniture

PLAN SECTION OF WALL FRAMING

Wall Mounting Heavy Pieces

If screws or nails are to be used to secure heavy wall furniture, they must be driven into the studs. Most studs are nominally 16 in. apart, but their location must be determined exactly by sounding—a smart rap with the knuckles or a block of wood will produce a hollow sound between studs, a "solid"

sound over them—or by trial and error. Frequently, inspection of the baseboard will reveal the places where nails were driven through it into the vertical studs.

Corner braces are often used in roughly finished rooms, such as cellars, garages, and workshops. They do not improve the appearance of furniture.

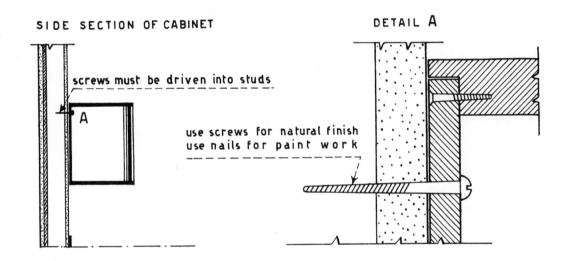

SIDE SECTION OF CABINET

screws must be driven into studs

A

use screws for natural finish
use nails for paint work

DETAIL A

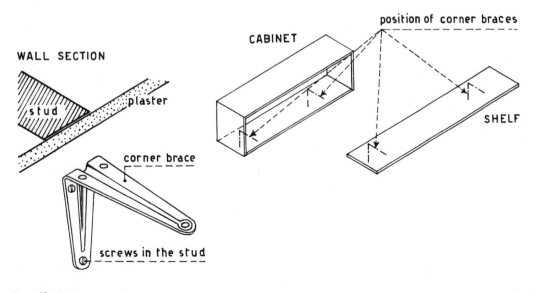

WALL SECTION

stud

plaster

corner brace

screws in the stud

position of corner braces

CABINET

SHELF

Wall Mounting with Braces

Flat metal braces give good light support, are simple to use, and have a neat appearance. As the drawings show, they can be used with either screws or toggle bolts. One end of the brace is attached to the furniture, and the other to the wall. Several possible uses are illustrated.

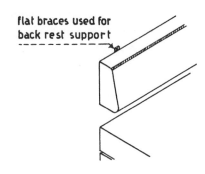

flat braces used for back rest support

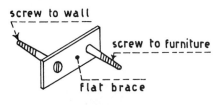

screw to wall

screw to furniture

flat brace

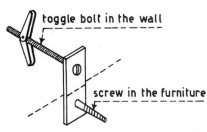

toggle bolt in the wall

screw in the furniture

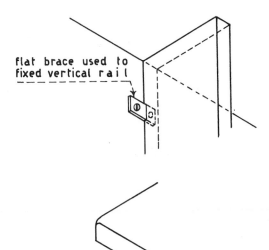

flat brace used to fixed vertical rail

for wall benches or heavy furniture use wood strips with flat braces for support

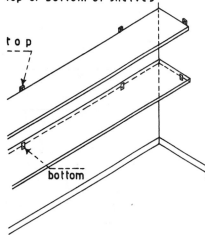

flat braces can be applied on top or bottom of shelves

top

bottom

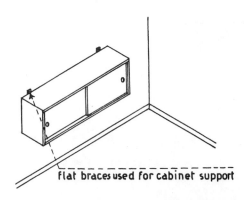

flat braces used for cabinet support

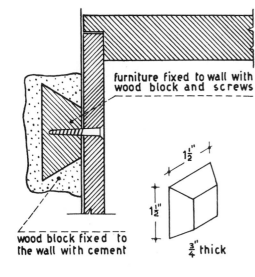

SIDE SECTION
apply screws in the studs

standard   shelf

bracket

SIDE SECTION

furniture fixed to wall with
wood block and screws

wood block fixed to
the wall with cement

$1\frac{1}{2}$"

$1\frac{1}{2}$"

$\frac{3}{4}$" thick

Wall Mounting of Shelves

The bracket shelf support at the left is the standard type used for large shelves in offices and stores. The standard is attached to the wall with screws or toggle bolts, and bracket and shelf are inserted.

Another strong shelf support can be provided by driving lag screws into the studs and removing the heads. Or a slot can be cut into the headless shaft and the lag screw driven with a screw driver. When the round shafts of the lag screws are inserted in holes bored in the shelf a very clean appearance is presented.

Masonry Walls

The most satisfactory method of installing built-ins against masonry walls is to insert a wooden block in the wall and attach the furniture to this block. Chisel a hole of the right size, wash it out, and set the block in concrete. Metal rods for furniture support can be inserted in a similar manner.

For lighter furniture, dowels, fiber tubes, or lead shields are inserted into drilled holes and expand when the screws are inserted. Molly bolts (see page 22) can also be used, and with cinder block walls these or masonry nails provide a very practical solution. Obviously any masonry wall subject to dampness must be waterproofed before furniture can be placed against it.

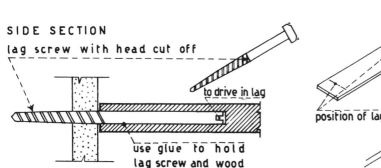

SIDE SECTION
lag screw with head cut off

to drive in lag

use glue to hold
lag screw and wood

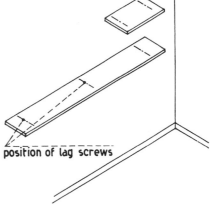

position of lag screws

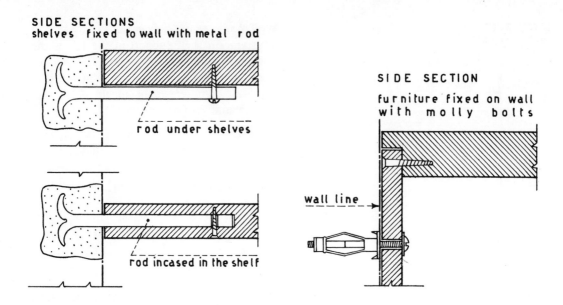

SIDE SECTIONS
shelves fixed to wall with metal rod

rod under shelves

rod incased in the shelf

SIDE SECTION

furniture fixed on wall
with molly bolts

wall line

Attaching Furniture to Ceiling

Furniture is less frequently attached to the ceiling than to floor or walls. The sketches show several methods that will assure complete stability.

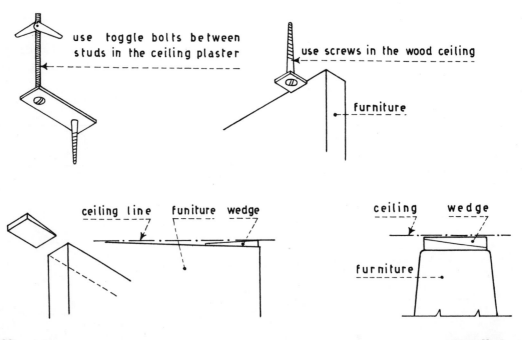

use toggle bolts between
studs in the ceiling plaster

use screws in the wood ceiling

furniture

ceiling line   funiture   wedge

ceiling   wedge

furniture

STANDARD DETAILS FOR DOOR INSTALLATION

Because the size of a door for any given opening will vary with the type of door used, the dimensions given in the lists of materials should be carefully checked to make sure that any necessary allowances are added for rabbetting, sliding door overlaps, or the like.

Doors with Butt Hinges

Standard doors are the most practical for use on furniture. These are easily hung on butt hinges by using a chisel and screwdriver.

The recessed door is most popular, because the recess hides any irregularity. Rabbet doors help to keep dust out of a cabinet. Offset hinges should be used to install heavy rabbet doors.

EXPLODED VIEW

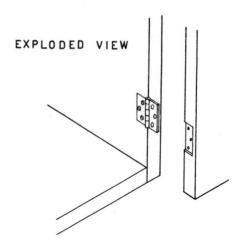

PLAN SECTIONS

flush doors

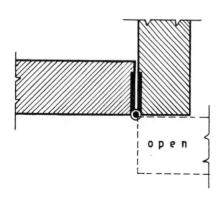

open

recessed doors

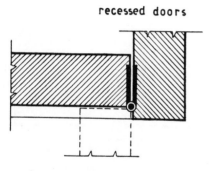

external doors

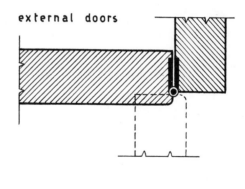

rabbet doors
add $\frac{3}{8}$" all around for rabbet

offset hinge

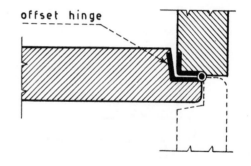

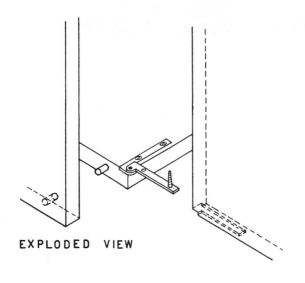

EXPLODED VIEW

Pivot Doors

Standard doors may be hung with pivots. Both methods illustrated—the corner pivot and the normal pivot—will give good results. The door works as if hung with hinges, and installation should present no difficulties.

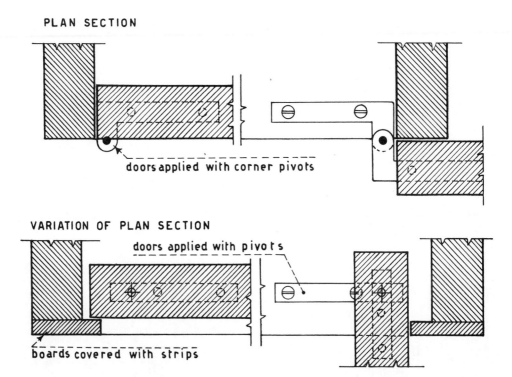

PLAN SECTION

doors applied with corner pivots

VARIATION OF PLAN SECTION

doors applied with pivots

boards covered with strips

Standard Details for Door Installation

space to remove the doors

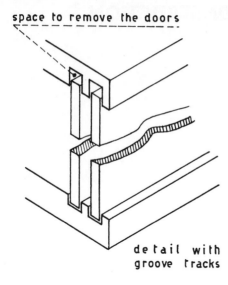

detail with
groove tracks

detail with metal tracks

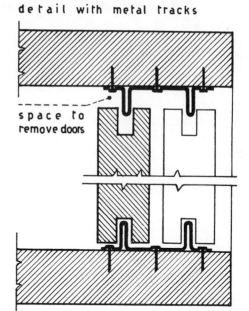

space to
remove doors

Sliding Doors

Sliding doors provide a good solution to the problem of opening doors where space is limited. Groove track, metal track, and track made with wood and metal strips can be used. Space must generally be left at the top for installation and removal, and doors should overlap when closed to help keep out dust. Sheaves should be used with heavy doors to ease sliding.

detail with wooden strips

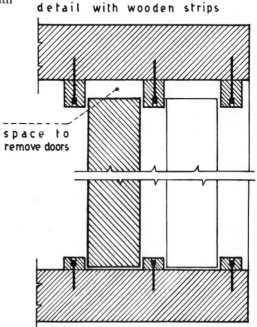

space to
remove doors

apply sheaves for heavy doors

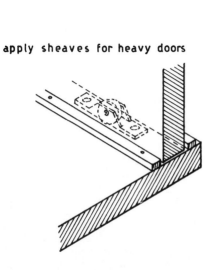

Standard Details for Door Installation

STANDARD DRAWER CONSTRUCTION

The construction of drawers is the most difficult operation in furniture building, and standard drawers cannot be constructed without the use of some woodworking machines. The drawer shown here, however, requires only a circular saw to make the grooves for the rabbet joints. The parts are joined with dowels, feather joints, and screws, as illustrated. An even simpler method is shown on the opposite page.

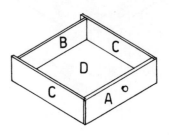

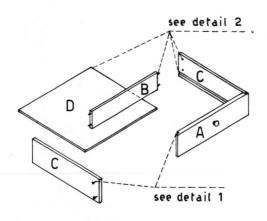

see detail 2

see detail 1

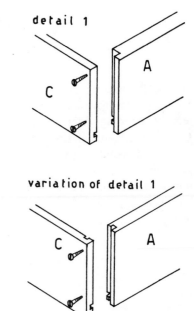

detail 1

variation of detail 1

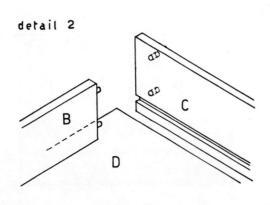

detail 2

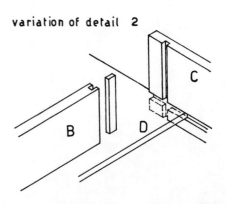

variation of detail 2

Simplified Drawer Construction

Here is a drawer adequate for normal use which can be made by hand. It is designed in the form of a box without cabinet joints, and is assembled with nails. The front is attached with screws driven from the inside, so that the visible portion is unbroken and resembles a standard drawer. A knob or pull can be attached in exactly the same way as for the more complicated type.

Drawer measurements in the lists of materials are intended for standard construction, but they can easily be adapted to this simplified design. Sides (C) and back (B) are the same for both methods. The simplified front is composed of two parts: (B), which is identical with the back piece, and (A), which is the same length and width as the corresponding piece for a standard drawer, but reduced 3/8 in. in thickness. The bottom (D) will be reduced in width to make it as wide as the back (B), but should be increased from 1/4 to 3/8 in. in thickness, to increase the holding power of nails.

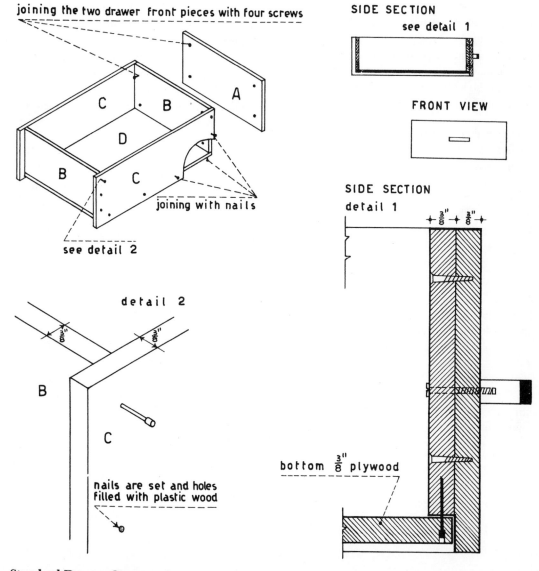

joining the two drawer front pieces with four screws

SIDE SECTION
see detail 1

FRONT VIEW

SIDE SECTION
detail 1

C B A

D

B C

joining with nails

see detail 2

detail 2

B

C

nails are set and holes
filled with plastic wood

bottom 3/8" plywood

STEREO CABINETS

The stereo cabinets on pages 58 and 62 are intended to house practically all standard-model receiver components, record players, and 12-in. independent speaker systems. Space for record storage, tapes, books, and accessories is also provided in both cabinets. (See manufacturers' instructions for purchasing of components.) It is best not to reduce any of the dimensions given, even though fit is not critical, because the space may be needed if other, larger components are substituted later. The extra shelves and compartments can be used for storage, or they can be adapted to house magnetic recorders, separate high-frequency "tweeters," or other adjuncts to the system.

The speaker enclosure front, or baffle, should be cut in accordance with manufacturer's instructions for the model being used. It is especially important that all joints of speaker enclosures be tightly fitted and glued, except that the front of the enclosure should be attached by closely spaced screws driven into the cleats behind, thus making a tight, soundproof joint that can be disassembled if it is ever necessary to change or service the equipment.

The interior of the enclosure (except for the baffle itself) should be lined with 1-in. insulating batting for sound absorption. Painting the front of the baffle a flat black will prevent the outline of the speaker or "bass-reflex" apertures from showing through the monk's cloth or other fabric that is used to cover it.

The fabric should be tightly and securely tacked along the edges of the baffle for maximum neatness and protection to the speaker cone. If the fabric is folded along the edges, it will be possible for the tacks to grip the fabric securely and still be covered by the ½-in. molding.

The position of components within the cabinet has been indicated in the drawings, but the exact arrangement will vary with the equipment being installed. Plywood shelves may be improvised and installed within the compartment to support components one above another. To avoid interfering with ventilation, such shelves should not be any deeper than is necessary to support the equipment.

The ventilation holes shown in the drawings are necessary for all compartments housing vacuum tubes, to avoid equipment breakdowns. The openings should be sized and spaced as liberally as possible; the easiest way to make them is with an expansion bit set at 1½ to 2 in.

Purists of sound reception may prefer to choose design No. 13 (page 58) and to separate the component units so that the speaker cabinet is at least 10 ft. distant from the tuner and amplifier euipment, thus avoiding any possibility of "feedback" vibration from the speaker to the tubes. Most listeners will be satisfied with the designs as they are, however.

SECTION 2: **Built-in furniture designs**

1 | LOW BOOKSHELF UNITS

This counter-height bookshelf wall is made up of two bookcases with solid doors, and a center unit containing a plant box.

List of Materials

PART	NO.	FUNCTION	thickness	width	length
			DIMENSIONS IN INCHES		
A	2	top	¾	12	33
B	6	side	¾	12	31¼
C	2	bottom	¾	12	31½
D	2	back	¼	31½	32½
E	4	shelf	¾	10½	31½
F	10	cleat	½	½	9½
G	4	door	¾	15¾	30½
H	1	top	¾	12	w_1
J	1	bottom	¾	12	$w_1 - 1½$
K	1	back	¼	31½	$w_1 - ½$
L	2	partition	¾	11¾	30½
M	1	shelf	¾	11¾	31½
O	1	shelf	¾	10½	31½
P	4	shelf	¾	11¾	$w_2 - ¾$
Q	1	drop door	¾	9¼	31½
R	2	door	¾	15¾	20½
S	1	toeplate	1	4	w
T	5	brace	1	4	10

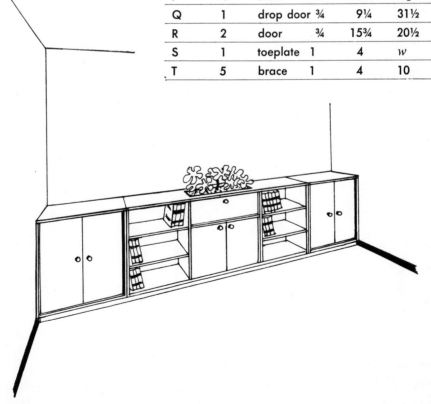

FRONT VIEW

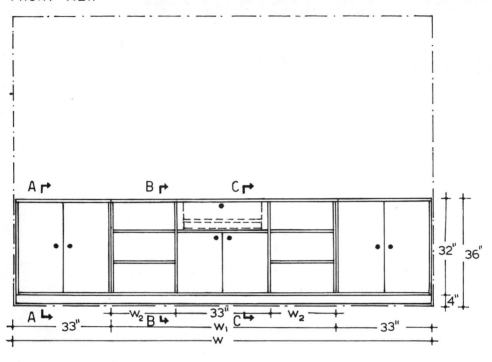

A → B → C →

32" 36"

4"

A ↳ W₂ B ↳ 33" C ↳ W₂

A ↳ 33" W₁ 33"

W

W = WIDTH OF THE ROOM
W₁ = WIDTH OF THE ROOM
    LESS 66"
2 x W₂ = W₁ LESS 33"

SECTION A A   B B   C C

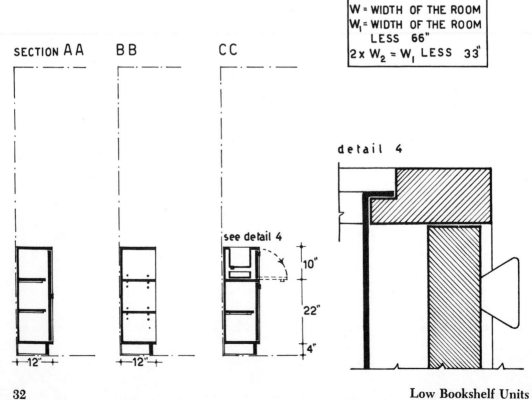

see detail 4

10"

22"

4"

←12"→   ←12"→

detail 4

Low Bookshelf Units

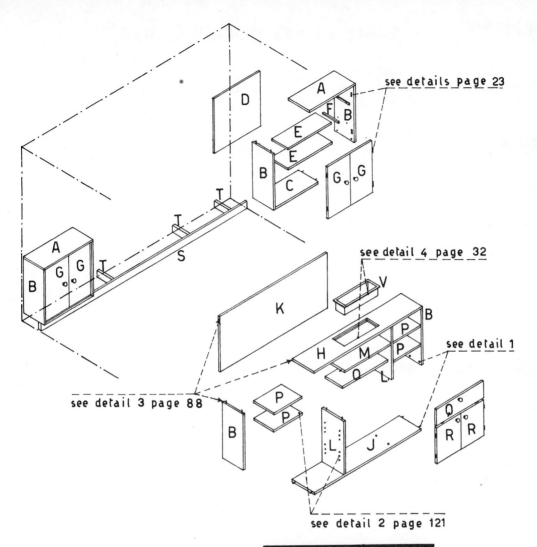

see details page 23

see detail 4 page 32

see detail 1

see detail 3 page 88

see detail 2 page 121

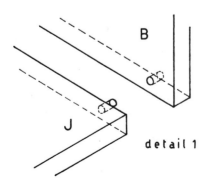

detail 1

Instructions for Assembly

Side Cabinets
1. Join sides (B) with top (A), bottom (C), and back (D).
2. Install cleats (F) and doors (G).
3. Insert shelves (E).

Center Unit
4. Cut hole in top (H) for box (V).
5. Join sides (B) and partitions (L) with top (H), bottom (J), and shelf (M).
6. Attach the back (K) and doors (Q), (R).
7. Insert shelves (O), (P).
8. Finish and place on base (S), (T).

Low Bookshelf Units

2 | WALL-HUNG BOOKSHELVES

These simply constructed bookshelves are suitable for a study, office, or living room.

List of Materials

PART	NO.	FUNCTION	DIMENSIONS IN INCHES thickness × width × length		
A	2	top, bottom	¾	12	w
B	6	partition	¾	12	18½
C	1	shelf	¾	12	w_1
D	2	shelves	¾	10½	16½
E	2	back	¼	17½	18½
F	2	doors	¾	16½	18½
G	8	cleat	½	½	16½

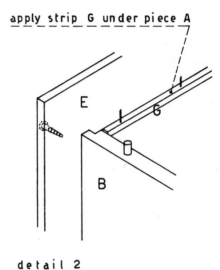

apply strip G under piece A

E

G

B

detail 2

Instructions for Assembly

1. Join top and bottom (A) with partitions (B) and cleats (G).
2. Attach back pieces (E) and doors (F).
3. Insert shelves (C) and (D).
4. Finish and attach to wall (see pages 11-19).

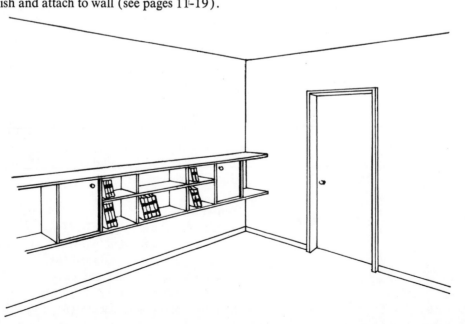

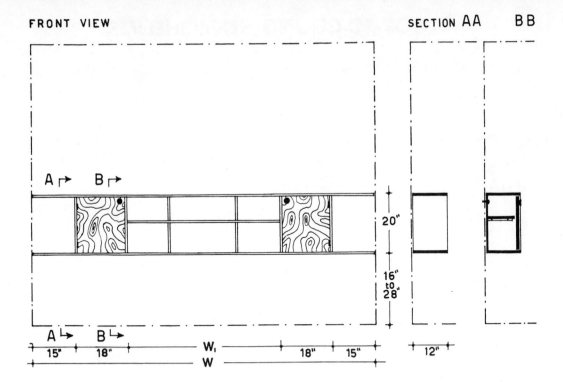

FRONT VIEW

A B

20"

16" to 28"

A B
15" 18" W₁
18" 15"
W

SECTION AA   BB

12"

W = WIDTH OF THE ROOM
W₁ = WIDTH OF THE ROOM
LESS 66"

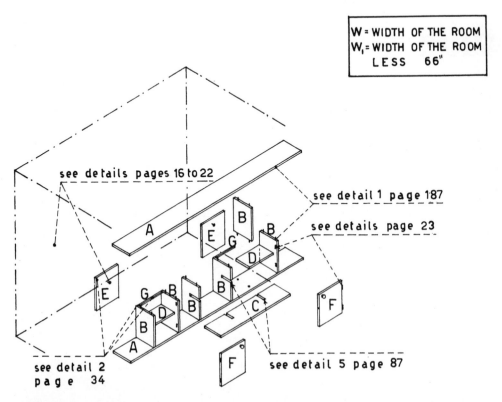

see details pages 16 to 22

see detail 1 page 187

see details page 23

A
E
B
B
G
D

E
G
B
B
D
B
B
A
C
F

see detail 2
page 34

F

see detail 5 page 87

Wall-hung Bookshelves

3 | FLOOR-TO-CEILING BOOKSHELVES

This series of shelves is ideal for the book collector. Construction is simple, and the inserted cabinets lend stability to the vertical rails.

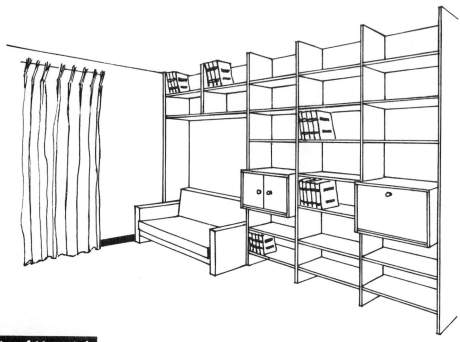

List of Materials

PART	NO.	FUNCTION	DIMENSIONS IN INCHES				
			thickness	×	width	×	length
A	5	side support	¾		12		h
B	1	partition	¾		12		$h - 71$
C	2	shelf	¾		12		w_1
D	10	shelf	¾		12		28½
E	7	shelf	¾		12		w_2
F	4	top, bottom	¾		15		28½
G	4	sides	¾		15		16½
H	2	back	¼		28		17½
J	1	shelf	¾		27		13½
K	2	door	¾		13½		16½
L	1	shelf	¾		27		13½
M	1	partition	¾		13		16½
O	3	shelf	½		10¼		13
P	1	door	¾		27		16½

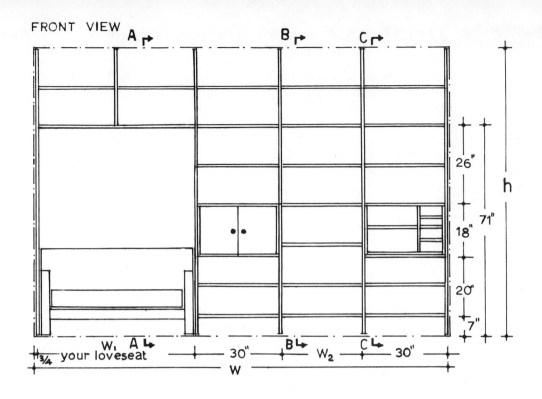

FRONT VIEW A → B → C →

26"

h

71"

18"

20"

7"

W₁ A your loveseat ₃/₄ 30" B W₂ C 30"

W

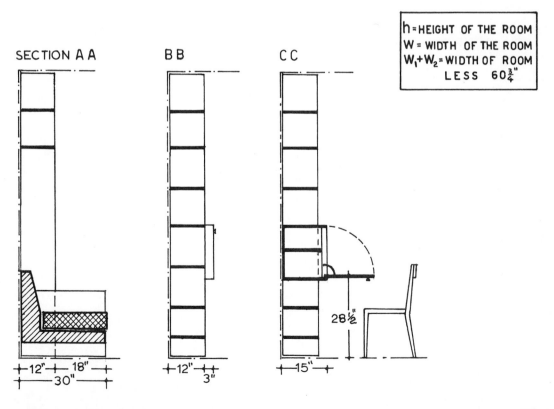

SECTION A A   B B   C C

h = HEIGHT OF THE ROOM
W = WIDTH OF THE ROOM
W₁+W₂ = WIDTH OF ROOM
          LESS 60¾"

28½"

12" 18"
30"

12"
3"

15"

Floor-to-Ceiling Bookshelves

37

Instructions for Assembly

1. Join top and bottom of cabinet (F) with sides (G), partition (M) and back (H).
2. Attach cabinet doors (K) and (P).
3. Insert cabinet shelves (J), (L), and (O).
4. Join vertical shelf supports (A) with sides of cabinet (G) and shelves (D).
5. Apply finish and set assembled shelves in place.
6. Join remaining shelf supports (A) with shelves (C) and (E), and partition (B) with shelf (C).
7. Place love seat in opening.

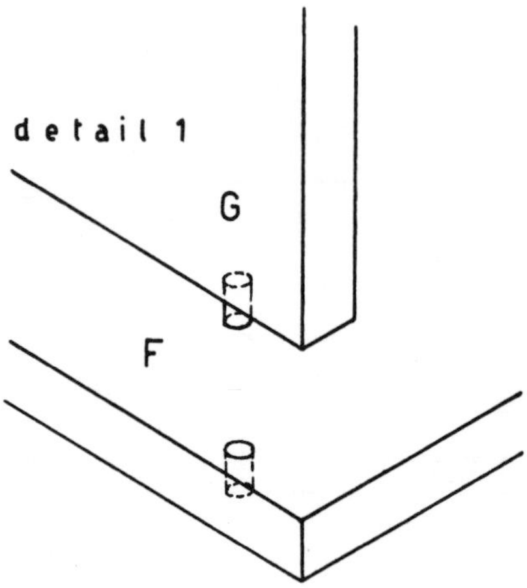

detail 1

G

F

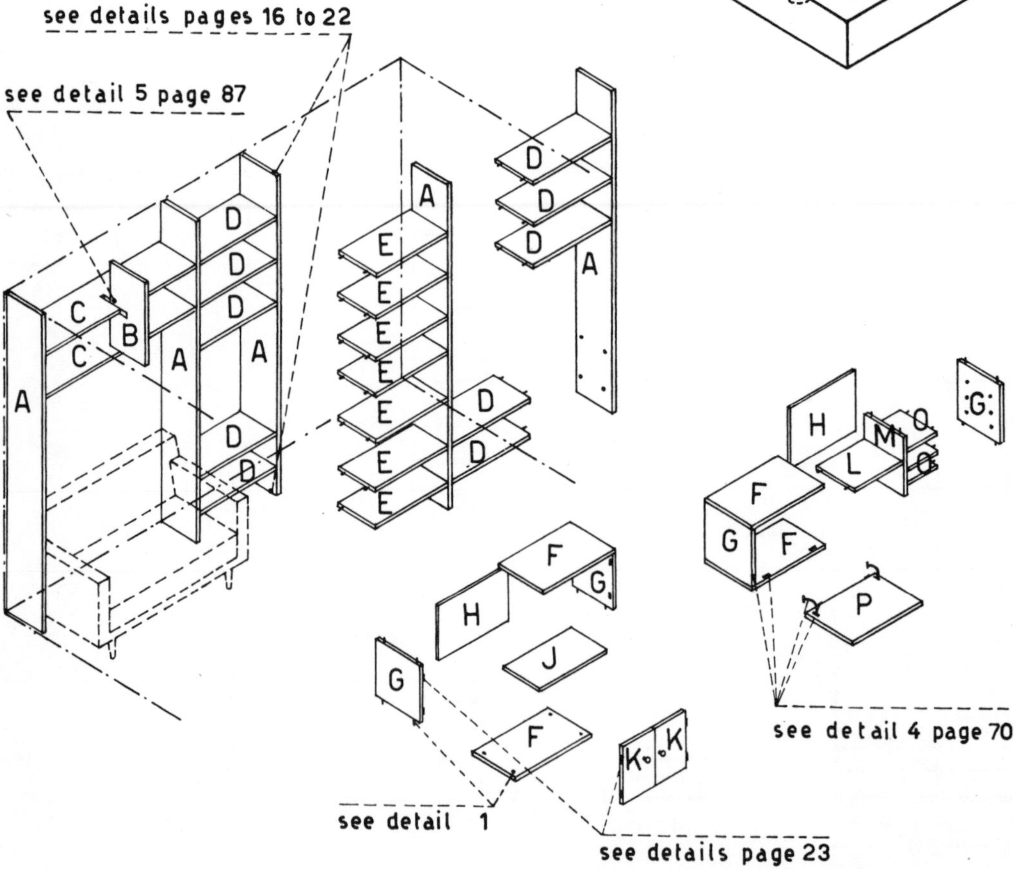

see details pages 16 to 22

see detail 5 page 87

see detail 4 page 70

see detail 1

see details page 23

Floor-to-Ceiling Bookshelves

4

DOUBLE-NOTCHED FLOOR-TO-CEILING BOOKCASE

This full-wall bookcase is made of planks joined by double-notched joints. The enclosed cabinets, with backs screwed in place, help to keep the shelves rigid. A drop door permits use of two adjoining cubicles as a desk, but this feature is optional.

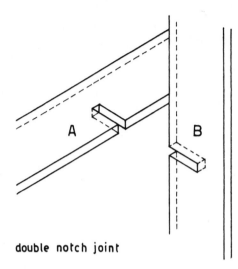

double notch joint

List of Materials

PART	NO.	FUNCTION	DIMENSIONS IN INCHES		
			thickness ×	width ×	length
A	5	shelf	¾	12	w
B	7	side support	¾	12	h
C	6	door	¾	20¼	20¼
D	10	shelf	¾	10½	20¼
E	8	back	½	20¼	20¼
F	16	shelf	¾	12	20¼
G	52	cleat	½	½	11
H	1	door	¾	41¼	20¼

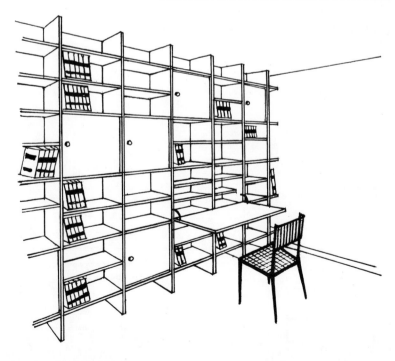

Double-Notched Floor-to-Ceiling Bookcase

FRONT VIEW

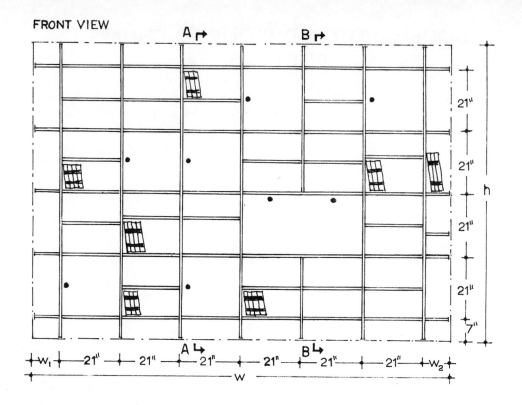

21"
21"
21"
21"
h
21"
7"

w₁   21"   21"   21"   21"   21"   21"   w₂

A   A

B   B

w

h = HEIGHT OF THE ROOM
W = WIDTH OF THE ROOM
W₁ + W₂ = WIDTH OF ROOM
LESS 10'-6"

SECTION AA   BB

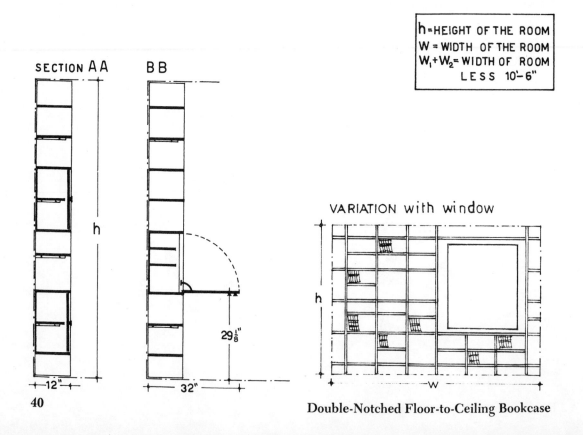

h

12"

29 1/8"

32"

VARIATION with window

h

w

40   Double-Notched Floor-to-Ceiling Bookcase

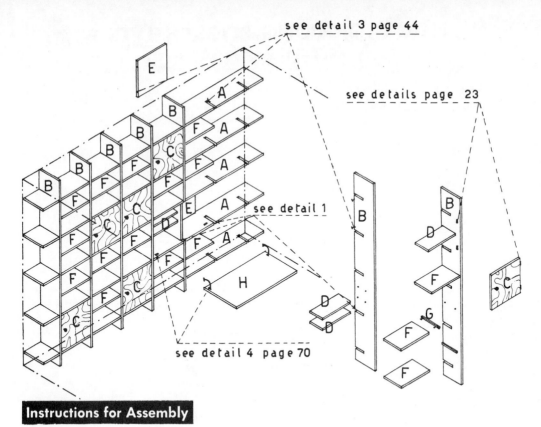

see detail 3 page 44

see details page 23

see detail 1

see detail 4 page 70

Instructions for Assembly

1. Join shelves (A) with side supports (B).
2. Attach back pieces (E).
3. Install cleats (G) on sides of shelf supports (B).
4. Set assembled shelves in place and join doors (C) and (H) with shelf supports (B).
5. Apply finish and insert shelves (D) and (F).

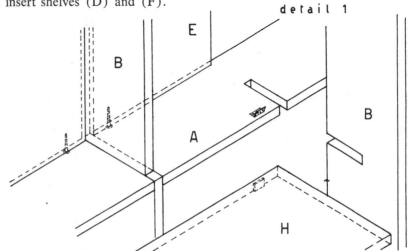

detail 1

Double-Notched Floor-to-Ceiling Bookcase

FLOOR-TO-CEILING BOOKSHELVES FOR LIMITED WALL SPACE

5

These double-notched bookshelves are designed to cover only part of a wall, particularly a wall divided by a door or window.

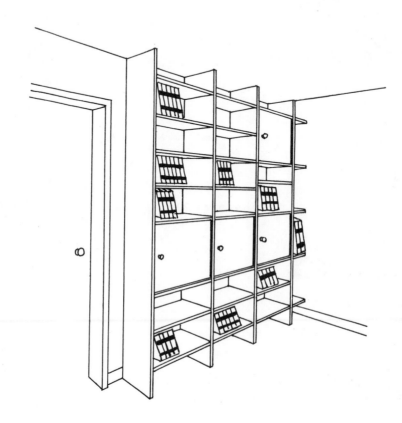

List of Materials

PART	NO.	FUNCTION	DIMENSIONS IN INCHES thickness × width × length		
A	5	shelf	¾	12	*w*
B	4	side support	¾	12	*h*
C	4	door	¾	20¼	20¼
D	4	shelf	¾	10½	20¼
E	4	back	½	20¼	20¼
F	8	shelf	¾	12	20¼
G	24	cleat	½	½	11

Floor-to-Ceiling Bookshelves for Limited Wall Space

FRONT VIEW

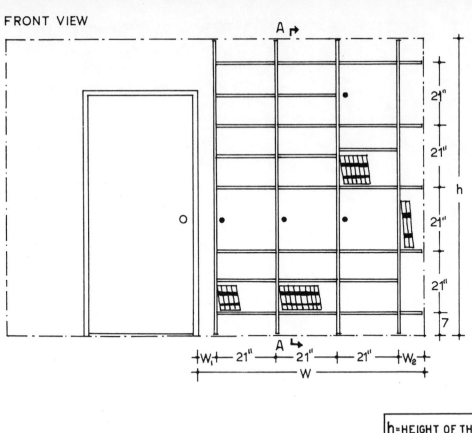

A

21"

21"

h

21"

21"

21"

7

A

+W₁+ — 21" — + — 21" — + — 21" — +W₂+

W

h = HEIGHT OF THE ROOM
W = WIDTH OF THE SPACE
W₁ + W₂ = WIDTH OF SPACE
LESS 63"

SECTION A A

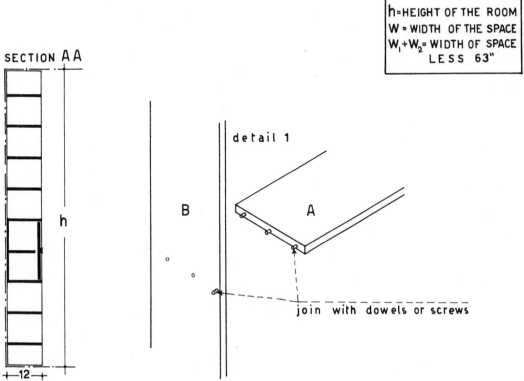

h

+—12—+

B

detail 1

A

join with dowels or screws

Floor-to-Ceiling Bookshelves for Limited Wall Space

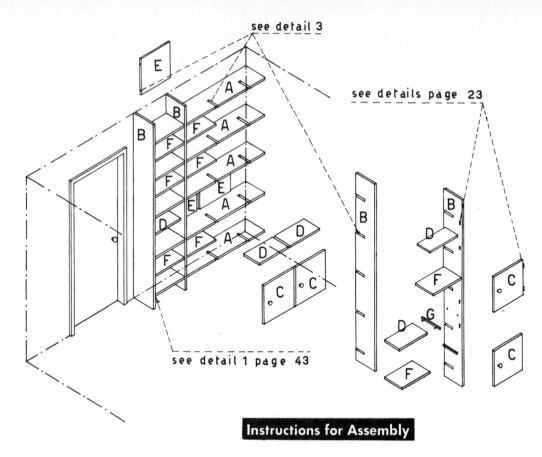

see detail 3

see details page 23

see detail 1 page 43

Instructions for Assembly

1. Join shelves (A) to shelf supports (B).
2. Attach back pieces (E).
3. Attach cleats (G) to side supports (B).
4. Attach doors (C) to shelf supports (B).
5. Apply finish and set assembled shelves in place.
6. Insert shelves (D) and (F).

detail 3

back
E

apply back with screws on side

$\frac{1}{4}" \times \frac{1}{4}"$ strip all around

A

B

Where space is limited, as in a small office or apartment, a table which can be folded against the wall when not in use is a great convenience. This design includes a shelf, which supports the table at one end and provides space for books, work materials, or serving dishes, as required.

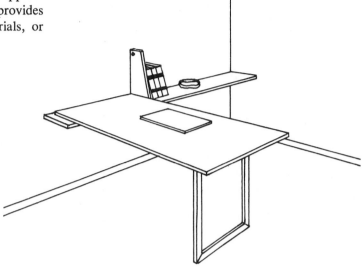

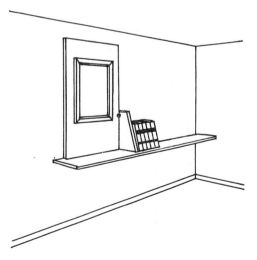

List of Materials

PART	NO.	FUNCTION	DIMENSIONS IN INCHES thickness × width × length		
			thickness	width	length
A	1	table top	¾	28	54
B	1	partition	¾	12	21¾
C	1	shelf	¾	12	75
D	2	supports	⅞	1½	28¼
E	2	supports	⅞	1½	20

FRONT VIEW   SIDE

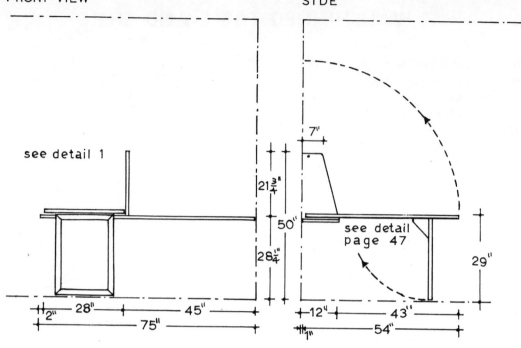

see detail 1

$21\frac{3}{4}''$

7"

50"

$28\frac{1}{4}''$

29"

2" — 28" — 45"

75"

12" — 43"

1" — 54"

see detail
page 47

detail 1

B

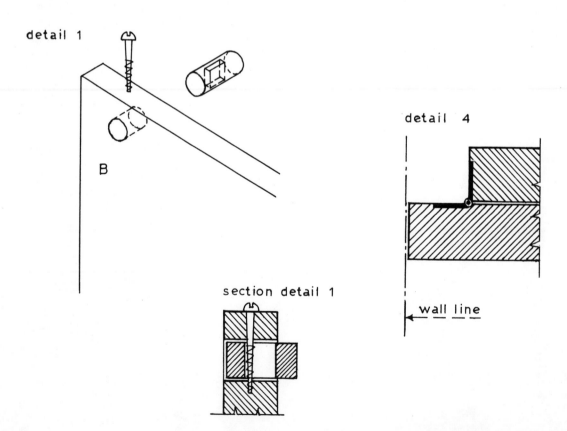

detail 4

wall line

section detail 1

                                   Wall-Hinged Table and Shelf

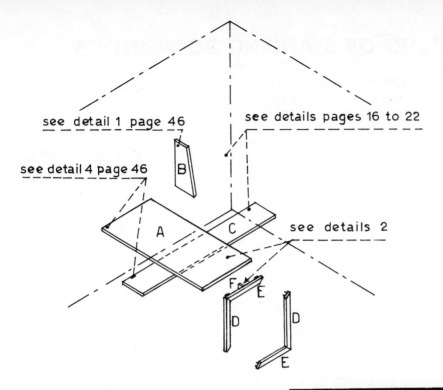

see detail 1 page 46

see details pages 16 to 22

B

see detail 4 page 46

A C

see details 2

F E

D D

E

Instructions for Assembly

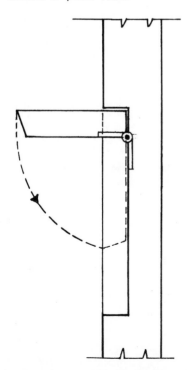

detail 2 plan view

1. Join partition (B) with shelf (C).
2. Join support (D) with support (F) and attach to top (A).
3. Apply finish and set shelf in place.
4. Attach table top (A) to shelf (C).

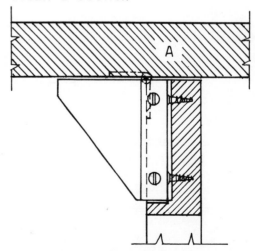

detail 2 section

A

Wall-Hinged Table and Shelf

This practical set of double-notched shelves can be installed with or without the base support. Doors can be added to any of the sections.

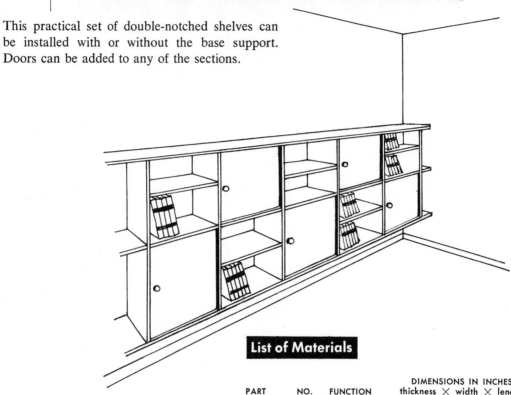

List of Materials

PART	NO.	FUNCTION	DIMENSIONS IN INCHES thickness × width × length		
A	3	shelf	¾	12	*w*
B	6	side	¾	12	41¼
C	5	door	¾	20¼	20¼
D	5	shelf	¾	10½	20¼
E	5	back	½	20¼	20¼
F	5	shelf	¾	12	20¼
G	20	cleat	½	½	11

VARIATION WITH BASE SUPPORT

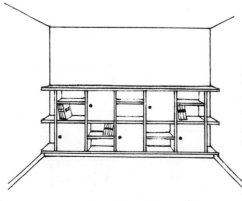

Instructions for Assembly

1. Join top, bottom, and center shelf (A) with sides (B).
2. Attach the backs (E).
3. Attach the cleats (G), to sides (B).
4. Attach doors (C) to (B).
5. Apply finish and set assembled shelves in place.
6. Insert shelves (D) and (F).

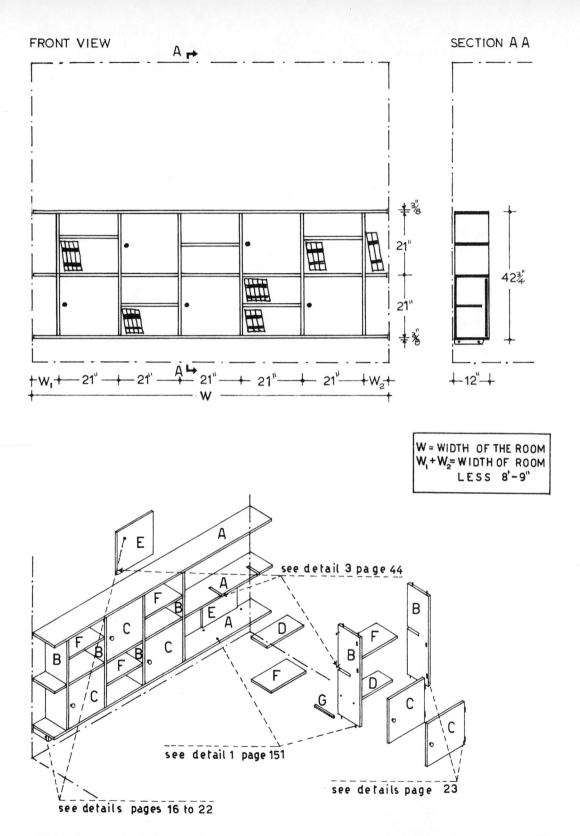

FRONT VIEW

A ➡

SECTION A A

$\frac{3}{8}$"

21"

21"

42$\frac{3}{4}$"

$\frac{3}{8}$"

A ↳

+W₁+— 21" —+— 21" —+ 21" —+— 21" —+— 21" —+W₂+

W

12"

W = WIDTH OF THE ROOM
W₁+W₂= WIDTH OF ROOM
LESS 8'-9"

E

A

see detail 3 page 44

F

A

B

E

C

A

F

B

B

B

F

C

D

F

C

B

F

B

B

D

C

G

F

C

C

see detail 1 page 151

see details page 23

see details pages 16 to 22

Hung or Standing Bookshelves

49

SHELVES FOR WALL RECESS

Building shelves like these into an existing wall recess will improve the appearance of a room and make use of space that might otherwise be wasted. The sketches on page 51 show how this design may be adapted for making a full wall of shelves around a window.

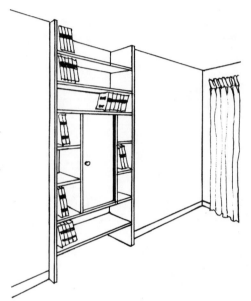

List of Materials

PART	NO.	FUNCTION	DIMENSIONS IN INCHES thickness × width × length		
A	2	side	¾	12	h
B	5	shelf	¾	12	$w - 1½$
C	2	partition	¾	12	39
D	4	shelf	¾	12	w_1
E	2	shelf	¾	10½	16½
F	1	back	¼	17½	39
G	1	door	¾	16½	39
H	6	cleat	½	½	16½

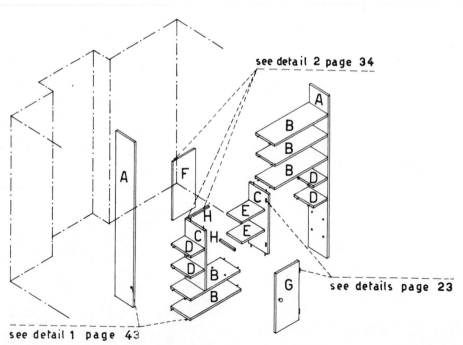

see detail 2 page 34

see details page 23

see detail 1 page 43

Shelves for Wall Recess

FRONT VIEW

SECTION A A

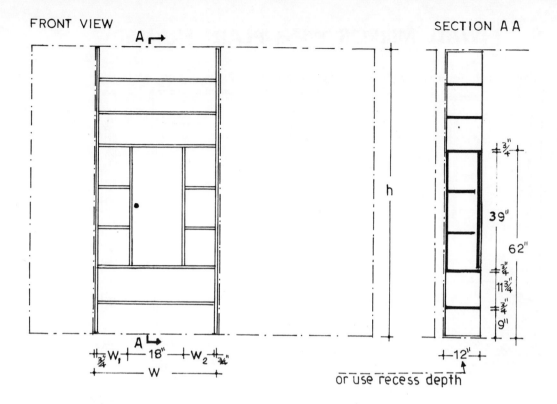

A→

h

A→

$\frac{3''}{4}$ W₁ — 18" — W₂ $\frac{3''}{4}$

W

$\frac{3''}{4}$

39"

62"

$\frac{3''}{4}$

11$\frac{3''}{4}$

$\frac{3''}{4}$

9"

+12"+

or use recess depth

Instructions for Assembly

1. Join shelves (B) with partitions (C).
2. Join sides (A) with shelves (B) and (D).
3. Attach the back (F) and cleats (H).
4. Attach door (G) to partition (C).
5. Apply finish and set furniture in position.
6. Insert shelves (E).

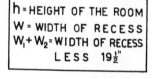

h = HEIGHT OF THE ROOM
W = WIDTH OF RECESS
W₁ + W₂ = WIDTH OF RECESS
LESS 19$\frac{1}{2}$"

VARIATION
FRONT VIEW

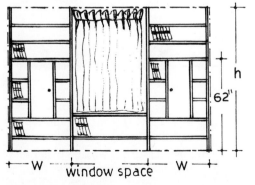

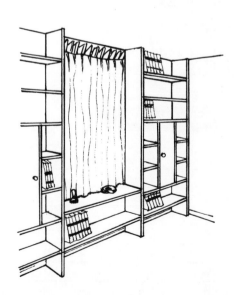

h

62"

— W — window space — W —

Shelves for Wall Recess

51

9 | WALL MIRROR WITH PLAIN FRAME

This type of mirror with a plain frame is indicated for halls.

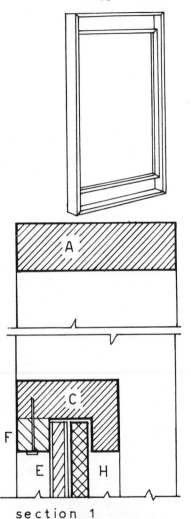

section 1

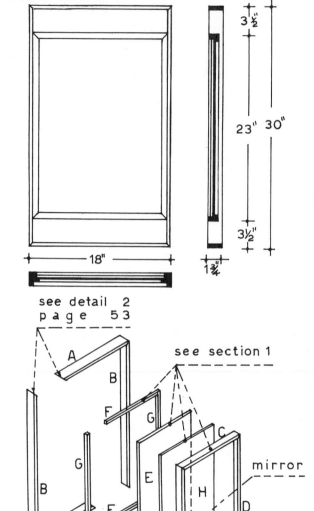

3½"

23" 30"

3½"

18"

1¾"

see detail 2
page 53

see section 1

mirror

List of Materials

PART	NO.	FUNCTION	DIMENSION IN INCHES thickness × width × length		
A	2	top and bottom	½	1¾	18
B	2	sides	½	1¾	30
C	2	rails	¾	1⅛	17
D	2	rails	¾	1⅛	23
E	1	panel	3/16	16⅛	22⅛
F	2	strips	⅜	⅜	16¼
G	2	strip	⅜	⅜	22¼
H	1	mirror	3/16	16⅛	22⅛

Instructions for Assembly

1. Join (A) with (B) and (C) with (D).
2. Attach (D) to (B) and apply finish.
3. Install mirror (H) and panel (E) and fasten with strips (F, G).

52   **Wall Mirror with Plain Frame**

10 | WALL MIRROR WITH DECORATIVE FRAME

More appropriate for the living-room area is a wall mirror with a decorative frame.

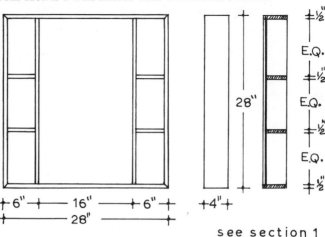

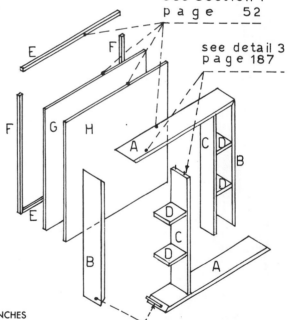

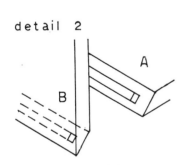

detail 2

see section 1
page 52

see detail 3
page 187

see detail 2

List of Materials

PART	NO.	FUNCTION	DIMENSION IN INCHES thickness × width × length		
A	2	top and bottom	½	4	28
B	2	sides	½	4	28
C	2	partitions	½	4	27
D	4	partitions	½	4	5
E	2	strips	¼	⅜	27½
F	2	strips	¼	⅜	27½
G	1	panel	³⁄₁₆	27⅜	27⅜
H	1	mirror		27⅜	27⅜

Instructions for Assembly

1. Join (A) with partitions (C).
2. Fasten (A, C) with (B) and (D) and apply finish.
3. Install mirror (H) and panel (G) and fasten with strips (E, F).

Wall Mirror with Decorative Frame

detail 2
metal knob and pull

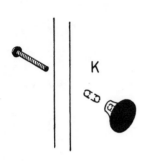

K

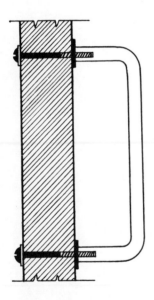

wood knob and pull

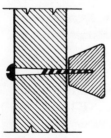

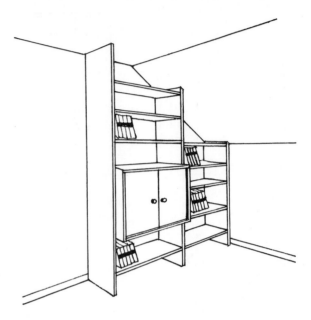

Rooms with sloping ceilings present problems of furniture placement. These bookshelves, especially designed for such a room, offer a practical solution.

List of Materials

PART	NO.	FUNCTION	DIMENSIONS IN INCHES thickness × width × length		
A	1	side	¾	12	h
B	1	side	¾	12	h_1
C	1	side	¾	12	h_2
D	9	shelf	¾	12	29
E	3	back	¾	4	29
F	1	top	¾	29	15
G	1	bottom	¾	27½	15
H	2	side	¾	26¼	15
J	1	back	¼	28½	26½
K	2	door	¾	13¾	25½
L	2	shelf	¾	27½	13
M	4	cleat	½	½	12

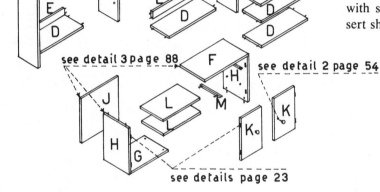

see detail 1 page 138

see detail 3 page 88

see detail 2 page 54

see details page 23

see detail 1 page 138
see detail 3 page 88
see detail 2 page 54
see details page 23

Instructions for Assembly

1. Join side pieces (A), (B), and (C) with shelves (D) and backs (E).
2. Join top (F) and bottom (G) of cabinet section, with sides (H) and back (J).
3. Attach doors (K) to sides (H) and cleats (M).
4. Apply finish and set shelves in place.
5. Join sides of cabinet section (H) with sides (A) and (B), and insert shelves (L).

h = HEIGHT OF THE ROOM
h_1, h_2 = HEIGHT TO THE SLOPING CEILING

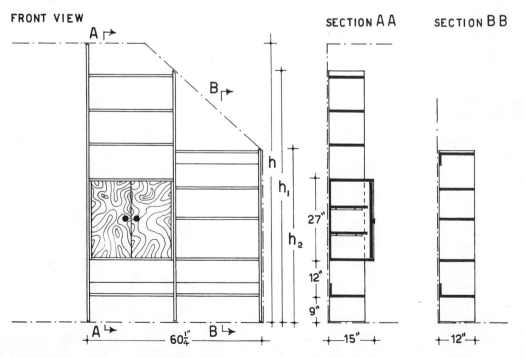

FRONT VIEW

SECTION AA   SECTION BB

Bookshelves Against Sloping Ceiling

This low bookcase could be installed in any room, but would be especially suitable for a child's use.

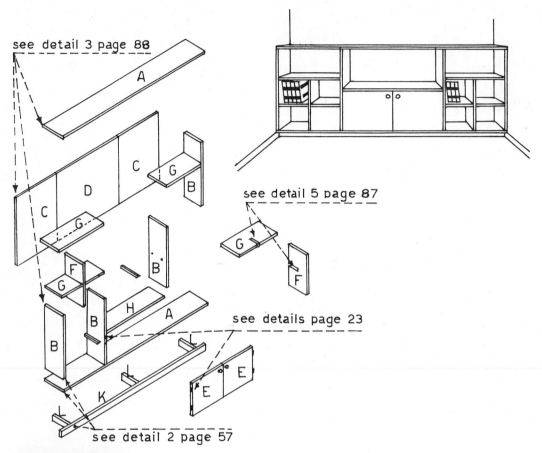

see detail 3 page 88

see detail 5 page 87

see details page 23

see detail 2 page 57

List of Materials

PART	NO.	FUNCTION	thickness	DIMENSIONS IN INCHES × width ×	length
A	2	top, bottom	¾	12	w
B	4*	end	¾	12	37
C	2	back	¼	37¾	w_1
D	1	back	¼	37¾	47¼
E	2	door	¾	17	23¼
F	2	partition	¾	11¾	24
G	4	shelf	¾	11¾	$w_1 - ¾$
H	1	shelf	¾	10	46½
J	6	cleat	½	½	10
K	1	toeplate	1	3½	w
L	3	base support	1	3½	9½

* For partition, trim width to 11¾ in.

FRONT VIEW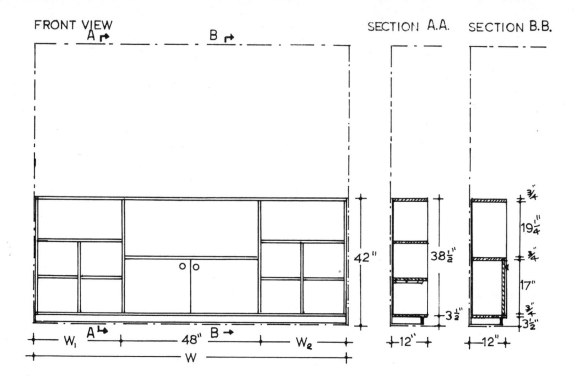

SECTION A.A.   SECTION B.B.

W = WIDTH OF THE ROOM
W₁+W₂ = WIDTH OF THE ROOM
LESS 48"

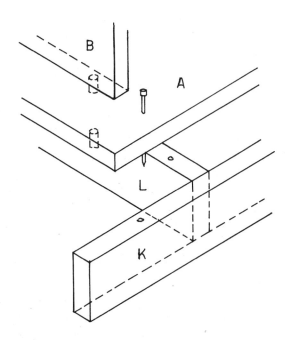

Instructions for Assembly

1. Join top and bottom (A) with ends (B).
2. Install backs (C) and (D).
3. Attach cleats (J) to ends (B).
4. Attach base supports (L) to toeplate (K).
5. Join base (L-K) to bottom (A).
6. Join shelf (G) and partition (F).
7. Attach (G-F) to (A-B).
8. Install doors (E).
9. Apply finish and insert removable shelf.

Child's Bookcase   57

STEREO CABINET I

This floor-to-ceiling cabinet for stereo components provides room for receiver, record player, storage for records, space for four speakers, and bookshelves. (See page 28 for additional instructions.)

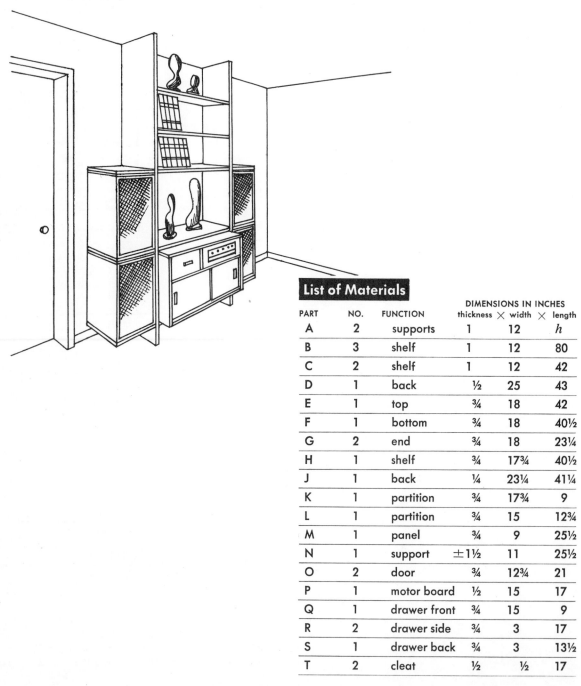

List of Materials

PART	NO.	FUNCTION	DIMENSIONS IN INCHES		
			thickness ×	width ×	length
A	2	supports	1	12	h
B	3	shelf	1	12	80
C	2	shelf	1	12	42
D	1	back	½	25	43
E	1	top	¾	18	42
F	1	bottom	¾	18	40½
G	2	end	¾	18	23¼
H	1	shelf	¾	17¾	40½
J	1	back	¼	23¼	41¼
K	1	partition	¾	17¾	9
L	1	partition	¾	15	12¾
M	1	panel	¾	9	25½
N	1	support	±1½	11	25½
O	2	door	¾	12¾	21
P	1	motor board	½	15	17
Q	1	drawer front	¾	15	9
R	2	drawer side	¾	3	17
S	1	drawer back	¾	3	13½
T	2	cleat	½	½	17

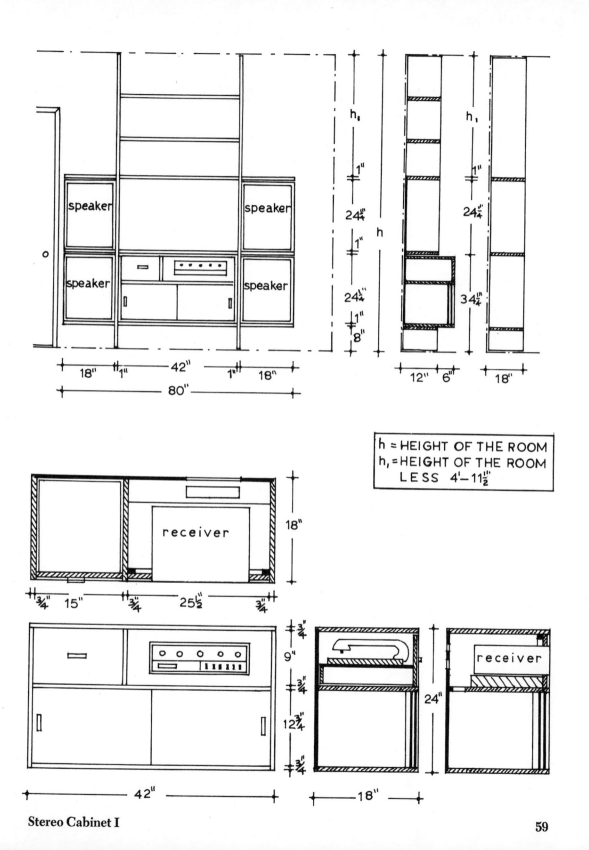

h = HEIGHT OF THE ROOM
h₁ = HEIGHT OF THE ROOM
    LESS 4'—11½"

Stereo Cabinet I

59

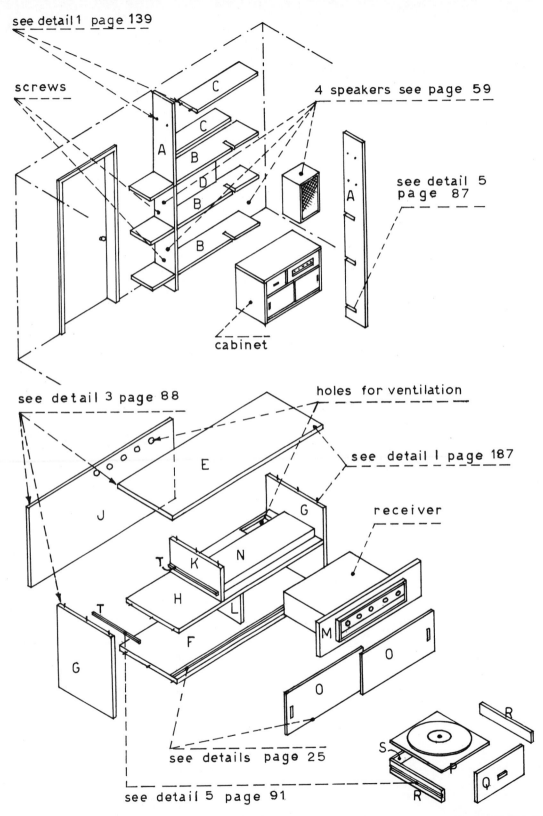

see detail 1 page 139

screws

4 speakers see page 59

C

C

A

B

D

B

B

see detail 5
page 87

A

cabinet

see detail 3 page 88

holes for ventilation

E

see detail 1 page 187

J

G

receiver

T

K

N

H

L

M

G

O

O

O

F

see details page 25

R

S

P

Q

R

see detail 5 page 91

Stereo Cabinet I

1. Join support (A) with shelves (B) and (C).
2. Attach back (D), apply finish, and place chase in the proper position.
3. Join top and bottom (E–F) with (G–H–K–L).
4. Attach back (J), cleats (T), and support (N).
5. Fasten receiver to front (M) and cabinet.
6. Join (R) with (Q–S) and motor board (P).
7. Apply finish and fasten cabinet to floor-to-ceiling chase with screws.
8. Insert record player and attach door (O) to the cabinet.

SPEAKER

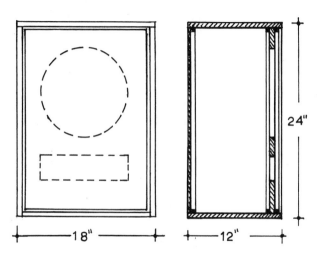

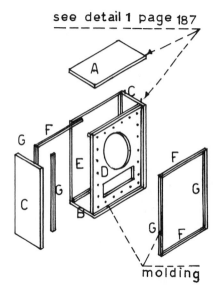

see detail 1 page 187

24"

18"

12"

molding

see detail 1 page 187

List of Materials

PART	NO.	FUNCTION	DIMENSIONS IN INCHES thickness × width × length		
			thickness	width	length
A	1	top	¾	12	18
B	1	bottom	¾	12	16½
C	2	sides	¾	12	23¼
D	1	front	¾	16½	22½
E	1	back	½	16½	22½
F	6	molding	½	½	16½
G	6	molding	½	½	22½

Instructions for Assembly

1. Join top (A) and bottom (B) with sides (C).
2. Attach cleats (F–G) and back (E).
3. Apply finish.
4. Line speaker enclosure with insulation.
5. Install equipment.
6. Install baffle (D).
7. Apply protective fabric over (D) and cover tacks with molding (F–G).

The four parts of this assembly, although planned to fit between two walls, may be separated to suit changing needs. (See page 28 for additional instructions.)

List of Materials

PART	NO.	FUNCTION	thickness	× width	× length
			DIMENSIONS IN INCHES		
A	1	top	¾	18	42
B	1	top	¾	16	20⅝
C	2	end	¾	18	27¼
D	1	bottom	¾	17¼	40½
E	1	back	½	24¼	41¼
F	1	partition	¾	16¾	23½
G	1	shelf	¾	16	19⅞
H	1	shelf	¾	16¾	19⅞
J	1	rail	¾	3	19⅞
K	1	panel	½	9¾	19⅞
L	4	door	¾	10⅛	24¼
M	1	toeplate	1	3	40½

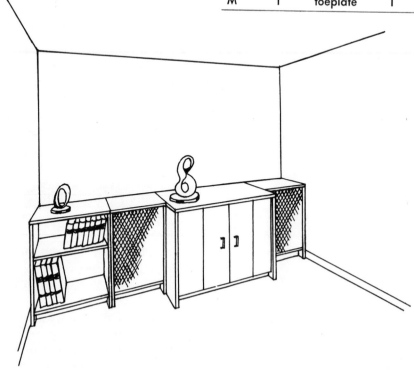

FRONT VIEW · SECTION A.A.

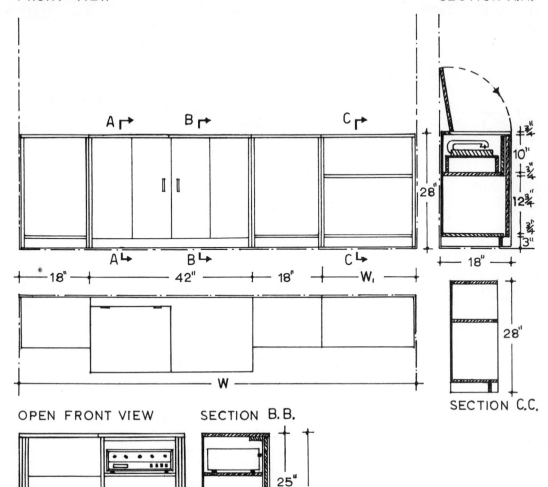

OPEN FRONT VIEW · SECTION B.B. · SECTION C.C.

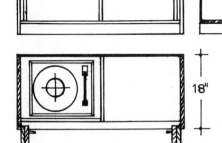

W = WIDTH OF THE ROOM
W₁ = WIDTH OF THE ROOM
LESS 6'-6"

Instructions for Assembly

1. Join top (A) and bottom (D) with partition (F). Also join together shelves (G–H), rail (J), panel (K), and ends (C).
2. Apply back (E) and toeplate (M) to the cabinet.
3. Attach folding top (B) to top (A).
4. Join together folding door (L) and fasten to the cabinet.
5. Apply finish.
6. Insert the stereo components.

Stereo Cabinet II

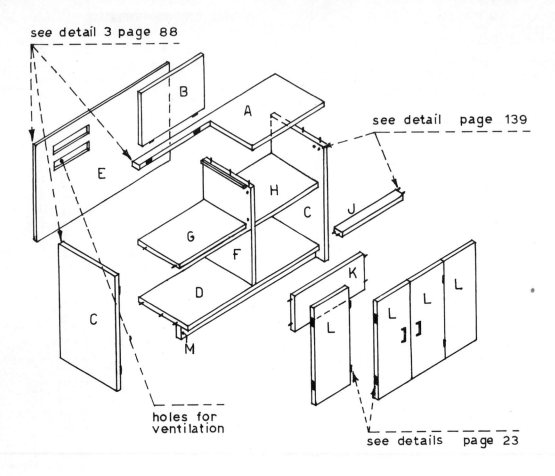

see detail 3 page 88

B

A

see detail page 139

E

H

C

J

G

F

K

D

C

L

L

L

L

M

holes for
ventilation

see details   page 23

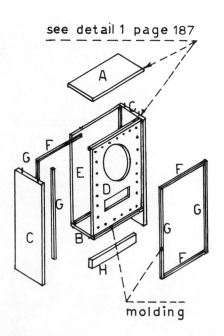

see detail 1 page 187

A

C

F

G

E

D

B

C

G

G

F

F

G

H

molding

SPEAKER

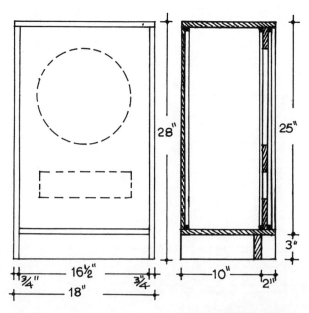

28"

25"

3"

3/4" 16½" 3/4"

18"

10" 2"

SPEAKER

see detail 3 page 88

List of Materials

PART	NO.	FUNCTION	thickness	DIMENSIONS IN INCHES width	length
A	1	top	¾	12	18
B	1	bottom	¾	12	16½
C	2	end	¾	12	27¼
D	1	front	¾	16½	23½
E	1	back	½	16½	23½
F	6	molding	½	½	16½
G	6	molding	½	½	23½
H	1	toeplate	1	3	16½

Instructions for Assembly

1. Join top (A) and bottom (B) with ends (C).
2. Attach cleats (F–G), back (E), and toeplate (H).
3. Apply finish.
4. Line speaker enclosure with insulation.
5. Install equipment.
6. Install baffle (D).
7. Apply protective fabric over (D) and cover tacks with molding (F–G).

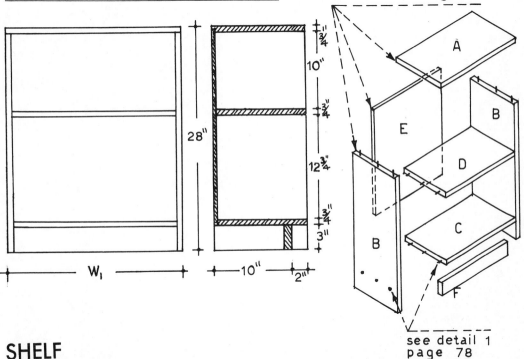

see detail 1 page 78

SHELF

List of Materials

PART	NO.	FUNCTION	thickness	DIMENSIONS IN INCHES width	length
A	2	top	¾	12	w_1
B	2	side	¾	12	27¼
C	1	bottom	¾	12	$w_1-1½$
D	1	shelf	¾	11¾	$w_1-1½$
E	1	back	¼	24¼	$w_1-¾$
F	1	toeplate	1	3	$w_1-1½$

Instructions for Assembly

1. Join top (A) and bottom (C) with shelf (D) and sides (B).
2. Attach back (E) and toeplate (F) to the cabinet.
3. Apply finish.
4. Set stereo cabinet, speakers, and shelf in respective places.

WALL HANGER

This is another simple piece to make. It is practical for use in the home or office.

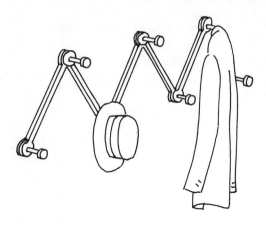

detail 1

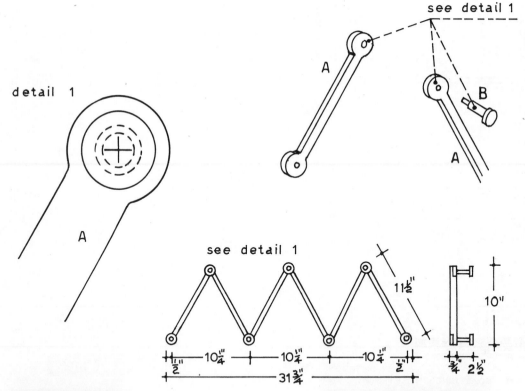

List of Materials					
PART	NO.	FUNCTION	DIMENSION IN INCHES		
			thickness × width × length		
A	6	rails	¾	1¼	11½
B	7	supports	1 (diam.)		3¼

Instructions for Assembly

1. Join rails (A) and insert supports (B).
2. Apply finish.

UMBRELLA STAND

Practical for the office or home, the example shown is easy to make.

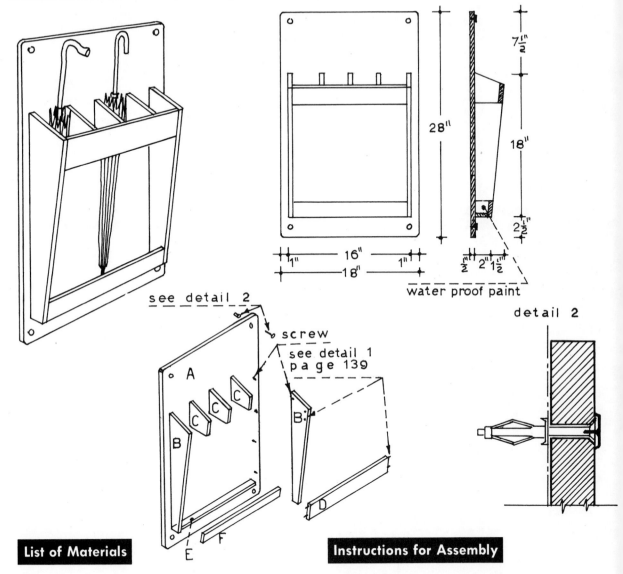

see detail 2

screw

see detail 1
page 139

water proof paint

detail 2

List of Materials

PART	NO.	FUNCTION	DIMENSION IN INCHES thickness × width × length		
A	1	back	½	18	28
B	2	sides	½	4	18
C	3	partitions	½	3½	3½
D	1	front	½	2½	15
E	1	bottom	½	2	15
F	1	front	½	2	15

Instructions for Assembly

1. Join sides (B) to fronts (D, F) and bottom (E).
2. Attach partitions (C) to front (D).
3. Fasten back (A) to sides (B), bottom (E) and partitions (C).
4. Apply finish and attach back (A) to wall with molly bolts.

This shelf, to be installed at table height, has a drawer front which opens to provide extra work space.

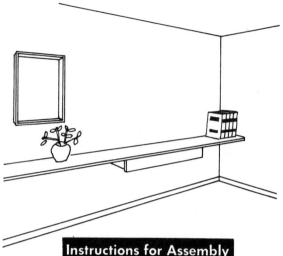

List of Materials

PART	NO.	FUNCTION	DIMENSIONS IN INCHES thickness × width × length		
A	1	shelf	1	12	w
B	1	drawer front	1	5½	40
C	1	drawer bottom	½	36	12
D	1	drawer back	½	4½	36
E	2	drawer side	½	5	12
F	1	partition	½	4½	11½
G	2	glide	⅜	½	12
H	2	track	1	1	12

Instructions for Assembly

1. Join bottom of drawer (C) with back and sides (D) and (E) and partition (F).
2. Attach glide (G) to side of drawer (E).
3. Attach track (H) to under side of shelf (A).
4. Attach drawer front (B) to shelf (A).
5. Apply finish and set shelf in place.

detail 4

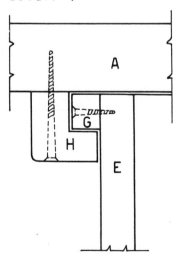

detail 2
open drawer front supported by drawer

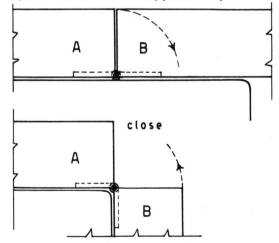

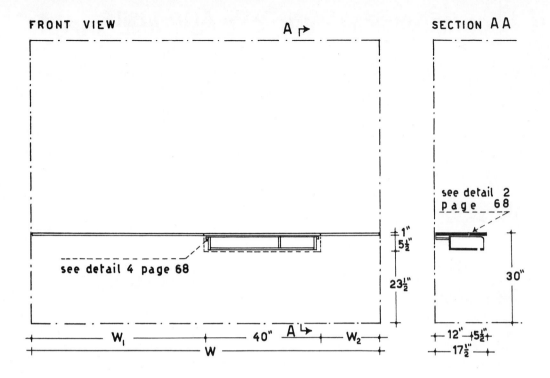

FRONT VIEW

A ⊢►

SECTION AA

see detail 2
page 68

1"
5½"

23½"

see detail 4 page 68

30"

W₁

40"

A ↳

W₂

12" 5½"

W

17½"

W = WIDTH OF THE ROOM
W₁ + W₂ = WIDTH OF ROOM
LESS 40"

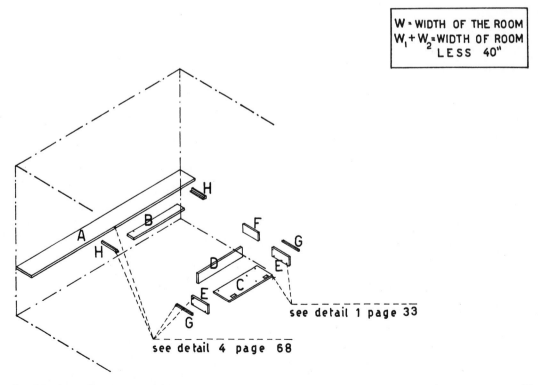

H

B

F

A

G

H

D

E

C

E

G

see detail 1 page 33

see detail 4 page 68

Combination Desk and Shelf

18 | COMBINATION DESK, CABINET, AND SHELF

This simple design is suitable for living room or study.

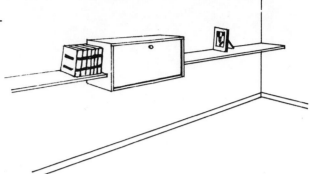

List of Materials

PART	NO.	FUNCTION	DIMENSIONS IN INCHES thickness × width × length		
A	1	shelf	1	12	w_1
B	1	shelf	1	12	w_2
C	1	top	¾	42	15
D	1	bottom	¾	40½	15
E	2	end	¾	20¼	15
F	1	back	¼	41½	20½
G	1	partition	¾	13½	19½
H	1	shelf	¾	13½	24
J	2	shelf	¾	13½	15¾
K	1	drop front	¾	40½	19½

Instructions for Assembly

1. Join ends of cabinet (E) and partition (G) with top of cabinet (C), bottom of cabinet (D), and shelves (H) and (J).
2. Attach back (F).
3. Install drop front from (K).
4. Apply finish and set cabinet and shelves in place.

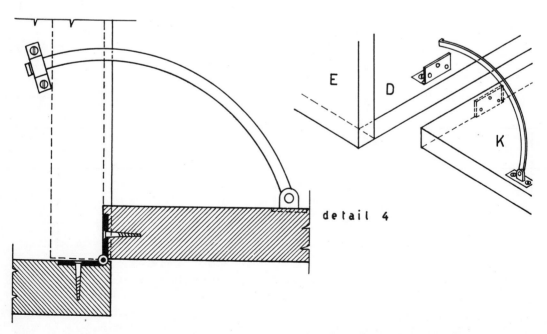

detail 4

Combination Desk, Cabinet, and Shelf

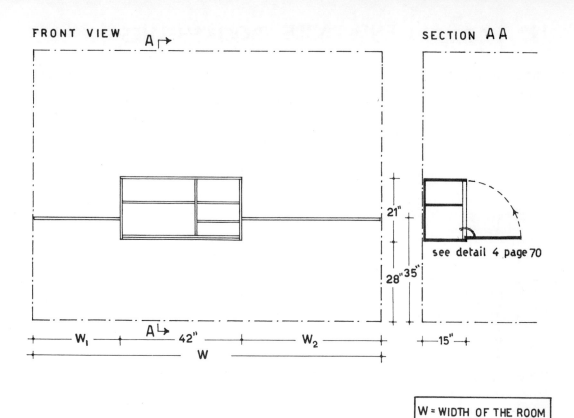

FRONT VIEW

A →

SECTION AA

21"

28" 35"

see detail 4 page 70

W₁   A →   42"   W₂

W

15"

W = WIDTH OF THE ROOM
W₁ + W₂ = WIDTH OF ROOM
LESS 42"

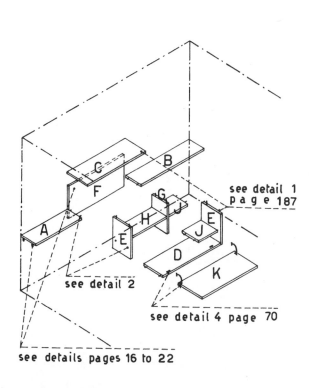

C   B

F

see detail 1
page 187

G

H

E

A   E   J

D

see detail 2   K

see detail 4 page 70

see details pages 16 to 22

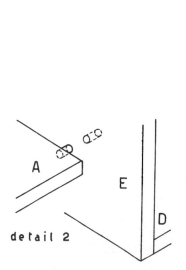

A

E

D

detail 2

Combination Desk, Cabinet, and Shelf

END TABLE—BOOKSHELVES

The space-saving feature of this project is that the two flanking units serve both as end tables and as bookshelves.

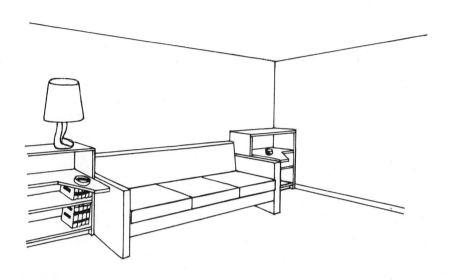

List of Materials

PART	NO.	FUNCTION	thickness	DIMENSIONS IN INCHES × width ×	length
A	2	toeplate	¾	2½	$w_1 - 1\frac{1}{2}$
B	4	side	¾	12	35¼
C	2	top	¾	12	w_1
D	2	shelf	¾	27	$w_2 - 1\frac{1}{2}$
E	4	shelf	¾	11¾	$w_2 - 1\frac{1}{2}$
F	2	back	¼	33	$w_2 - \frac{1}{2}$

Instructions for Assembly

1. Attach sides (B) to tops (C) and shelves (D, E).
2. Attach backs (F).
3. Attach toeplates (A) to bottom shelves (E).
4. Apply finish and set sofa in place.

End Table—Bookshelves

FRONT VIEW   SECTION A.A.

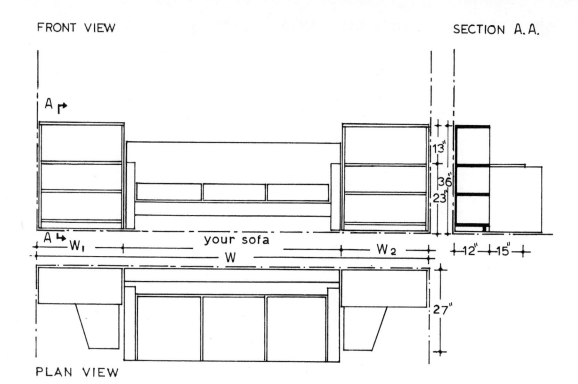

A

A   W₁   your sofa   W₂   12" 15"
                              W
13"
36"
23"

PLAN VIEW   27"

W = WIDTH OF THE ROOM
W₁ + W₂ = WIDTH OF ROOM
LESS YOUR SOFA

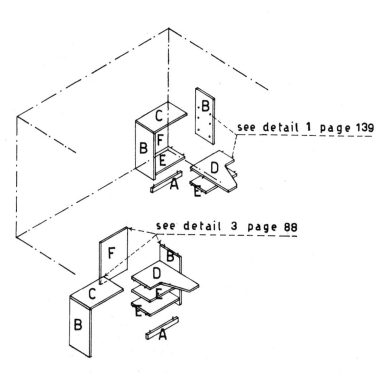

see detail 1 page 139

see detail 3 page 88

End Table—Bookshelves

This hinged table doubles as the door of a china cabinet, but might also be used in a study, workroom, or recreation room.

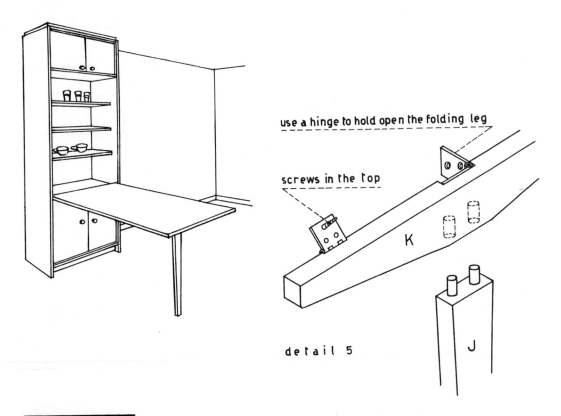

use a hinge to hold open the folding leg

screws in the top

K

detail 5

J

List of Materials

PART	NO.	FUNCTION	thickness	× width	× length
A	2	side	¾	12	h
B	4	top, bottom	¾	12	32½
C	1	back	¼	33½	h − 4½
D	4	shelf	¾	10½	32½
E	8	cleat	½	½	10
F	2	door	¾	16¼	h − 78¾
G	2	door	¾	16¼	23¾
H	1	table top	¾	32½	48
J	1	leg	1	2¼	26
K	1	brace	1	2¼	18
L	1	toeplate	1	3	32½

DIMENSIONS IN INCHES

Instructions for Assembly

1. Attach top and bottom pieces (B) to side pieces (A).
2. Attach back (C).
3. Install cleats (E) on side pieces (A), and attach toeplate (L) to bottom piece (B).
4. Join table leg (J) with brace (K), and (K) with table top (H).
5. Attach doors (F), (G), and (H) to horizontal members (B).
6. Apply finish and set assembled parts in place.
7. Insert shelves (D).

Cabinet with Hinged Table

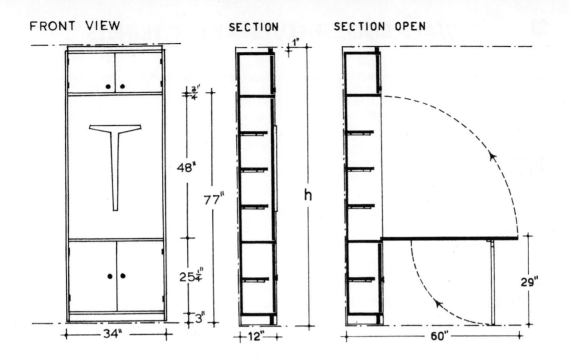

FRONT VIEW

SECTION

SECTION OPEN

$\frac{3}{4}$"

48"

77"

$25\frac{1}{4}$"

3"

34"

1"

h

12"

h

29"

60"

h =HEIGHT OF THE ROOM

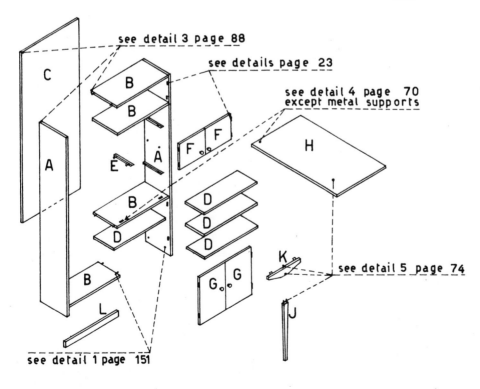

see detail 3 page 88

see details page 23

see detail 4 page 70
except metal supports

C

B

B

F F

H

A

E

A

B

D

D

D

B

D

K

see detail 5 page 74

G G

J

L

see detail 1 page 151

Cabinet with Hinged Table

21 | WALL BOOKSHELVES AND CABINETS

The repeating design offers a practical solution to storage problems in the office or home.

List of Materials

PART	NO.	FUNCTION	thickness	DIMENSIONS IN INCHES		
				× width ×		length
A	8	top	¾		15	22½
B	8	side	¾		15	60
C	4	back	¼		23½	59½
D	4	door	¾		22½	58½
E	16	shelf	¾		13	22½
F	62	cleat	½		½	12
G	15	shelf	¾		12	w_1
H	1	support	¾		17	w
J	3	cross toeplate	¾		9¼	15½
K	2	toeplate	¾		9¼	w

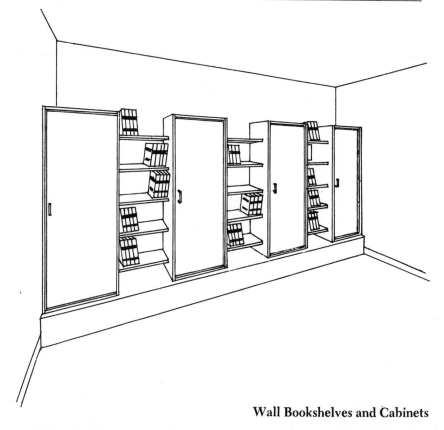

Wall Bookshelves and Cabinets

FRONT VIEW

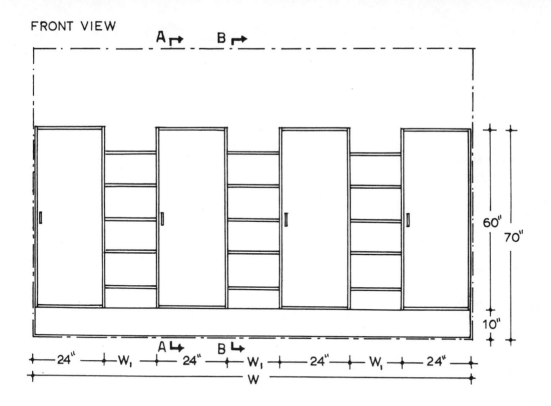

A → B →

60"
70"
10"

|← 24" →|← W₁ →|← 24" →|← W₁ →|← 24" →|← W₁ →|← 24" →|

|← W →|

A ↳ B ↳

SECTION A A   SECTION B B

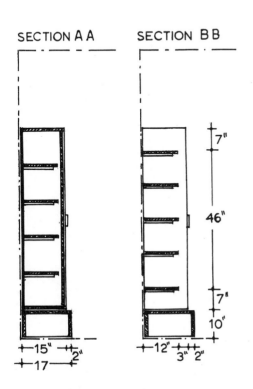

7"

46"

7"
10"

|← 15" →|← 2" →|
|← 17 →|

|← 12" →|← 3" →|← 2" →|

W = WIDTH OF THE ROOM
3XW₁ = WIDTH OF THE
ROOM LESS 96"

Instructions for Assembly

1. Attach top pieces (A) to sides (B).
2. Attach backs (C).
3. Mount cleats (F) on sides (B).
4. Hang doors (D) on sides (B).
5. Join toeplate (K) with (J) and support (H).
6. Apply finish and set in place.
7. Insert shelves (E) and (G).

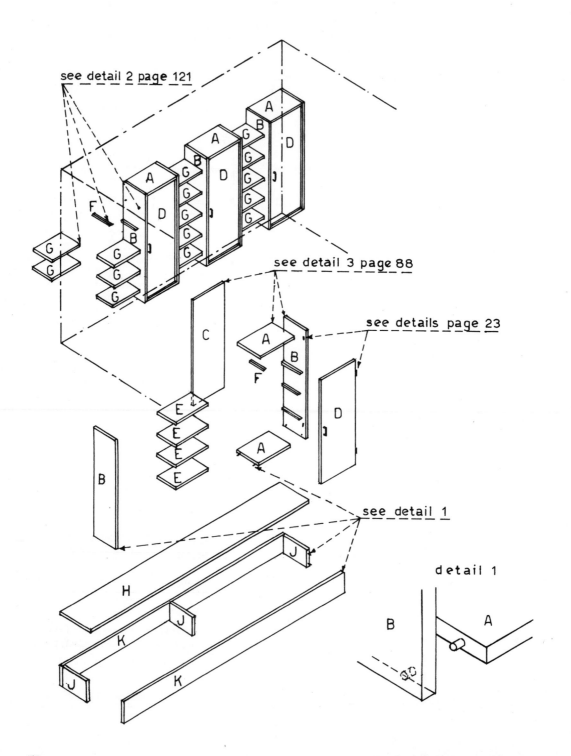

see detail 2 page 121

see detail 3 page 88

see details page 23

see detail 1

detail 1

Wall Bookshelves and Cabinets

SHELVES

Both examples shown are practical for any home. They will also improve the look of the walls when they are attached. You will find them easy to make and install.

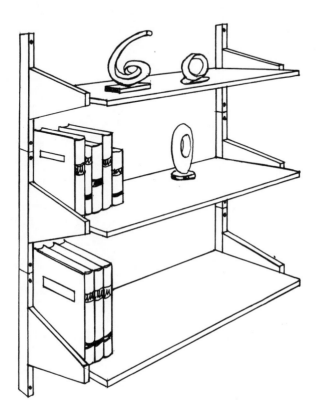

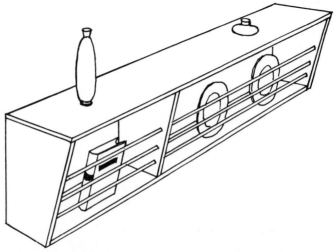

List of Materials

PART	NO.	FUNCTION	DIMENSION IN INCHES thickness × width × length		
A	1	shelf	¾	12	28½
B	2	sides	¾	6	8
C	2	supports	¾	1	12

Instructions for Assembly

1. Join sides (B) to supports (C) and shelf (A) to sides (B).
2. Apply finish and fasten the supports (C) to wall with toggle bolts.

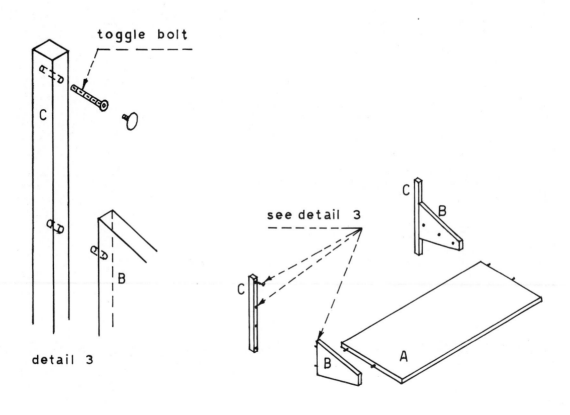

toggle bolt

C

B

detail 3

see detail 3

C B

C B

A

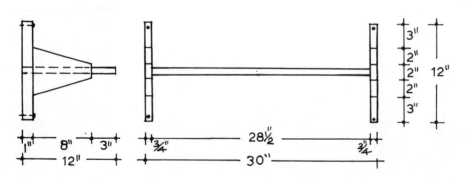

Shelves

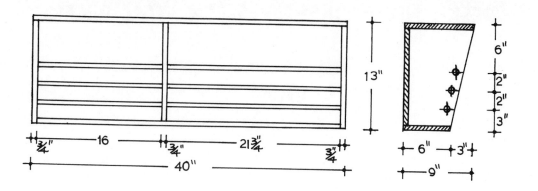

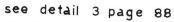
see detail 3 page 88

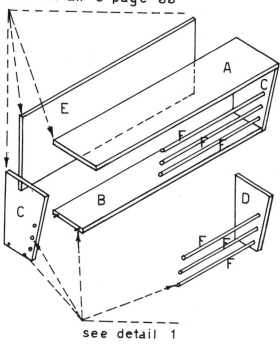
see detail 1

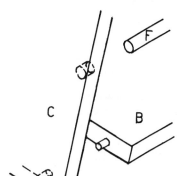
detail 1

List of Materials

PART	NO.	FUNCTION	DIMENSION IN INCHES thickness × width × length		
A	1	top	¾	9	40
B	1	bottom	¾	6⅛	38½
C	2	sides	¾	9	12¼
D	1	partition	¾	8½	11½
E	1	back	½	12¼	39¼
F	3	dowels	½ (diam.)		39½

Instructions for Assembly

1. Insert dowels (F) in partition (D).
2. Join partition (D) to top (A), bottom (B) and sides (C).
3. Attach back (E) to (A, B, C).
4. Apply finish.

Shelves

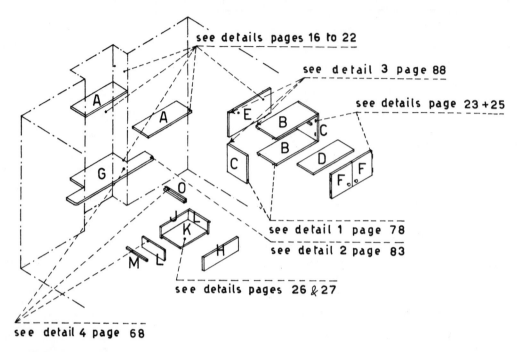

see details pages 16 to 22

see detail 3 page 88

see details page 23 + 25

see detail 1 page 78

see detail 2 page 83

see details pages 26 & 27

see detail 4 page 68

This design makes full use of a wall recess, and the work surface is made more generous with extensions to right and left.

List of Materials

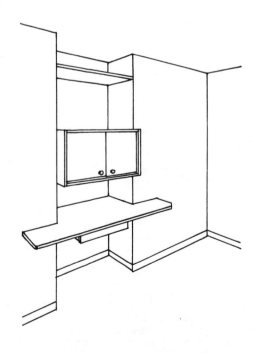

PART	NO.	FUNCTION	DIMENSIONS IN INCHES thickness × width × length		
			thickness	width	length
A	2	shelf	¾	d	w
B	2	top, bottom	¾	15	$w - 1½$
C	2	side	¾	15	18
D	1	shelf	¾	13½	$w - 1½$
E	1	back	¼	17½	$w - ½$
F	2	door	¾	16½	to fit
G	1	shelf	¾	$d + 8$	60
H	1	drawer front	¾	4	24
J	1	drawer back	⅜	3½	22½
K	1	drawer bottom	¼	22⅞	15½
L	2	drawer side	⅜	4	15½
M	2	cleat	⅜	½	15½
O	2	glide	1	1	15½

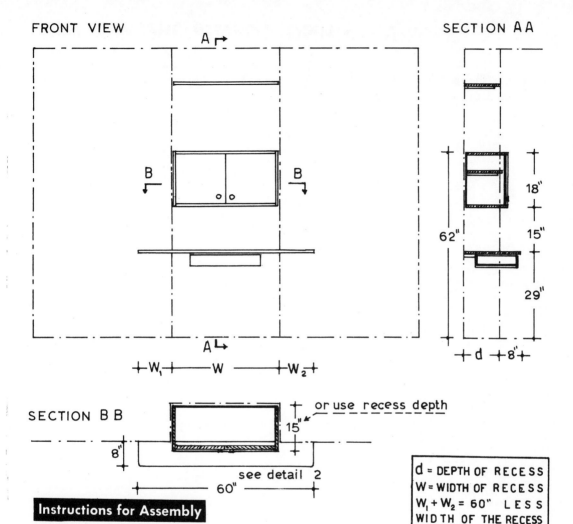

FRONT VIEW

SECTION AA

A

B B

62"

18"

15"

29"

+ d + 8" +

+ W₁ + —— W —— + W₂ +

SECTION B B

or use recess depth

15"

8"

see detail 2

60"

Instructions for Assembly

d = DEPTH OF RECESS
W = WIDTH OF RECESS
W₁ + W₂ = 60" LESS
WIDTH OF THE RECESS

1. Join top and bottom of cabinet (B) with sides (C) and back (E).
2. Install doors (F) and shelf (D).
3. Join front of drawer (H) with back (J) and sides (L).
4. Join bottom of drawer (K) to front (H) and sides (L), and attach glides (M) to sides of drawer (L).
5. Attach track (O) to under side of desk surface (G).
6. Apply finish and set pieces, cabinet shelves, and desk in place.

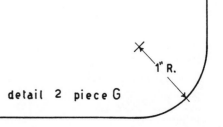

1" R.

detail 2 piece G

Desk and Bookshelves for Wall Recess

83

These corner shelves are designed to fill an entire corner from floor to ceiling.

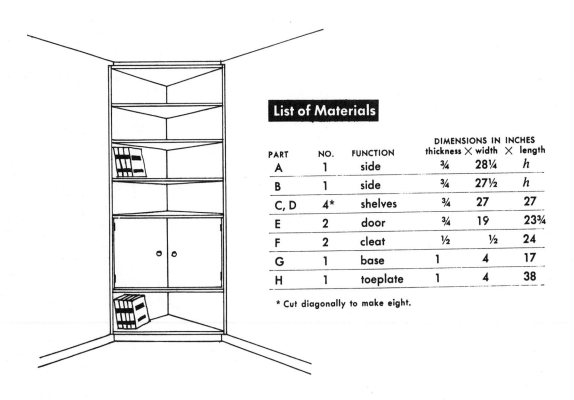

List of Materials

PART	NO.	FUNCTION	DIMENSIONS IN INCHES thickness × width × length		
			thickness	width	length
A	1	side	¾	28¼	h
B	1	side	¾	27½	h
C, D	4*	shelves	¾	27	27
E	2	door	¾	19	23¾
F	2	cleat	½	½	24
G	1	base	1	4	17
H	1	toeplate	1	4	38

* Cut diagonally to make eight.

Instructions for Assembly

1. Attach shelves (C) to side pieces (A) and (B).
2. Attach cleat (F) to side pieces (A) and (B).
3. Attach brace (G) to toeplate (H), and fasten combined (G) and (H) to bottom shelf (C).
4. Fasten doors (E) to side pieces (A) and (B).
5. Apply finish and set cabinet in place.
6. Insert interior shelf (D).

detail 4

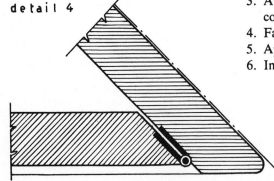

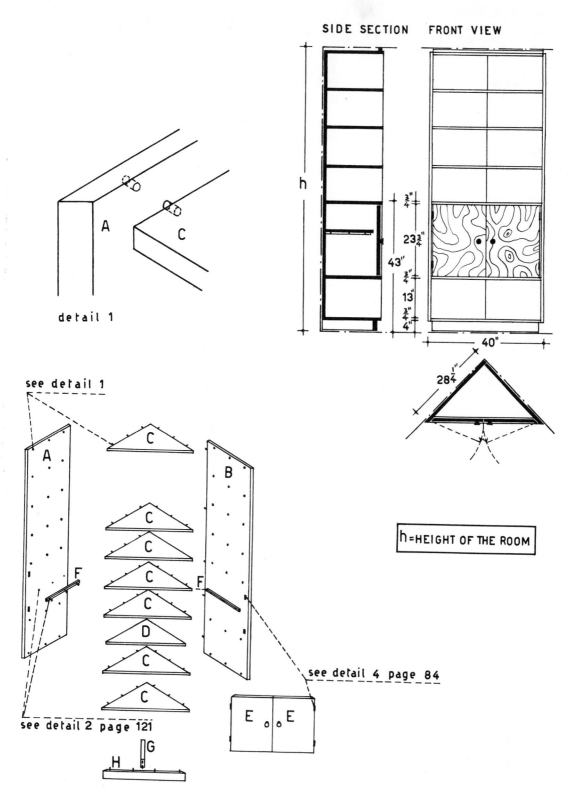

SIDE SECTION   FRONT VIEW

detail 1

h

$\frac{3}{4}$"
$23\frac{3}{4}$"
43"
$\frac{3}{4}$"
13"
$\frac{3}{4}$"
$\frac{3}{4}$"

40"

$28\frac{1}{4}$"

h=HEIGHT OF THE ROOM

A   C

see detail 1

A   C   B

C
C
C
C
D
C
C
F   F

see detail 4 page 84

E o o E

see detail 2 page 121

G
H

Floor-to-Ceiling Corner Shelves

25 | CABINETS AND COUNTER FOR DINING ROOM

The frame provides support for the cabinets and a counter surface that may be used as either a shelf or a serving aid.

List of Materials

PART	NO.	FUNCTION	DIMENSIONS IN INCHES thickness × width × length		
A	1	counter	1	12	w
B	2	sides	1	12	h
C	2	top	¾	15	60
D	2	bottom	¾	15	58½
E	2	end	¾	15	17¼
F	2	shelf	¾	13	58½
G	1	back	¼	17½	59½
H	1	door	¾	16¼	29¼
J	1	door	¾	16¼	30
K	2	end	¾	15	21¼
L	1	back	¼	21½	59½
M	1	door	¾	20¼	29¼
O	1	door	¾	20¼	30

Instructions for Assembly

Upper Cabinet
1. Join end pieces (E), top (C) and bottom (D).
2. Attach back (G).

Lower Cabinet
3. Join end pieces (K) with top (C) and bottom (D).
4. Attach back (L).
5. Apply finish.

Combined Pieces
6. Attach counter (A) and sides (B) to wall and install cabinets.
7. Install shelves (F) and doors (H), (J), (M), and (O).

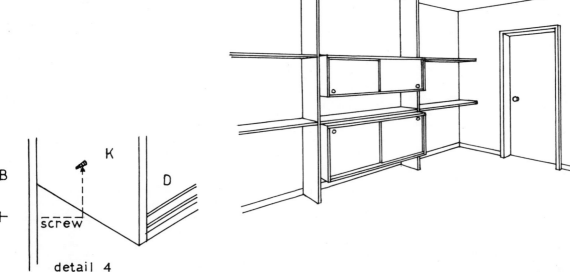

detail 4

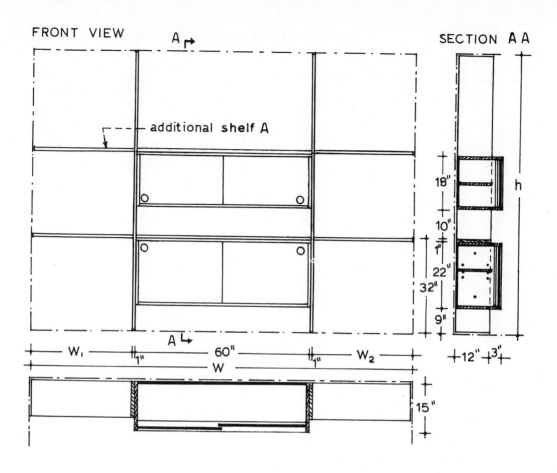

FRONT VIEW

SECTION A A

additional shelf A

18"
10"
1"
22"
32"
9"
h

W₁ 60" W₂
1" 1"
W

15"

12" 3"

h = HEIGHT OF THE ROOM
W = WIDTH OF THE ROOM
W₁ + W₂ = WIDTH OF ROOM
LESS 62"

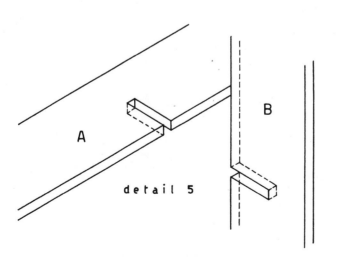

A

B

detail 5

Cabinets and Counter for Dining Room

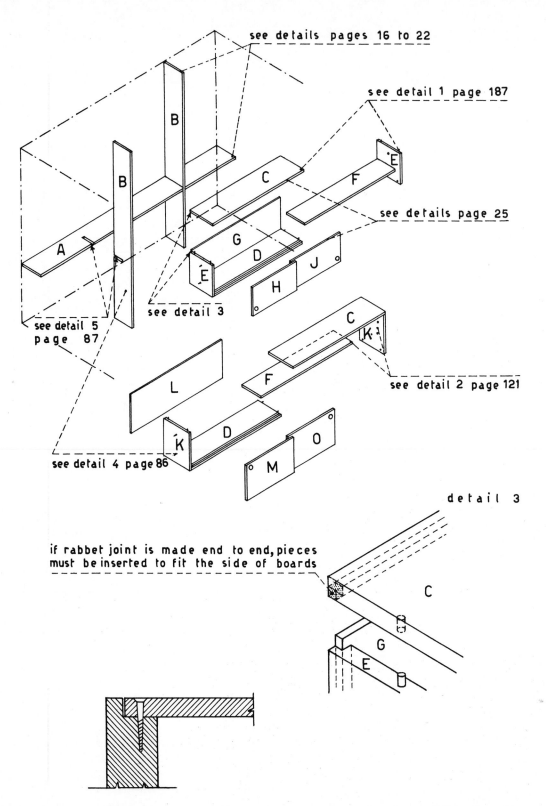

see details pages 16 to 22

see detail 1 page 187

B

B

see details page 25

C

F

E

A

G

D

J

H

E

see detail 3

see detail 5
page 87

C

K

F

see detail 2 page 121

L

D

K

O

M

see detail 4 page 86

detail 3

if rabbet joint is made end to end, pieces
must be inserted to fit the side of boards

C

G

E

Cabinets and Counter for Dining Room

This series of wall cabinets contains both drawer and shelf units.

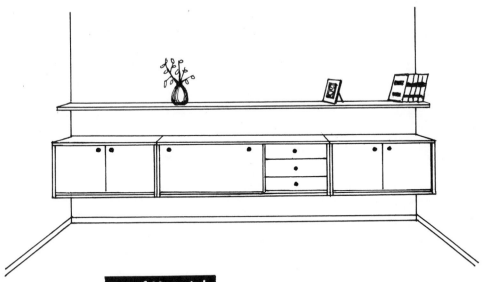

← see detail 3

List of Materials

PART	NO.	FUNCTION	DIMENSIONS IN INCHES thicknes	× width	× length
A	1	shelf	1	12	w
B	2	top	¾	15	w_1
C	2	bottom	¾	15	$w_1 - 1½$
D	6	side	¾	15	17¼
E	2	back	¼	17½	$w_1 - ½$
F	2	shelf	¾	13	$w_1 - 1½$
G	4	door	¾	16½	to fit
H	1	top	¾	15	60
J	1	bottom	¾	15	58½
K	1	back	¼	17½	59½
L	1	drop door	¾	16½	35¾
M	1	partition	¾	14¾	16½
O	1	partition	¾	13½	16½
P	2	shelf	¾	13½	21
Q	6	cleat	¼	½	14¼
R	3	drawer front	¾	5½	22
S	6	drawer side	⅜	5½	14⅜
T	3	drawer back	⅜	5	21⅛
V	3	drawer bottom	¼	21½	14¼

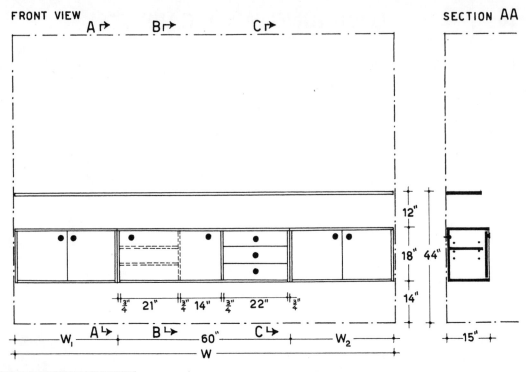

FRONT VIEW

SECTION AA

W = WIDTH OF THE ROOM
W₁ + W₂ = WIDTH OF ROOM
LESS 60"

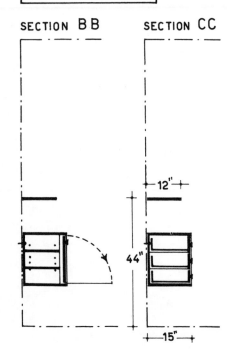

SECTION BB

SECTION CC

Instructions for Assembly

Side Cabinets
1. Join top (B) and bottom (C) with sides (D) and back (E).
2. Attach doors (G).

Center Cabinet
3. Join top (H) and bottom (J) with sides (D) and partitions (O) and (M).
4. Attach back (K).
5. Join sides of drawer (S) with front (R) and back (T), and bottom of drawer (U) with sides (S) and front (R).
6. Attach drop door (L) with bottom of cabinet (J), and fix cleat (Q) to partition (M) and sides (D).
7. Apply finish and set cabinets in place.
8. Insert shelves (F) and (P) and install drawers.
9. Install shelf (A).

Low-hung Wall Cabinets

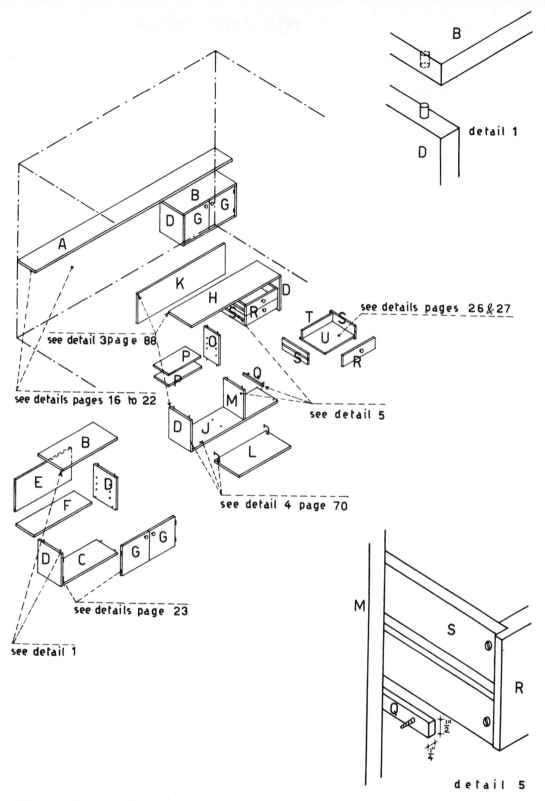

B

detail 1

D

B
D G G

A

K
H D
see details pages 26&27
R
T S
S
U
R

see detail 3 page 88

O

P
P

Q

M

see detail 5

see details pages 16 to 22

D J

D

L

see detail 4 page 70

B

E D

F

D C G G

see details page 23

see detail 1

M

S

R

Q

detail 5

Low-hung Wall Cabinets   91

This cover is easily constructed to fit any radiator. The inner surfaces should be primed or painted to protect the wood from warpage.

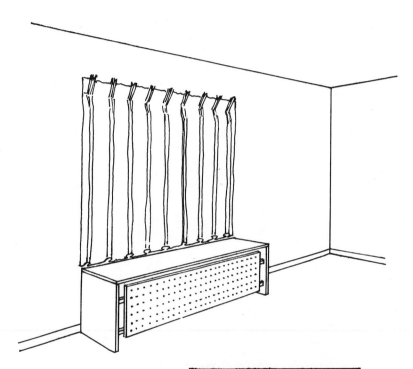

Instructions for Assembly

1. Join sides (B) with top (A) and rails (C).
2. Apply finish and set cover in place.
3. Attach front (D) to rails (C).

VARIATION IN SIZE

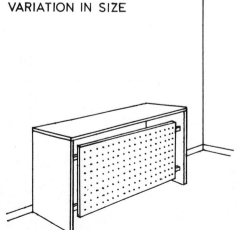

List of Materials

PART	NO.	FUNCTION	DIMENSIONS IN INCHES thickness × width × length		
A	1	top	¾	d	w
B	2	side	¾	d	$h - ¾$
C	2	rail	1	2	$w - 1½$
D	1	front*	⅛	$h - 3¼$	$w - 4$

* Perforated hardboard.

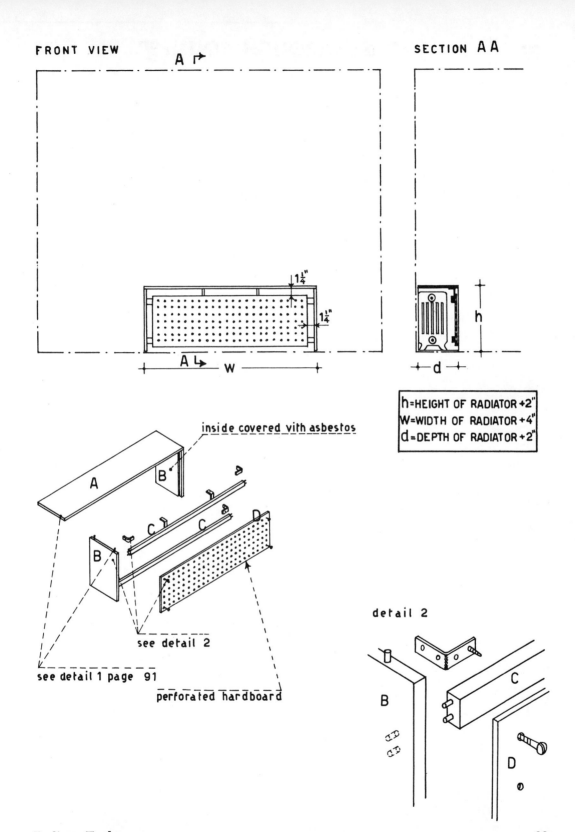

FRONT VIEW

A ↱

SECTION AA

$1\frac{1}{4}$"

$1\frac{1}{4}$"

A ↳ W

d

h

| h=HEIGHT OF RADIATOR +2" |
| W=WIDTH OF RADIATOR +4" |
| d=DEPTH OF RADIATOR +2" |

inside covered with asbestos

A

B

B

C

C

D

see detail 2

see detail 1 page 91

perforated hardboard

detail 2

B

C

D

PASS-THROUGH COUNTER

An opening of this sort can save many steps between kitchen and dining area. It can be painted to match woodwork in each room.

List of Materials

PART	NO.	FUNCTION	thickness	×	DIMENSIONS IN INCHES width	×	length
A	3	molding	½		1¼		29½
B	4	molding	½		1¼		16
C	2	side	¾		16¾		d
D	1	top	¾		28½		d
E	1	bottom	¾		39		d + 12½
F	2	sliding door	¼		16½		14

Instructions for Assembly

1. Join sides (C), top (D), and bottom (E).
2. Insert frame in wall.
3. Attach molding (A) and (B) to frame (C) and (D).
4. Apply finish and install sliding doors (F).

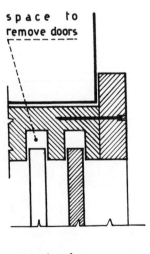

space to remove doors

detail 1

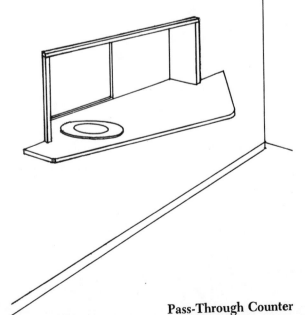

FRONT VIEW

SIDE SECTION

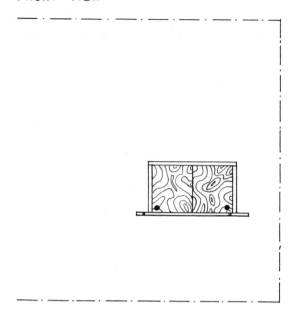

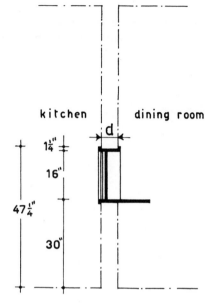

kitchen   dining room

d

$1\frac{1}{4}$"

16"

$47\frac{1}{4}$"

30"

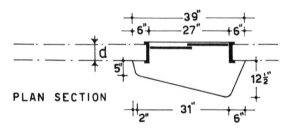

39"
6" | 27" | 6"

d

5"

$12\frac{1}{2}$"

PLAN SECTION

2" | 31" | 6"

d = THICKNESS OF WALL

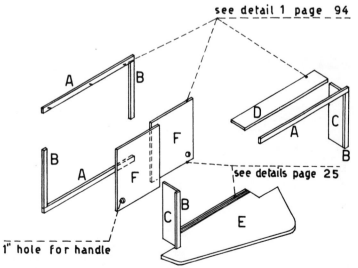

see detail 1 page 94

A   B

D
A   C
B

B
A

F
F

F

see details page 25

C   B

C

E

1" hole for handle

Pass-Through Counter

95

29 | PASS-THROUGH WINDOW

This simple window, with a sliding plate glass panel, is easily constructed and installed. It offers a solution for many office arrangement problems.

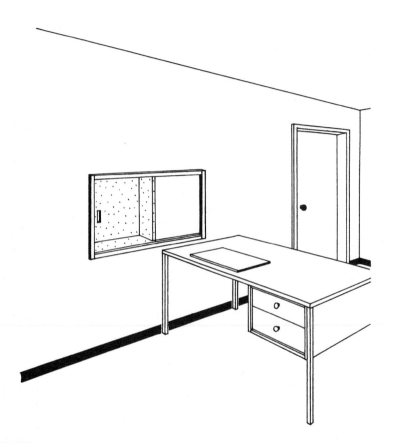

List of Materials

PART	NO.	FUNCTION	DIMENSIONS IN INCHES thickness × width × length		
A	2	frame	¾	13½	d
B	2	frame	¾	16½	d
C	1	glass*	¼	12¾	17
D	4	molding	¾	1¼	19
E	2	molding	¾	1¼	12
F	2	molding	¾	1¼	24¾

* Plate glass with pull.

Instructions for Assembly

1. Join top and bottom of frame (A) with sides (B).
2. Attach molding (D), (E), to one side of frame (A-B).
3. Insert frame in wall.
4. Attach molding (F) to top of frame (A) and wall.
5. Attach molding (D) to sides of frame (B) and wall.
6. Apply finish and insert plate glass.

FRONT VIEW

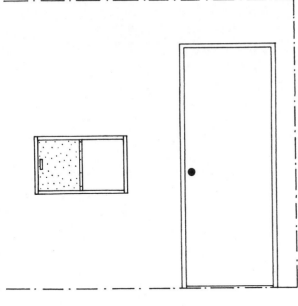

SIDE SECTION

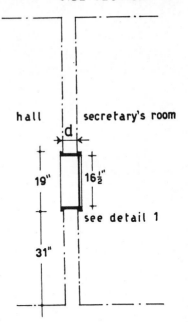

hall   secretary's room

d

19"   16½"

see detail 1

31"

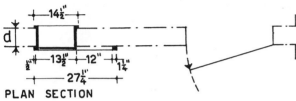

14½"

d

½"   13½"   12"   1¼"

27¼"

PLAN SECTION

d =THICKNESS OF WALL

detail 1

space to
remove door

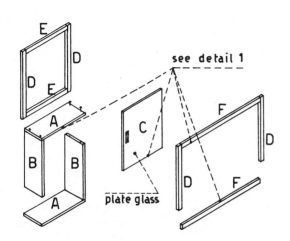

E
D
D   E
A
B   B
A

see detail 1

C

F
D
D
F

plate glass

Pass-Through Window

A telephone shelf makes it possible for one instrument to be used in either of two rooms. This arrangement may be a convenience in either home or office.

List of Materials

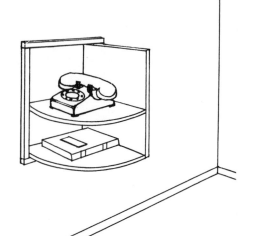

PART	NO.	FUNCTION	thickness	× width	× length
A	2	frame	¾	18½	d
B	2	frame	¾	20	d
C	1	side	¾	16¼	20
D	1	side	¾	17	20
E	2	shelf	¾	16¼	16¼
F	4	molding	½	1¼	19½
G	4	molding	½	1¼	22½

DIMENSIONS IN INCHES

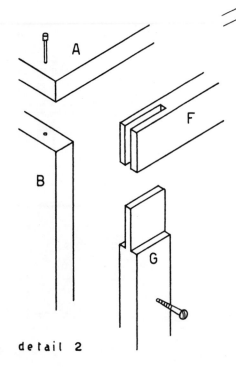

detail 2

Instructions for Assembly

1. Join top and bottom of frame (A) with sides (B).
2. Attach molding (F) and (G) to one side of frame (A) and (B). (*Note:* molding can also be made with miter joints.)
3. Insert frame in wall opening and attach molding (F) and (G) to other side of frame (A) and (B).
4. Attach shelves (E) to side pieces (C) and (D).
5. Attach side (D) to side of frame (B).
6. Apply finish.

FRONT VIEW

SIDE VIEW

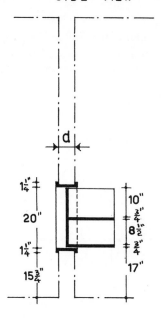

d

$1\frac{1}{4}"$
$20"$
$1\frac{1}{4}"$
$15\frac{3}{4}"$

$10"$
$\frac{3}{4}"$
$8\frac{1}{2}"$
$\frac{3}{4}"$
$17"$

$1\frac{1}{4}"$ 17" $1\frac{1}{4}"$

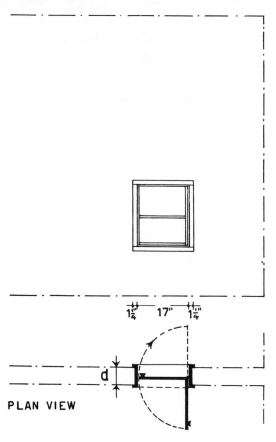

d

PLAN VIEW

d = THICKNESS OF WALL

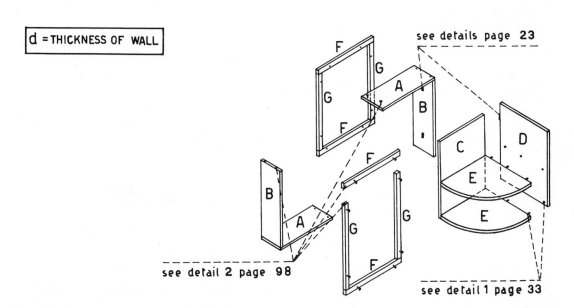

see details page 23

see detail 2 page 98

see detail 1 page 33

Telephone Shelf

WALL BENCH

A board attached to the wall at the proper height makes a good bench for plants or a shelf for books. One end can be used for extra seating; two rails attached to the wall make a simple back rest.

List of Materials

PART	NO.	FUNCTION	DIMENSIONS IN INCHES		
			thickness ×	width ×	length
A	2	back rest	¾	3	48
B	1	top	1	22	w
C	2	leg	1¾ (round)		18

Instructions for Assembly

1. Attach legs (C) to top (B).
2. Apply finish.
3. Attach supports to wall and set bench in place.
4. Fasten back rest rails (A) to wall.

FRONT VIEW

SIDE

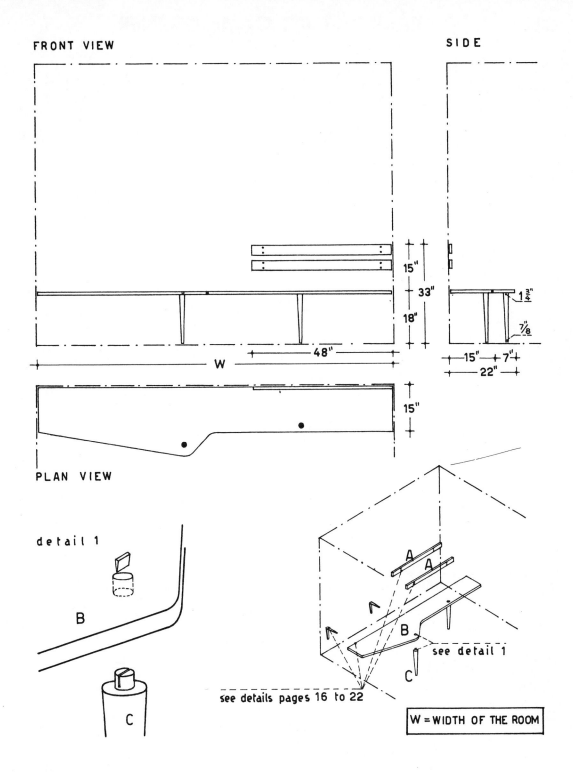

15"

33"

18"

48"

W

1¾"

⅞"

15" 7"

22"

15"

PLAN VIEW

detail 1

B

C

A

A

B

C

see detail 1

see details pages 16 to 22

W = WIDTH OF THE ROOM

This group can be built for use in kitchen, living room, or game room. Choice of finish and upholstery material will depend on intended use.

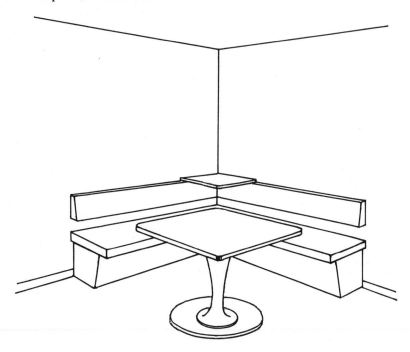

List of Materials

detail 3

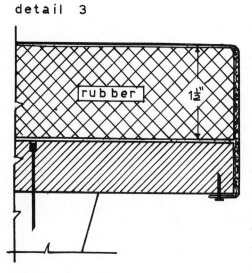

rubber

1½"

PART	NO.	FUNCTION	DIMENSIONS IN INCHES		
			thickness ×	width ×	length
A	1	back	¾	9	56
B	1	back	¾	9	55¼
C	1	seat	¾	17	39
D	1	seat	¾	17	56
E	2	support	¾	13	14½
F	1	support	¾	15¼	54
G	1	support	¾	15¼	45
H	1	corner shelf	¾	17	17
J	1	table top	¾	31	31
K	4	molding	½	1½	32
L	1	support	¾	16 (diam.)	
M	1	column	10 (diam.)		25½
N	1	base	1	25 (diam.)	

FRONT VIEW

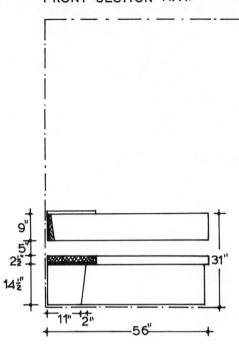

28"

├─17"─┼─7"─┼──32"──┤

FRONT SECTION A.A.

9"
5"
2½"
14½"

31"

├─11"─┼2"┤
├────────56"────────┤

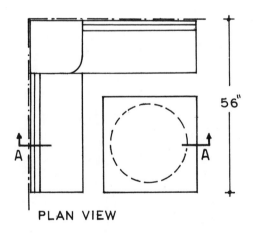

56"

A ──►   ◄── A

PLAN VIEW

detail 4

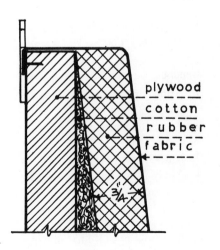

plywood
cotton
rubber
fabric

¾"

Breakfast or Game Corner

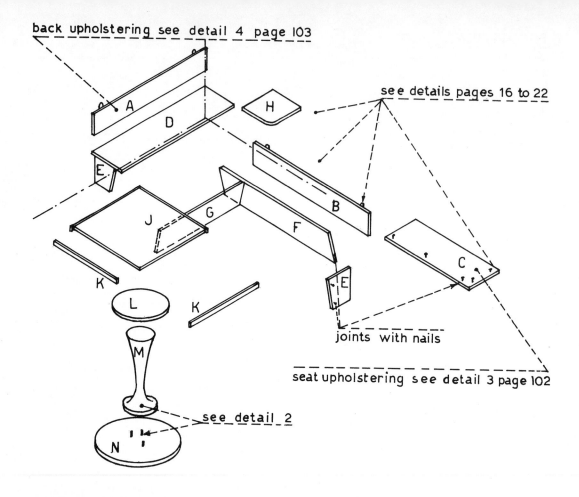

back upholstering see detail 4 page 103

A

D

H

see details pages 16 to 22

E

J G

K

B

F

E

C

joints with nails

L

K

K

M

seat upholstering see detail 3 page 102

see detail 2

N

Instructions for Assembly

Foam rubber and fabric must be cut to fit seats
(C) and (D), and backs (A) and (B).

Benches:

1. Apply upholstery to pieces (A) and (B) and
   seats (C) and (D).
2. Attach end supports (E) to front supports (F)
   and (G).
3. Join (F) and (G).
4. Apply finish and set bench frame, seat, corner
   and back in place.
5. Attach column (M) to support (L) and base
   (N).
6. Join moldings (K) to table top (J).
7. Attach combined legs support to table top (K).
8. Apply finish.

detail 2

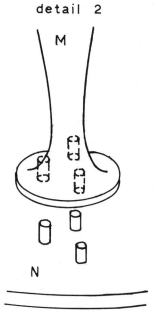

M

N

Breakfast or Game Corner

33

TABLE BAR

It is the pride of every woman to have an elegant-looking bar in the home. The husband can build one very easily and save money.

List of Materials

PART	NO.	FUNCTION	DIMENSION IN INCHES		
			thickness ×	width ×	length
A	1	top	½	8½	23½
B	1	bottom	½	8½	22½
C	2	sides	½	8½	16
D	1	back	¼	15½	23
E	4	tops and bottoms	½	3	11¾
F	4	sides	½	3	16
G.	2	doors	½	12	16½
H	4	shelves	⅜	3	10¾
J	4	strips	⅜	1	10¾
K	1	toe plate	2	2	23½
L	2	toe plates	1	2	10

Instructions for Assembly

1. Join sides (C) with top and bottom (A, B) and attach back (D).
2. Fasten toe plate (K) with (L) and attach base to bottom (B).
3. Join (E) with (F), attach doors (G) and install shelves (H) and strips (J).
4. Fasten sides (F) to sides (C) with hinges.
5. Apply finish.

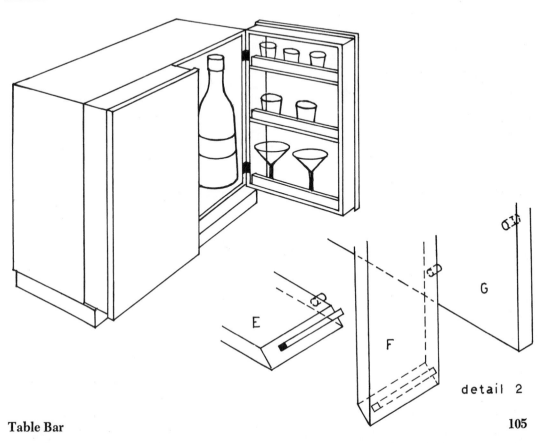

detail 2

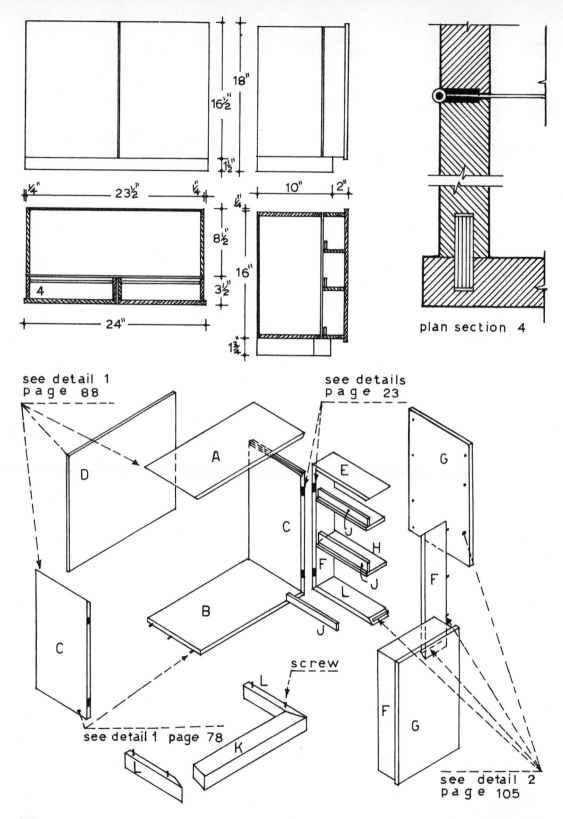

18"

16½"

1½"

¼" 23½" ¼"

8½"

4

3½"

24"

10" 2"

¼"

16"

1¾"

plan section 4

see detail 1
page 88

see details
page 23

D

A

E

G

C

J

H

C

F

J

B

L

J

F

F

G

screw

L

see detail 1 page 78

K

L

see detail 2
page 105

Table Bar

34

BAR AND BOOKSHELVES

This unit can be used as a room divider between living and dining areas.

List of Materials

PART	NO.	FUNCTION	thickness	×	width	×	length
A	2	side	¾		15		h
B	6	shelf	¾		15		46½
C	2	back, drop door	¾		17¼		46½
D	1	back	¾		23½		46½
E	3	shelf	¾		13		46½
F	2	toeplate	1		4		46½
G	6	cleat	½		½		12½
H	2	door	¾		23¼		23½

DIMENSIONS IN INCHES

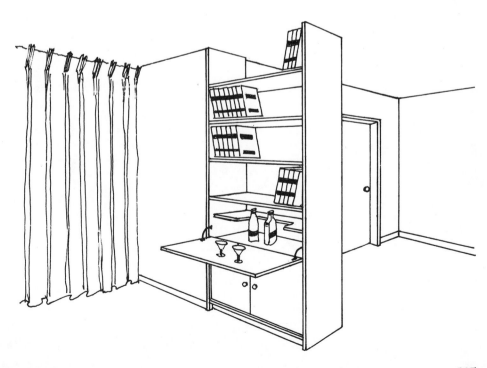

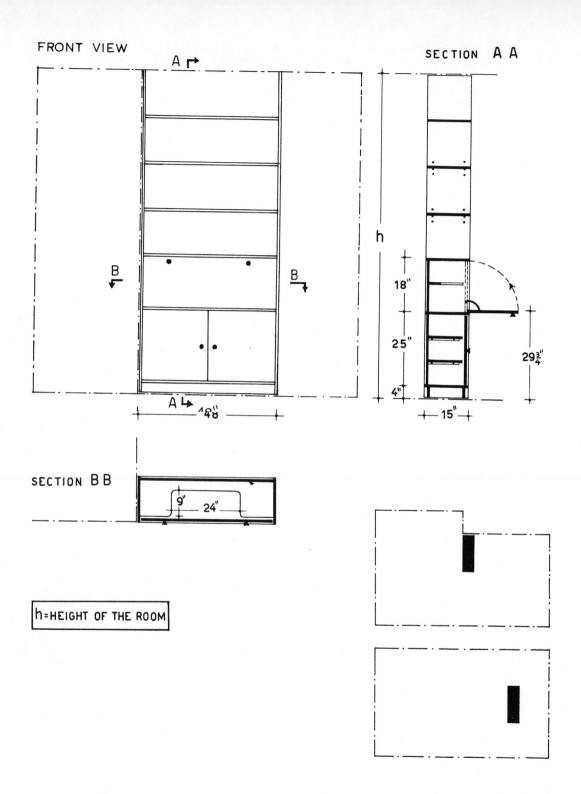

FRONT VIEW

SECTION A A

h

18"

25"

4"

$29\frac{3}{4}$"

15"

48"

SECTION BB

9" 24"

h=HEIGHT OF THE ROOM

bar can be placed in various positions in the room

Bar and Bookshelves

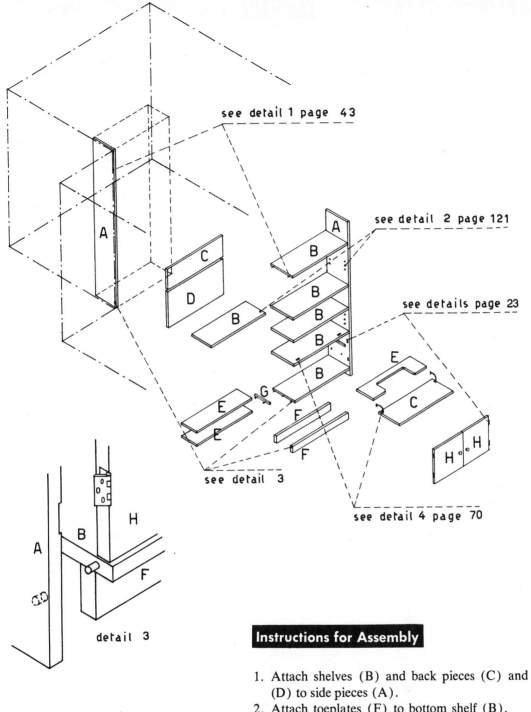

see detail 1 page 43

see detail 2 page 121

see details page 23

see detail 3

see detail 4 page 70

detail 3

Instructions for Assembly

1. Attach shelves (B) and back pieces (C) and (D) to side pieces (A).
2. Attach toeplates (F) to bottom shelf (B).
3. Attach cleats (G) to side pieces (A).
4. Install doors (H) and drop door (C).
5. Apply finish and set pieces in place.
6. Install shelves (B) and (E).

Bar and Bookshelves

35

SERVICE BAR

This bar, intended for the home recreation room, is complete with swinging door. Stools, of course, are not built-in. A surfacing material can be applied to the table top, as shown on page 225.

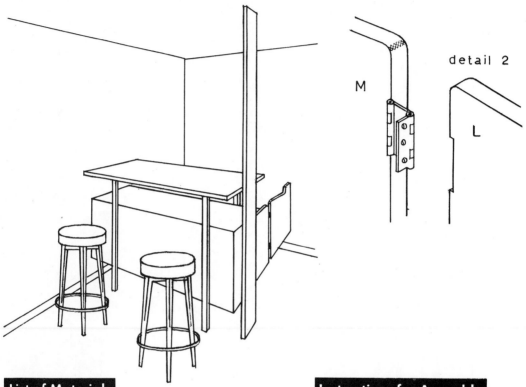

detail 2

M

L

List of Materials

| PART | NO. | FUNCTION | DIMENSIONS IN INCHES |||
			thickness ×	width ×	length
A	1	table top	¾	24	60
B	2	top, bottom	¾	17¼	60
C	2	side	¾	17¼	22½
D	1	back	¾	60	24
E	1	shelf	¾	15	58½
F	1	door	¾	30	22¼
G	1	door	¾	29¼	22¼
H	4	framing piece	1	1¾	41¼
J	2	framing piece	1	1¾	18
K	1	stanchion	1	12	*h*
L	1	partition	¾	11	24
M	1	door	¾	21	24

Instructions for Assembly

1. Join sides (C) and back (D) of cabinet with top and bottom pieces (B).
2. Join framing pieces (H) with framing pieces (J), top and bottom of cabinet (B), and front of cabinet (D).
3. Attach top of bar (A) to framing pieces (J).
4. Install shelf (E) and doors (F) and (G).
5. Set bar in place.
6. Attach partition (L) to stanchion (K) and combined (K-L) to side of cabinet (C) and top of bar (A).
7. Install swinging door (M).

FRONT VIEW   A →

SECTION A A

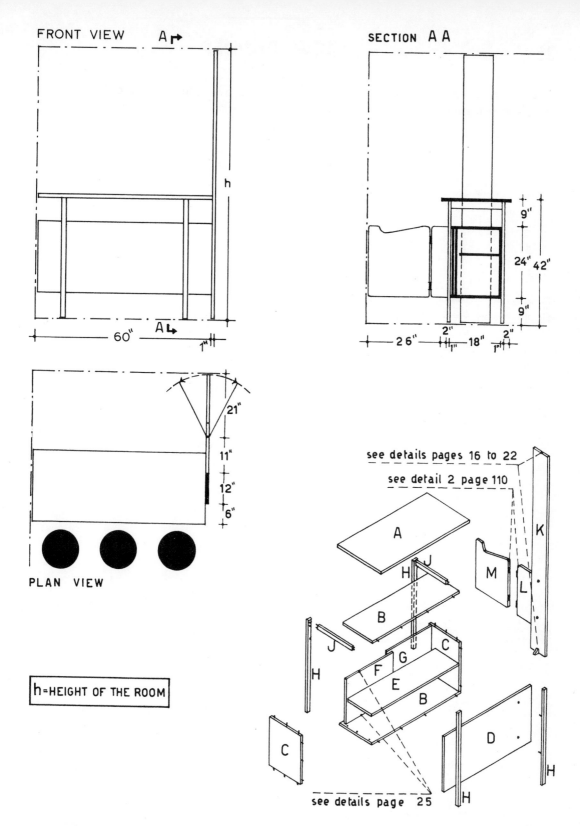

h = HEIGHT OF THE ROOM

PLAN VIEW

see details pages 16 to 22

see detail 2 page 110

see details page 25

Service Bar

This divider is composed of two plywood panels attached to the solid wood frame of a bookcase. The partition is removable.

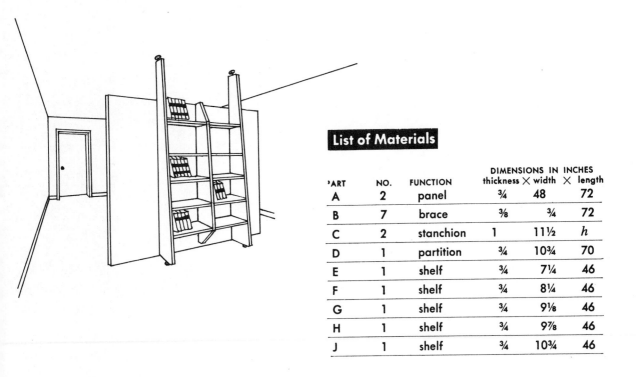

List of Materials

PART	NO.	FUNCTION	DIMENSIONS IN INCHES thickness × width × length		
A	2	panel	¾	48	72
B	7	brace	⅜	¾	72
C	2	stanchion	1	11½	*h*
D	1	partition	¾	10¾	70
E	1	shelf	¾	7¼	46
F	1	shelf	¾	8¼	46
G	1	shelf	¾	9⅛	46
H	1	shelf	¾	9⅞	46
J	1	shelf	¾	10¾	46

Instructions for Assembly

1. Join sides (C) with shelves (E), (F), (G), (H), and (J).
2. Insert partition (D).
3. Join panel (A) with stanchions (C) and partition (D).
4. Attach braces (B) with panel (A).
5. Apply finish and set divider in place.

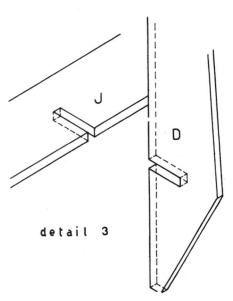

detail 3

FRONT VIEW

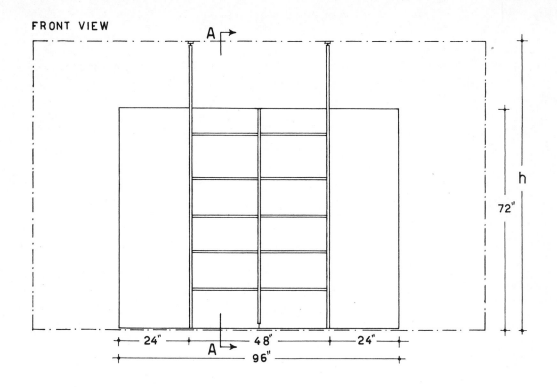

A →

h

72"

← 24" →|← 48" →|← 24" →
A →
96"

SIDE

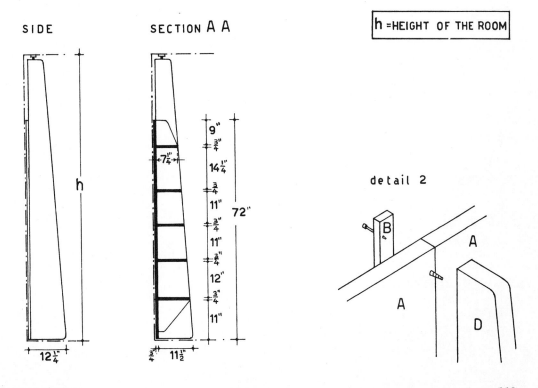

SECTION A A

h = HEIGHT OF THE ROOM

9"
¾"
14¼"
←7¼"→
¾"
11"
¾"
11"
¾"
12"
¾"
11"

72"

h

12¼"

¾" 11½"

detail 2

B

A

A

D

Room Divider

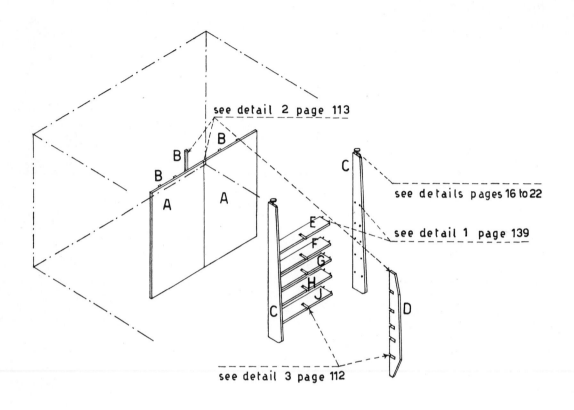

see detail 2 page 113

B B B B A A

C

see details pages 16 to 22

see detail 1 page 139

E F G H J

C

D

see detail 3 page 112

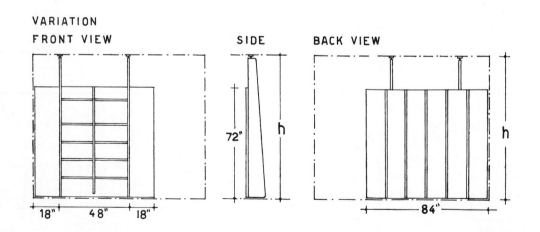

VARIATION
FRONT VIEW

SIDE

BACK VIEW

72"

h

18" 48" 18"

84"

h

Room Divider

This simple partition is designed for setting off a dining area from the living room, but it could find uses in any part of the house where a visual separation is desired without loss of ventilation.

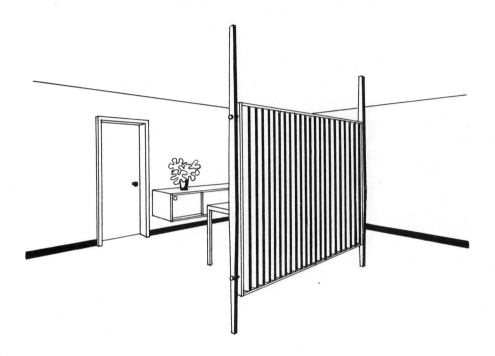

VARIATION

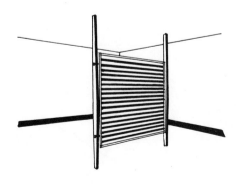

List of Materials

PART	NO.	FUNCTION	DIMENSIONS IN INCHES		
			thickness × width	×	length
A	2	stanchion	1	3	h
B	2	rail	1	2	69
C	2	frame	1	2	60
D	25	louver fin	½	3¼	58
	4	bolts, cap nuts ¼ (round)			3¼

FRONT VIEW   SIDE

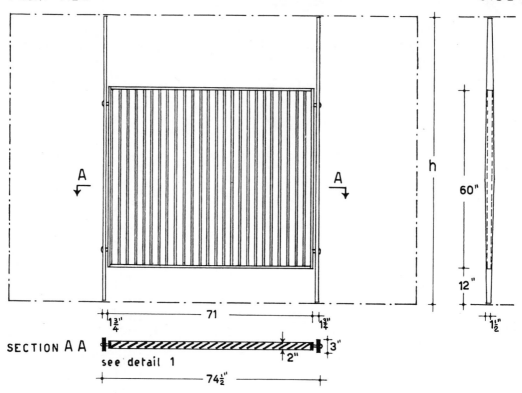

A   A

SECTION A A   3"
see detail 1   2"

$1\frac{3}{4}$"   71 $1\frac{3}{4}$" $1\frac{1}{2}$"

$74\frac{1}{2}$"

h

60"

12"

h = HEIGHT OF THE ROOM

detail 1

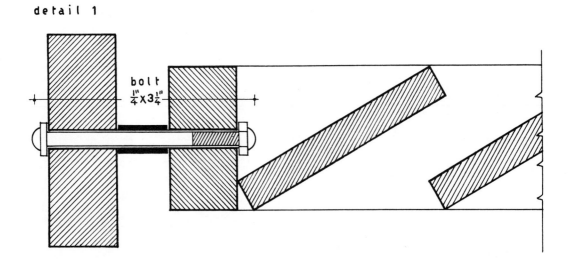

bolt
$\frac{1}{4}$" x $3\frac{1}{4}$"

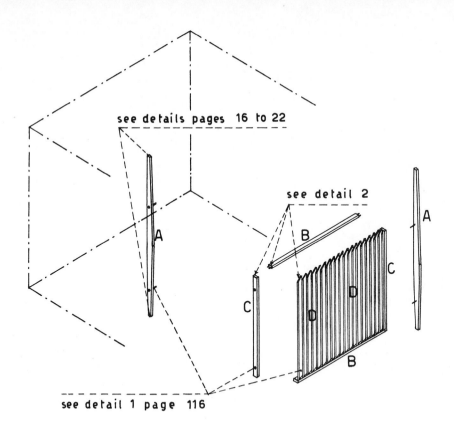

see details pages 16 to 22

see detail 2

B

A

C

C

D

D

A

B

see detail 1 page 116

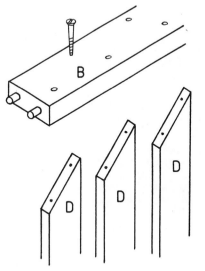

detail 2

B

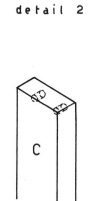

C

D

D

D

Instructions for Assembly

1. Attach louver fins (D) to rails (B).
2. Attach sides of frame (C) to top and bottom (B).
3. Bolt stanchion (A) to side of frame (C).
4. Apply finish and set partition in position.

Louver Partition

117

To make a room more attractive, the walls can be covered—partially or totally—with plywood panels.

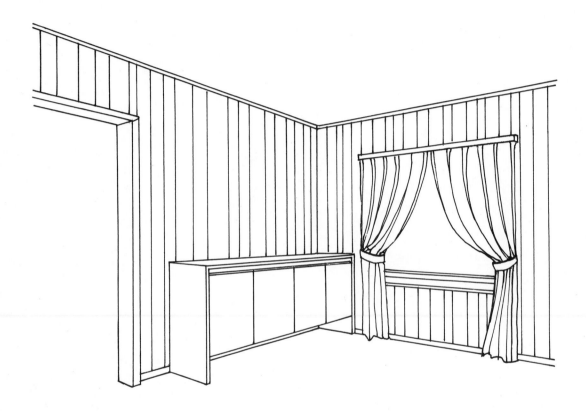

List of Materials

PART	FUNCTION	DIMENSIONS IN INCHES		
		thickness ×	width ×	length
A	panel	3/16	48	96
B	strip	3/4	1½	as required
C	molding	½	½	as required
D	toeplate	½	3	as required
E	molding	½	1½	as required
F	door sill	½	width and length as required	

Instructions for Assembly

1. Fasten strip (B) to wall with nails.
2. Attach plywood panels (A) to strip (B).
3. Apply door sill (F) and molding (E) to wall and panels (A).
4. Attach molding (C) and toeplate (D) to panels (A) with brads.
5. Apply finish.

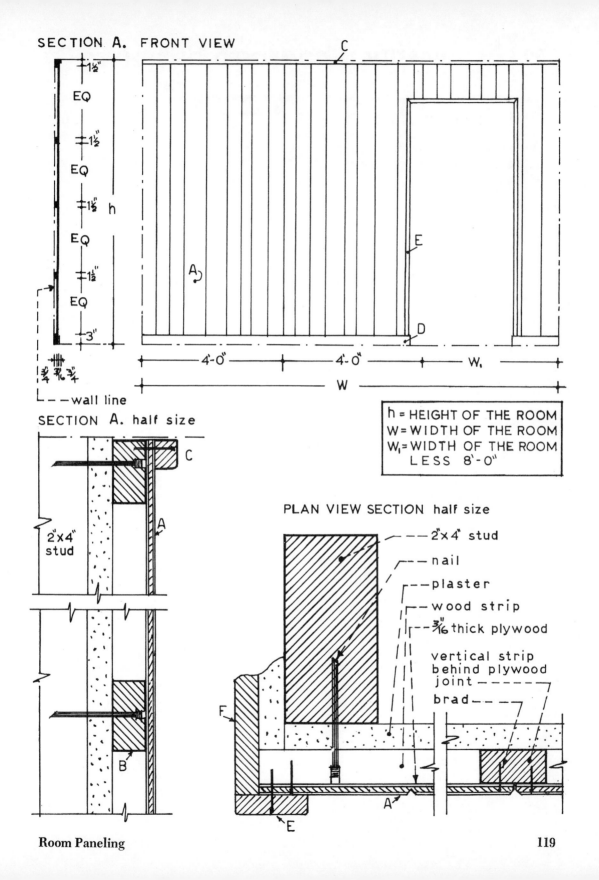

SECTION A. FRONT VIEW

$1\frac{1}{2}"$

EQ

$1\frac{1}{2}"$

EQ

$1\frac{1}{2}"$

EQ

$1\frac{1}{2}"$

EQ

3"

h

C

E

A

D

$\frac{3}{4}"$ $\frac{3}{16}"$ $\frac{3}{4}"$

wall line

4'-0"   4'-0"   W₁

W

SECTION A. half size

2"x4"
stud

C

A

B

h = HEIGHT OF THE ROOM
W = WIDTH OF THE ROOM
W₁ = WIDTH OF THE ROOM
       LESS 8'-0"

PLAN VIEW SECTION half size

2"x4" stud

nail

plaster

wood strip

$\frac{3}{16}"$ thick plywood

vertical strip
behind plywood
joint

brad

F

E

A

Room Paneling

This partition is a combination of four independent bookcase elements, two opening into each room. Other arrangements may be made of these same elements, as for example a floor-to-ceiling wall bookcase.

PART	NO.	FUNCTION	DIMENSIONS IN INCHES thickness × width × length		
A	8	top, bottom	$\frac{3}{4}$	12	$28\frac{1}{2}$
B	4	side	$\frac{3}{4}$	12	h_1
C	2	back	$\frac{1}{2}$	$28\frac{1}{2}$	$h_1 - 2\frac{1}{2}$
D	10	shelf	$\frac{3}{4}$	$11\frac{3}{8}$	$28\frac{1}{2}$
E	4	side	$\frac{3}{4}$	12	72
F	2	back	$\frac{1}{2}$	$28\frac{1}{2}$	68
G	2	shelf	$\frac{3}{4}$	10	$28\frac{1}{2}$
H	4	door	$\frac{3}{4}$	$14\frac{1}{4}$	18
J	4	toeplate	1	$2\frac{1}{2}$	$28\frac{1}{2}$

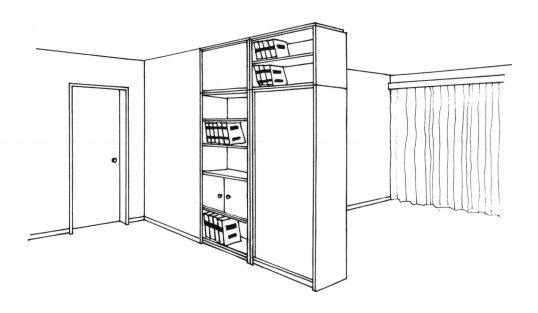

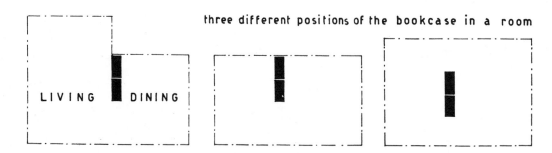

three different positions of the bookcase in a room

LIVING | DINING

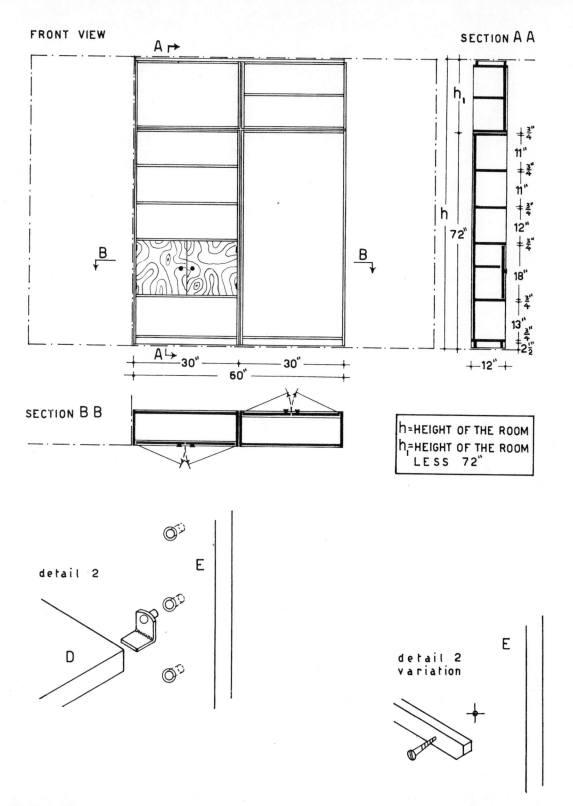

FRONT VIEW

SECTION A A

A

h_1

h
72"

A

B

B

¾"
11"
¾"
11"
¾"
12"
¾"
18"
¾"
13"
¾"
2½"

30" ———— 30"

60"

12"

SECTION B B

h=HEIGHT OF THE ROOM
h_1=HEIGHT OF THE ROOM
LESS 72"

detail 2

E

D

detail 2
variation

E

Partition Composed of Shelves

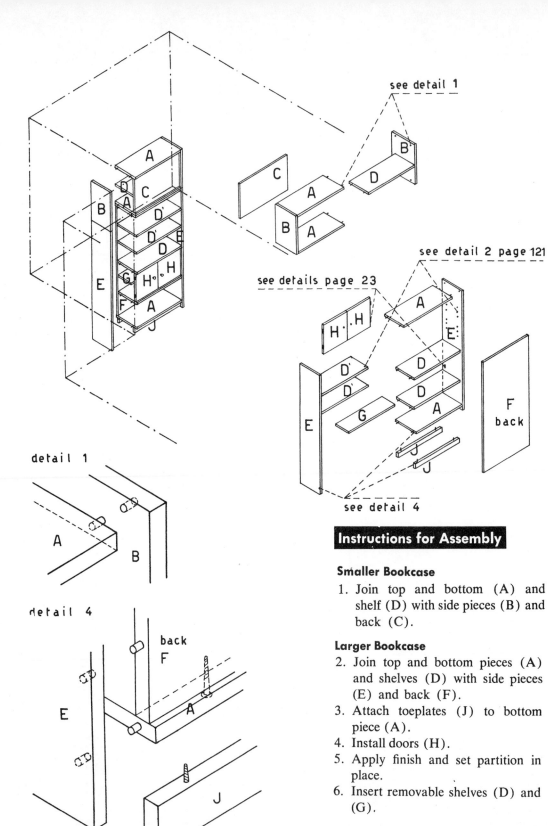

see detail 1

see detail 2 page 121

see details page 23

see detail 4

detail 1

detail 4

back
F

Instructions for Assembly

Smaller Bookcase

1. Join top and bottom (A) and shelf (D) with side pieces (B) and back (C).

Larger Bookcase

2. Join top and bottom pieces (A) and shelves (D) with side pieces (E) and back (F).
3. Attach toeplates (J) to bottom piece (A).
4. Install doors (H).
5. Apply finish and set partition in place.
6. Insert removable shelves (D) and (G).

Partition Composed of Shelves

40

PARTITION COMPOSED OF CABINETS

This partition can be very useful as a divider between living and dining areas, with cabinets that can be built to include a coat closet and bar (or desk) for the living room and china or glassware storage for the dining room.

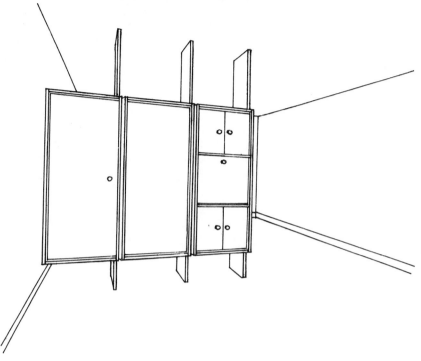

List of Materials

PART	NO.	FUNCTION	DIMENSIONS IN INCHES		
			thickness	× width	× length
A	3	stanchion	1	11	*h*
B	6	side	¾	18	60
C	6	top, bottom	¾	23½	18
D	3	back	½	23½	58½
E	7	shelf	¾	16	23½
F	16	cleat	½	½	15
G	2	door	¾	23½	58½
H	1	shelf	¾	8	23½
J	2	top, bottom	¾	17⅜	23½
K	1	drop door	¾	22	23½
L	4	door	¾	17½	11¾
M	1	hanger bar	1 (round)		16

Partition Composed of Cabinets

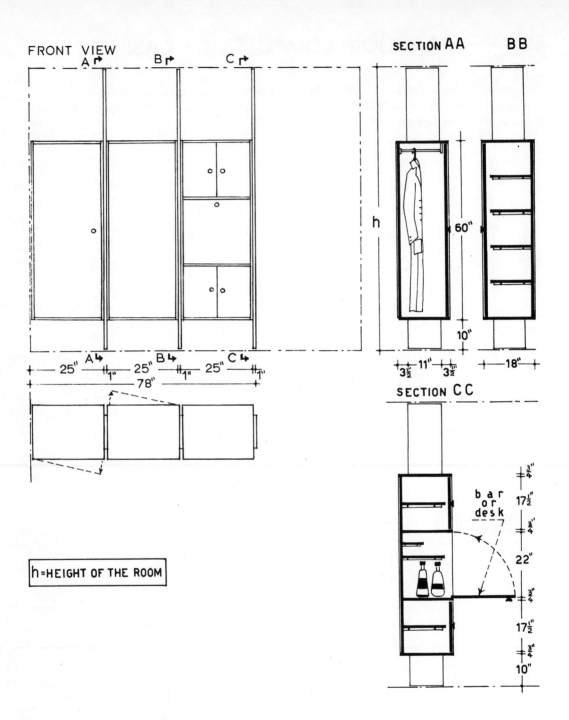

FRONT VIEW

SECTION AA   BB

h

60"

10"

25"   25"   25"
1"   1"   1"
78"

A   B   C

3½" 11" 3½"   18"

SECTION CC

bar
or
desk

¾"
17½"
¾"
22"
¾"
17½"
¾"
10"

h=HEIGHT OF THE ROOM

Partition Composed of Cabinets

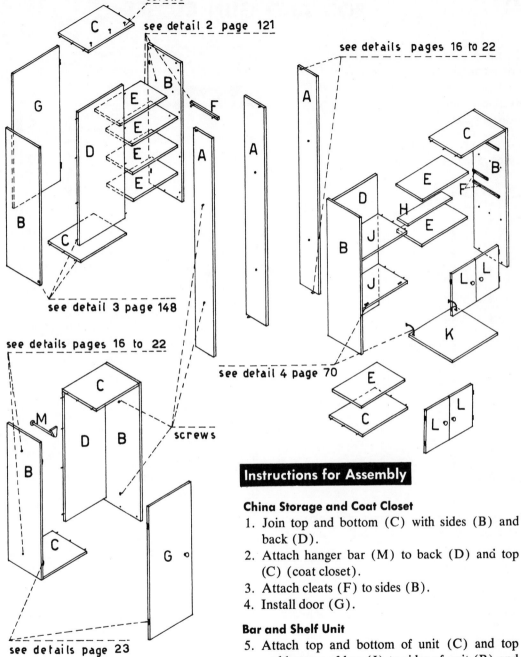

screws

see detail 2 page 121

see details pages 16 to 22

see detail 3 page 148

see details pages 16 to 22

screws

see detail 4 page 70

see details page 23

Instructions for Assembly

China Storage and Coat Closet

1. Join top and bottom (C) with sides (B) and back (D).
2. Attach hanger bar (M) to back (D) and top (C) (coat closet).
3. Attach cleats (F) to sides (B).
4. Install door (G).

Bar and Shelf Unit

5. Attach top and bottom of unit (C) and top and bottom of bar (J) to sides of unit (B) and back (D).
6. Attach brackets (F) to sides of unit (B).
7. Install drop door (K) and doors (L).
8. Apply finish and set furniture in place, using stanchions (A) as shown.
9. Insert shelves (E) and (H) and retouch finish.

Partition Composed of Cabinets

41

ROD AND GUN CLOSET

This closet is designed to display and protect hunting and fishing equipment. Shelves, drawers, gun rack, and an overhead cabinet provide a variety of storage space.

Glass panes can be measured and cut after cabinet is assembled.

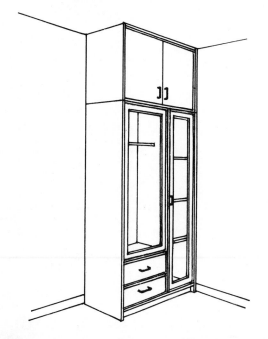

List of Materials

PART	NO.	FUNCTION	thickness	$\times$ width	$\times$ length
			DIMENSIONS IN INCHES		
A	4	top, bottom	¾	12	34½
B	2	side	¾	12	$h_1 - 1$
C	1	back	¼	35½	$h_1 - 1½$
D	1	shelf	¾	10½	34½
E	2	door	¾	17¼	$h_1 - 2½$
F	2	cleat	½	½	10
G	2	side	¾	12	72
H	1	partition	¾	11¾	67½
J	2	floor	¾	20¼	11¾
K	1	gun rack	¾	6	20¼
L	1	gun rack	¾	3	20¼
M	1	back	¼	35½	68½
O	1	toeplate	1	3	34½
P	2	frame	1	1¾	51½
Q	2	rail	1	1¾	16¾
R	2	frame	1	1¾	67½
S	2	rail	1	1¾	10
T	3	door frame	1	1	11
U	2	drawer bottom	¼	19¾	11⅜
V	2	drawer front	¾	7¼	20¼
W	2	drawer back	⅜	6¾	19⅜
X	4	drawer side	⅜	7¼	11⅜

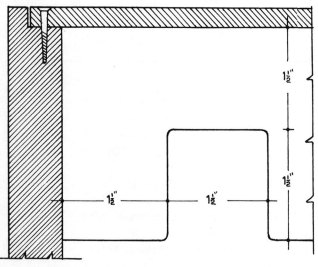

detail 2

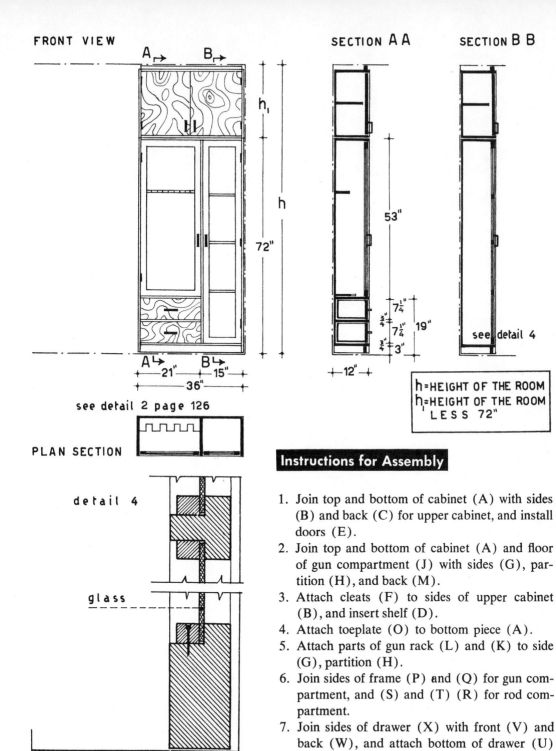

FRONT VIEW

SECTION A A

SECTION B B

h_1

h

72"

53"

$7\frac{1}{4}"$

$\frac{3}{4}"$

$7\frac{1}{4}"$ 19"

$\frac{3}{4}"$

3"

A B

21" 15"

36"

12"

h = HEIGHT OF THE ROOM
h₁ = HEIGHT OF THE ROOM
LESS 72"

see detail 2 page 126

PLAN SECTION

detail 4

glass

Instructions for Assembly

1. Join top and bottom of cabinet (A) with sides (B) and back (C) for upper cabinet, and install doors (E).

2. Join top and bottom of cabinet (A) and floor of gun compartment (J) with sides (G), partition (H), and back (M).

3. Attach cleats (F) to sides of upper cabinet (B), and insert shelf (D).

4. Attach toeplate (O) to bottom piece (A).

5. Attach parts of gun rack (L) and (K) to side (G), partition (H).

6. Join sides of frame (P) and (Q) for gun compartment, and (S) and (T) (R) for rod compartment.

7. Join sides of drawer (X) with front (V) and back (W), and attach bottom of drawer (U) to sides (X) and front (V).

8. Attach sides of door frames (P) and (R) to sides of cabinet (G) and install glass.

9. Apply finish and set cabinet in place.

Rod and Gun Closet

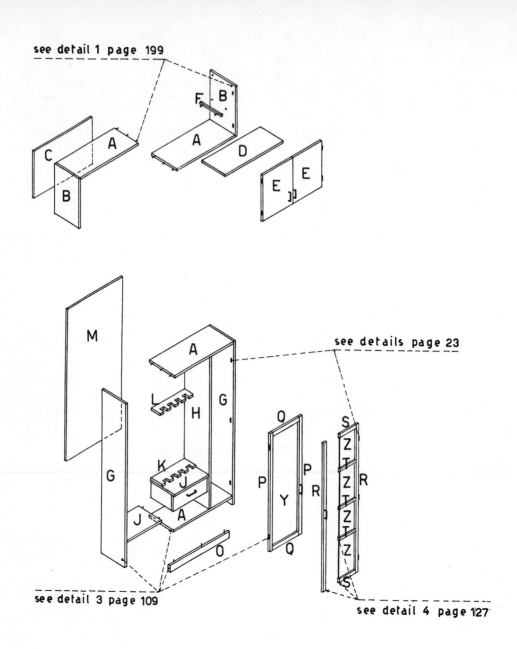

see detail 1 page 199

see details page 23

see detail 3 page 109

see detail 4 page 127

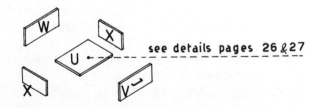

see details pages 26 & 27

Rod and Gun Closet

42

FLOWER STANDS

If you are a flower lover you will be interested in these two practical flower stands. Both are easy to make. The one on page 130 can be changed from floor to ceiling.

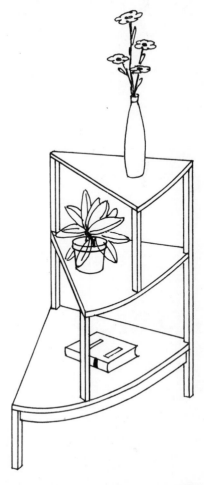

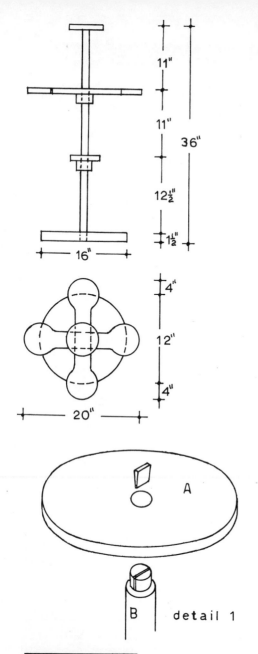

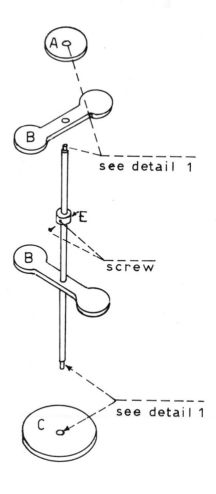

see detail 1

screw

E

see detail 1

detail 1

List of Materials

PART	NO.	FUNCTION	DIMENSION IN INCHES thickness × width × length		
A	1	top	¾	6 (diam.)	
B	2	supports	¾	5½	20
C	1	base	1½	14 (diam.)	
D	1	dowel	1½ (diam.)		36
E	2	supports	1½	3 (diam.)	

Instructions for Assembly

1. Insert supports (B) in dowel (D) and fasten with glue and screws.
2. Join top (A) and base (C) to dowel (D).
3. Apply finish.

Flower Stands

List of Materials

PART	NO.	FUNCTION	DIMENSION IN INCHES thickness × width × length		
			thickness	width	length
A	1	top	¾	9	18
B	1	shelf	¾	15	18
C	1	shelf	¾	18	18
D	2	legs	1⅛	1⅛	25¼
E	2	supports	1⅛	1⅛	9
F	1	leg	1⅛	1⅛	5¾
G	1	rail	1½	6	25

Instructions for Assembly

1. Join rail (G) to legs (D, F).
2. Fasten shelves (B, C) to legs (D, F) and supports (E).
3. Attach top (A).
4. Apply finish.

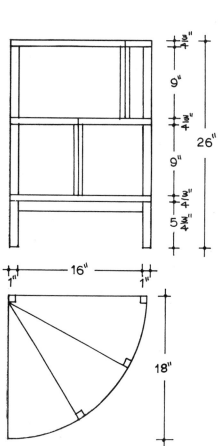

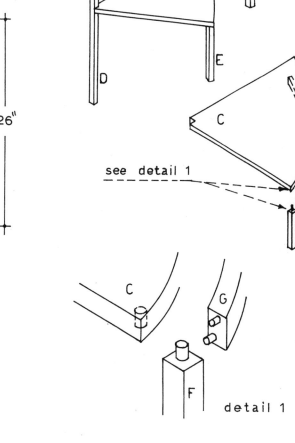

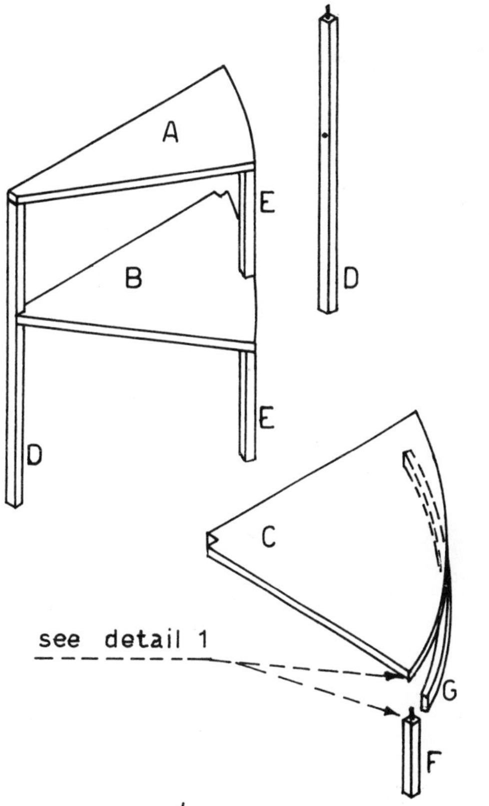

see detail 1

detail 1

Flower Stands

Vines in a vestibule provide a gay accent as well as a screen. This simple design has both a plant box and a trellis.

List of Materials

PART	NO.	FUNCTION	DIMENSIONS IN INCHES thickness × width × length		
A	2	stanchions	1¼	2½	h
B	15	dowel	1 (round)		48
C	2	box side	¾	7	34½
D	2	box end	¾	8	7
E	1	box bottom	¾	6½	34½
F	1	base	1	6	34

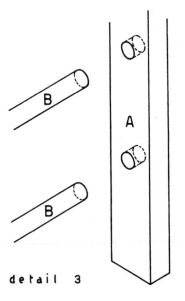

detail 3

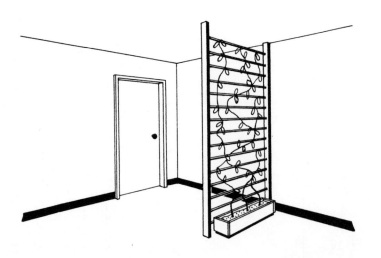

FRONT VIEW

SIDE

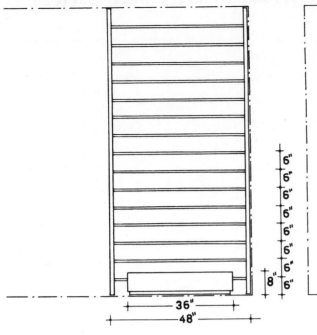

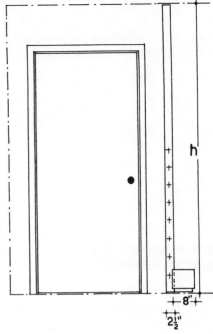

6"
6"
6"
6"
6"
6"
6"
8" 6"

36"
48"

h

8"
2½"

h = HEIGHT OF THE ROOM

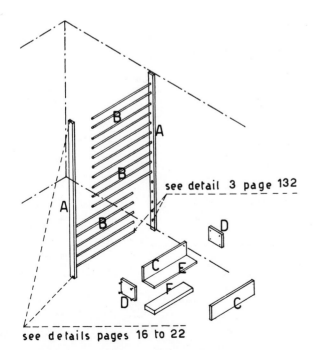

see detail 3 page 132

see details pages 16 to 22

Vestibule Partition with Planting

Instructions for Assembly

1. Attach dowels (B) to stanchions (A).
2. Join sides of plant box (C) with bottom (E).
3. Join ends of box (D) with sides (C).
4. Attach base (F) to bottom (E).
5. Apply a layer of asphalt inside the box.
6. Apply exterior finish and set partition in place.

There are many advantages in setting off the entrance from the living area. The partition shown also provides a coat closet and bookshelf.

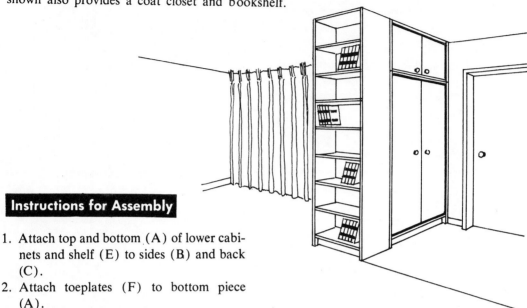

Instructions for Assembly

1. Attach top and bottom (A) of lower cabinets and shelf (E) to sides (B) and back (C).
2. Attach toeplates (F) to bottom piece (A).
3. Secure bar (G) to sides (B).
4. Attach top and bottom of upper cabinet (A) to sides (H) and back (K).
5. Install doors (D) and (J).
6. Attach shelves (O) to side supports (L).
7. Attach toeplate (P) to bottom shelf (O)
8. Apply finish and set furniture in place.

detail 4

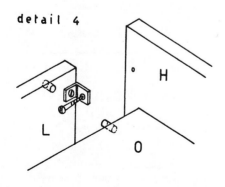

List of Materials

PART	NO.	FUNCTION	DIMENSIONS IN INCHES		
			thickness $\times$ width	$\times$	length
A	4	top, bottom	¾	24	46½
B	2	side	¾	24	72
C	1	back	½	46½	67½
D	2	door	¾	23¼	67½
E	1	shelf	¾	20	46½
F	2	toeplate	1	3	46½
G	1	hanger bar	1 (round)		46½
H	2	side	¾	24	$h_1 - 1$
J	2	door	¾	23¼	$h_1 - 2\frac{1}{2}$
K	1	back	½	46½	$h_1 - 2\frac{1}{2}$
L	2	side	¾	12	h
O	9	shelf	¾	12	22½
P	1	toeplate	1	3	22½

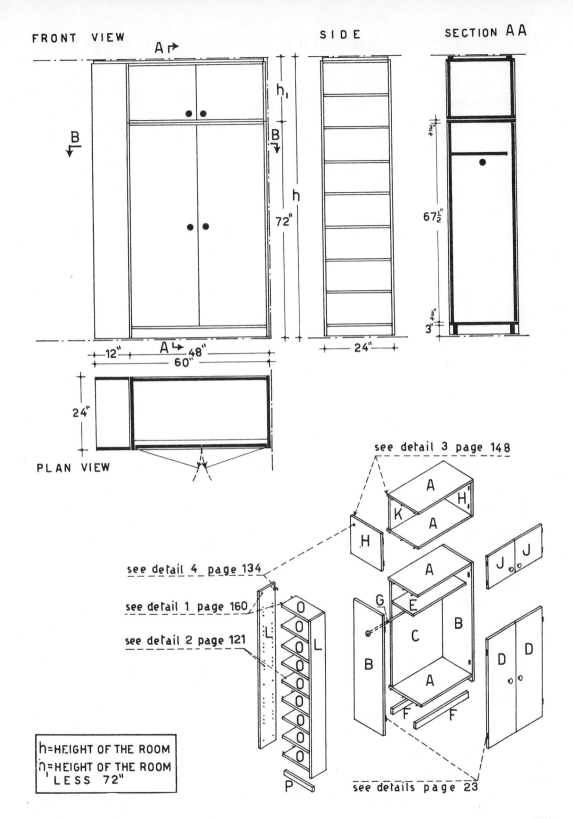

FRONT VIEW

A →

h_1

B →

B →

h

72"

PLAN VIEW

12"   A →   48"
60"

24"

SIDE

24"

SECTION AA

$67\frac{1}{2}"$

3"

see detail 3 page 148

see detail 4 page 134

see detail 1 page 160

see detail 2 page 121

see details page 23

h=HEIGHT OF THE ROOM
h_1=HEIGHT OF THE ROOM
LESS 72"

Vestibule Partition with Coat Closet

135

An unused corner near the front door can be used to house this coat closet, or it can be modified to serve as a linen closet elsewhere in the home.

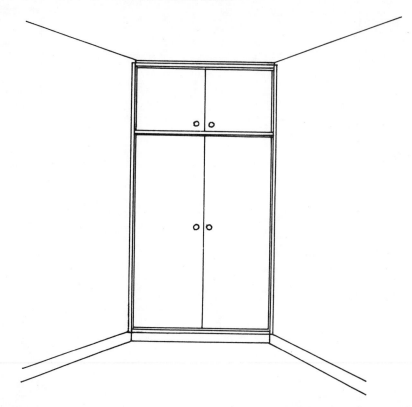

List of Materials

PART	NO.	FUNCTION	DIMENSIONS IN INCHES		
			thickness × width	×	length
A	2*	top, bottom	¾	27	27
B	1*	shelf	¾	24	24
C	1	left side	¾	28¼	h
D	1	right side	¾	27½	h
E	2	door	¾	19	64½
F	2	door	¾	19	$h_1 - 1\frac{3}{4}$
G	6	hanger	¾	1¼	2½
H	6	pin	¾ (round)		2
J	2	base	1	4	11
K	1	toeplate	1	4	38

* Cut diagonally to make two of (B) and three of (A).

Instructions for Assembly

1. Attach top, bottom, and shelves (A, B) to sides (C, D.)
2. Attach hangers (G) to pins (H); mount assemblies on sides (C, D) and doors (E).
3. Connect base pieces (J) to toeplate (K).
4. Join base assembly (J-K) to bottom (A).
5. Hang doors (E, F).
6. Install umbrella stand.
7. Apply finish and set closet in place.

FRONT VIEW   SIDE SECTION

detail 2

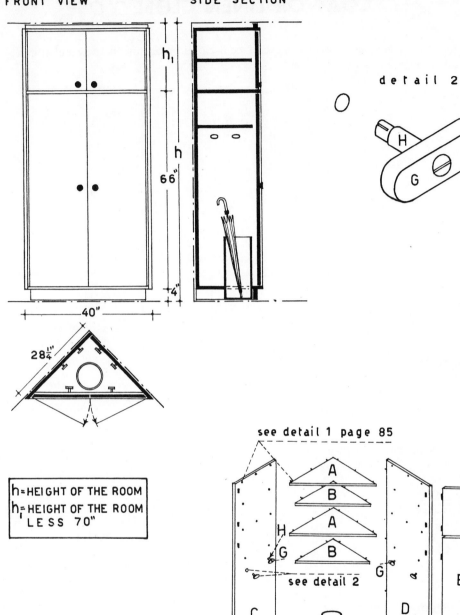

h₁

h

66"

4"

40"

28¼"

h = HEIGHT OF THE ROOM
h₁ = HEIGHT OF THE ROOM
LESS 70"

see detail 1 page 85

A
B
A
B

H
G

see detail 2

G

C

D

F F

E E

umbrella stand

see detail 4 page 84

A

J J K

Corner Coat or Linen Closet

With a bar for hangers this design makes a useful coat closet; substitute shelves and it can be used as a linen closet.

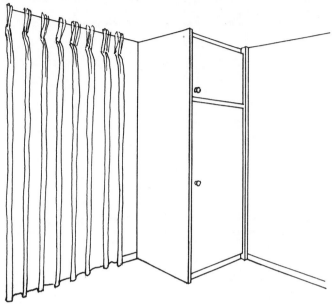

List of Materials

PART	NO.	FUNCTION	DIMENSIONS IN INCHES thickness × width × length		
A	2	side	¾	24	h
B	3	top, bottom	¾	23	23⅛
C	1	back	¼	24	$h - 5½$
D	5	shelf	¾	23	22
E	10	cleat	½	½	21
F	3	cornice	¾	2½	23
G	1	door	¾	23	$h_1 - 2½$
H	1	door	¾	23	67½

detail 3

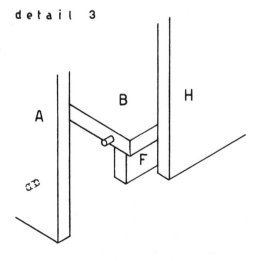

Instructions for Assembly

1. Attach cornice (F) to top (B) of cabinets.
2. Attach combined (B-F) to sides (A).
3. Install back (C).
4. Attach cleats (E) to sides (A).
5. Install doors (G) and (H).
6. Apply finish and set closet in place.
7. Insert shelves (D).

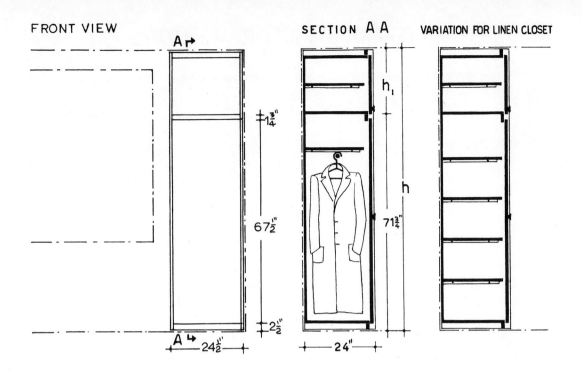

FRONT VIEW

SECTION AA

VARIATION FOR LINEN CLOSET

h_1

$1\frac{3}{4}$"

$67\frac{1}{2}$"

h

$71\frac{3}{4}$"

$2\frac{1}{2}$"

$24\frac{1}{2}$"

24"

h = HEIGHT OF THE ROOM
h_1 = HEIGHT OF THE ROOM
LESS $71\frac{3}{4}$"

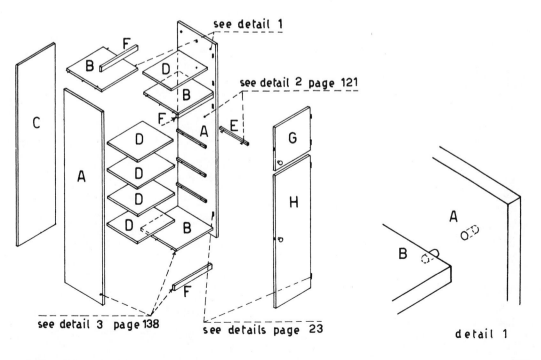

see detail 1

F

B

D

C

B

A

D

E

see detail 2 page 121

F

A

G

D

D

D

H

D

B

see detail 3 page 138

F

see details page 23

A

B

detail 1

Coat or Linen Closet

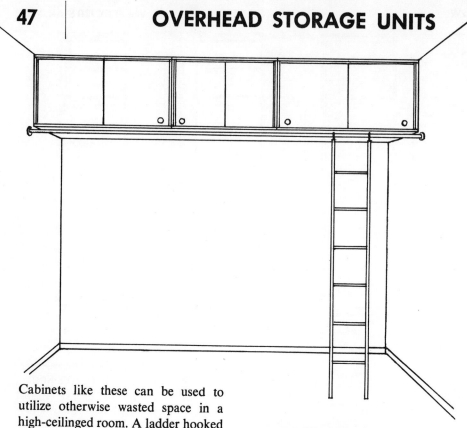

Cabinets like these can be used to utilize otherwise wasted space in a high-ceilinged room. A ladder hooked into a permanent rail makes the stored articles easily accessible.

Instructions for Assembly

1. Join top and bottom (A) to sides (B) and back (D) for larger cabinets.
2. Join top and bottom (G) to sides (B) and back (L) for smaller cabinet.
3. Attach cleats (M) to sides (B).
4. Install track for sliding doors.
5. Apply finish and set cabinets in place.
6. Insert shelves (C) and (H).
7. Attach rungs (O) to sides of ladder (P).
8. Install wall-to-wall metal pipe (Q).

List of Materials

PART	NO.	FUNCTION	DIMENSIONS IN INCHES thickness × width × length		
A	4	top, bottom	¾	18	48
B	6	side	¾	18	22½
C	2	shelf	¾	15½	46½
D	2	back	¼	47½	23½
E	2	door	¾	24	22¼
F	2	door	¾	23¼	22¼
G	2	top, bottom	¾	18	w_1
H	1	shelf	¾	15½	$w_1 - 1½$
J	1	door	¾	22¼	to fit
K	1	door	¾	22¼	to fit
L	1	back	¼	23½	$w_1 - ½$
M	6	cleat	½	½	15
O	6	rung	¾ (round)		11
P	2	ladder side	1	2	to fit
Q	1	ladder bar	1¼-in. pipe		w

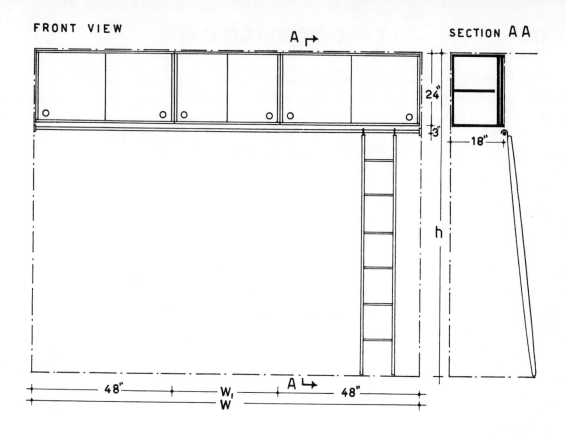

SECTION A A

A →

24"

3"

h

18"

A →

48"   W₁   48"
W

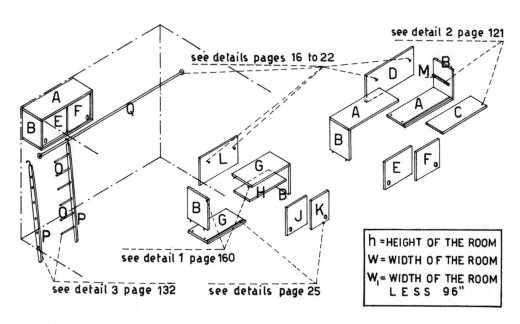

see detail 2 page 121

see details pages 16 to 22

A   D   M   B

A   C

B

E   F₀

A
B   E   F

Q

D

Q   P

P

see detail 1 page 160

see detail 3 page 132   see details page 25

L

G
H   B

B   G

J   K₀

| h = HEIGHT OF THE ROOM |
| W = WIDTH OF THE ROOM |
| W₁ = WIDTH OF THE ROOM LESS 96" |

Overhead Storage Units

Cabinets of this type can often be incorporated into the walls of an attic room before the room is plastered, but they can also be installed in a finished room.

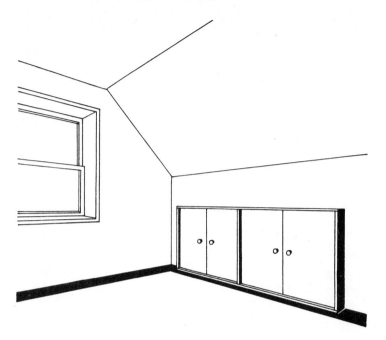

List of Materials

PART	NO.	FUNCTION	DIMENSIONS IN INCHES		
			thickness ×	width ×	length
A	2	top, bottom	¾	21	96
B	3	side	¾	21	28½
C	1	back	¼	96	30
D	2	shelf	¾	46⅞	18
E	4	cleat	½	½	17
F	4	door	¾	23½	28½

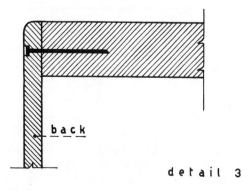

back

detail 3

Instructions for Assembly

1. Attach top and bottom of cabinet (A) to sides (B).
2. Attach back (C) to top and bottom (A).
3. Attach cleats (E) to sides (B).
4. Install doors (F).
5. Apply finish and set cabinet in wall.
6. Insert shelf (D).

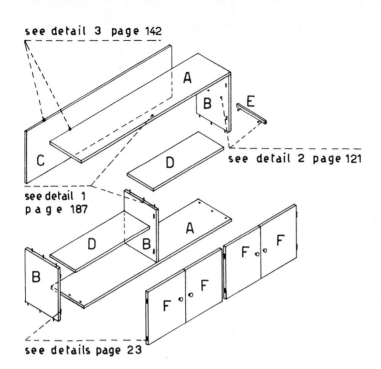

see detail 3 page 142

A

B

E

C

D

see detail 2 page 121

see detail 1
page 187

D

A

B

B

F F F

F F

see details page 23

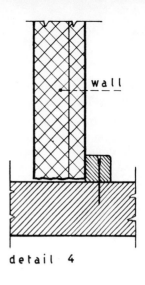

wall

detail 4

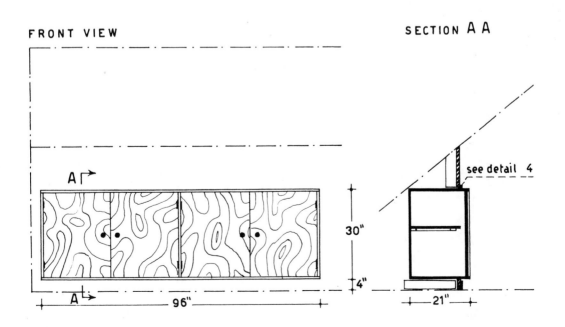

FRONT VIEW

SECTION A A

A

A

30"

4"

see detail 4

96"

21"

This closet design has a number of variations. It may be constructed with shelves only, or with a bar for hanging clothing in the lower portion. If desired, an upper unit may be added to extend the closet to the ceiling. Any number of these units may be grouped together. Materials are listed for three large cabinets and three overhead units, as shown on page 145.

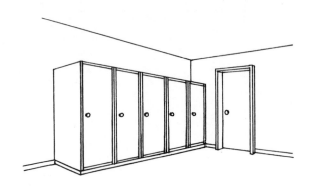

Instructions for Assembly

1. Join top and bottom (B) with sides (A) and back (C), for large cabinet.
2. Join top and bottom (B) with sides (G) and back (H), for small cabinet.
3. Attach cleats (F) to sides (A) and (G).
4. Install doors (J) and (D).
5. Attach ends of base (K) to toe-plate (L).
6. Apply finish and set furniture in place.
7. Insert shelves (E).

List of Materials

PART	NO.	FUNCTION	DIMENSIONS IN INCHES thickness × width × length		
			thickness	width	length
A	6	side	¾	24	68
B	12	top, bottom	¾	24	22½
C	3	back	¼	23½	67½
D	3	door	¾	22½	66½
E	9	shelf	¾	22½	22
F	18	cleat	½	½	21
G	6	side	¾	24	$h_1 - 1$
H	3	back	¼	23½	$h_1 - 1½$
J	3	door	¾	22½	$h_1 - 2½$
K	3	base end	1	4	21
L	2	toeplate	1	4	70
	2	clothes bar	1-in. pipe		22½

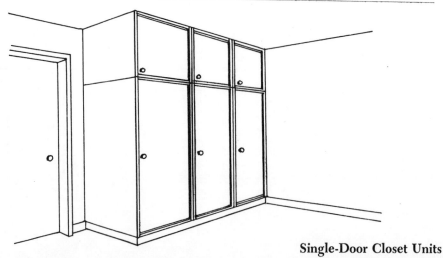

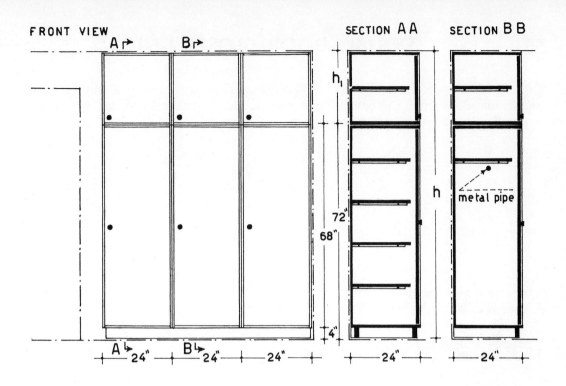

FRONT VIEW

A→ B→

SECTION AA SECTION BB

h_1

metal pipe

h

72"
68"

4"

A↳ 24" B↳ 24" 24"

24" 24"

h = HEIGHT OF THE ROOM
h_1 = HEIGHT OF THE ROOM
LESS 72"

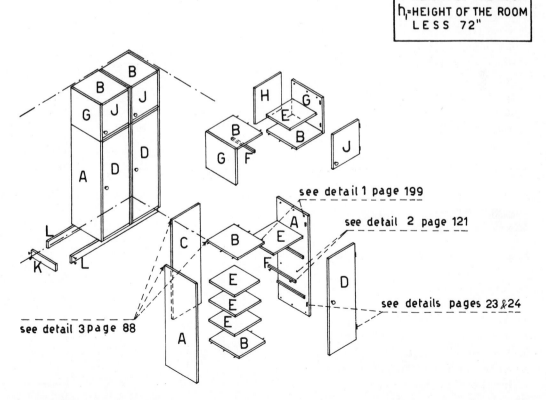

see detail 1 page 199

see detail 2 page 121

see details pages 23 & 24

see detail 3 page 88

Single-Door Closet Units

Like the previous design, these closet units can be constructed with shelves only or with shelves and clothes bar, and optional units may be added to make a floor-to-ceiling storage wall. List of materials is for two units, as shown on page 147.

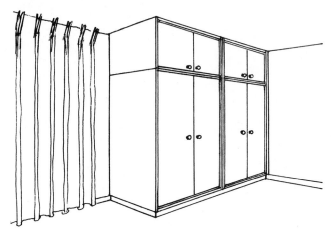

List of Materials

PART	NO.	FUNCTION	thickness	×	width	×	length
A	4	side	¾		24		68
B	8	top, bottom	¾		24		46½
C	2	back	¼		47½		67½
D	4	door	¾		23¼		66½
E	7	shelf	¾		22		46½
F	14	cleat	½		½		21
G	4	side	¾		24		$h_1 - 1$
H	2	back	¼		47½		$h_1 - 1\frac{1}{2}$
J	4	door	¾		23¼		$h_1 - 2\frac{1}{2}$
K	3	base end	1		4		21
L	2	toeplate	1		4		94
	1	clothes bar	1-in. pipe				46½

DIMENSIONS IN INCHES

Instructions for Assembly

1. Join sides (A) with top and bottom (B) and back (C).
2. Join sides (G) with top and bottom (B) and back (H).
3. Attach cleats (F) to (A) and (G).
4. Install doors (D) and (J).
5. Join base (K) to toeplate (L).
6. Apply finish and set closet in place.
7. Insert shelves (E).

VARIATION

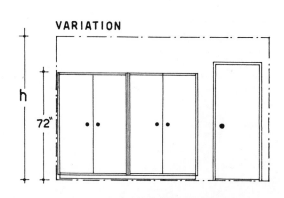

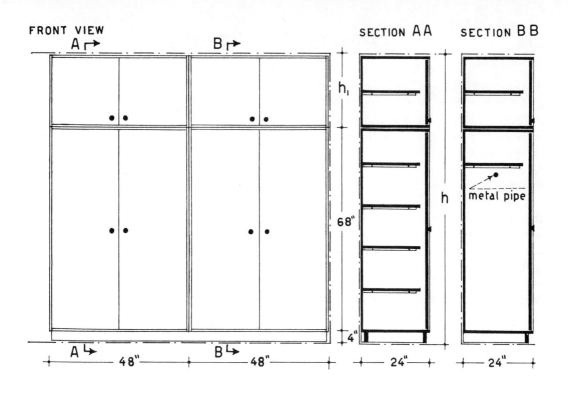

FRONT VIEW

SECTION AA   SECTION BB

h_1

68"

h

metal pipe

4"

A ⟶ 48" ⟶ B ⟶ 48"

24"   24"

h = HEIGHT OF THE ROOM
h_1 = HEIGHT OF THE ROOM
LESS 72"

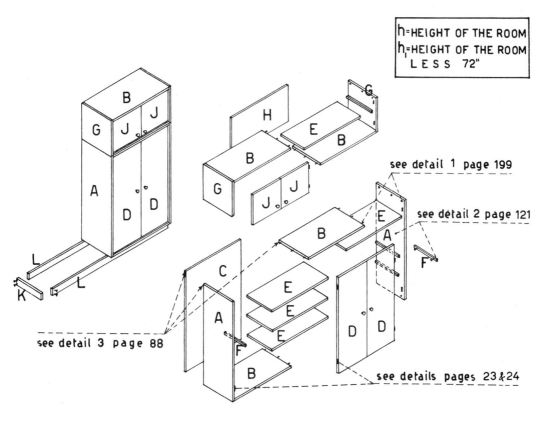

see detail 1 page 199

see detail 2 page 121

see detail 3 page 88

see details pages 23 & 24

Double-Door Closet Units

CLOSETS AS PARTITIONS

The sketches on page 149 show several ways that closets may be arranged as room partitions. The design shown is similar to the two preceding closets, except that the back must be more carefully finished because it will be visible. Consult the design on page 146 for instructions and parts, except that the parts shown in the list of materials below should be substituted for backs (C) and (H) for each closet to have its back exposed.

See page 146 and Detail 3, this page.

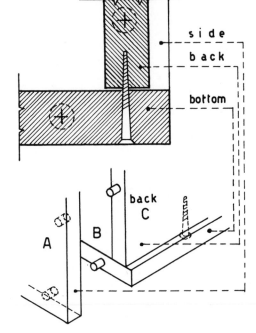

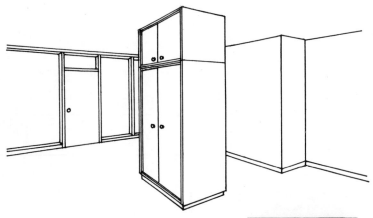

List of Materials

PART	NO.	FUNCTION	DIMENSIONS IN INCHES thickness × width × length		
C	1	back	½	46½	66½
H	1	back	½	46½	$h_1 - 2½$

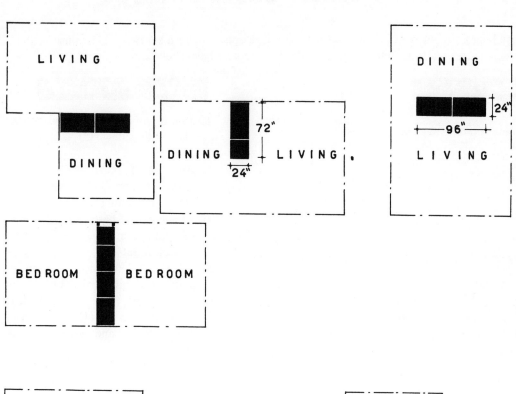

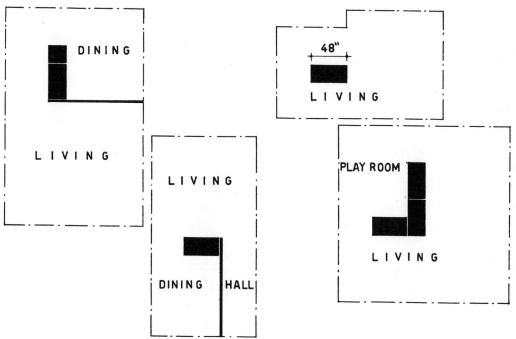

Installing a row of closets is a good way to utilize space under a stairway. The tallest of the closets illustrated is designed as a coat closet; the others have shelves.

List of Materials

PART	NO.	FUNCTION	DIMENSIONS IN INCHES thickness × width × length		
A	1	top	¾	24	to fit
B	1	bottom	¾	24	$w - ¾$
C	1	side	¾	24	h
D	1	side	¾	23¾	to fit
E	1	side	¾	23¾	to fit
F	1	side	¾	24	to fit
G	1	back	¼	71½	$h - 4½$
H	6	shelf	¾	23	22
J	12	cleat	½	½	21
K	1	hangar bar	1 (round)		23
L	2	brace	¾	1	to fit
M	1	panel	¾	w_1	to fit
O	1	door	¾	23	to fit
P	1	door	¾	23	to fit
Q	1	door	¾	23	to fit
R	1	toeplate	1	4	$w - ¾$
S	3	base end	1	4	21

Instructions for Assembly

1. Join top of closet (A) and bottom (B) with sides (C), (D), (E), and (F).
2. Attach back (G).
3. Attach cleats (J) to sides (C), (D), (E), and (F).
4. Attach end of base (S) to toeplate (R), and combined (S-R) to bottom of closet (B).
5. Set closets in place and install brace (L) and panel (M).
6. Install doors (O), (P), and (Q).
7. Install hanger bar (K).
8. Apply finish and insert shelves (H).

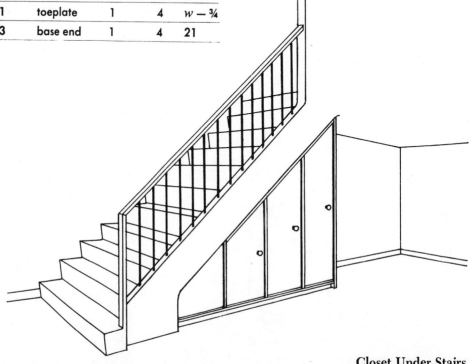

FRONT VIEW

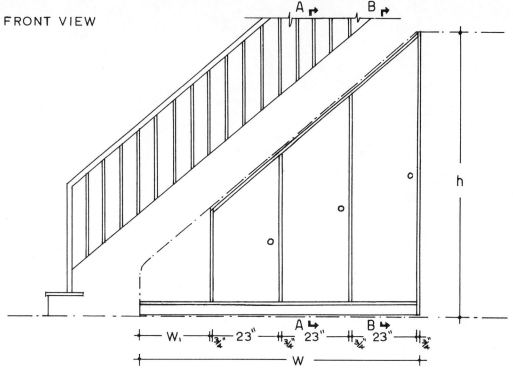

A
B

h

W₁   ¾" 23" ¾" 23" ¾" 23" ¾"
A   B
W

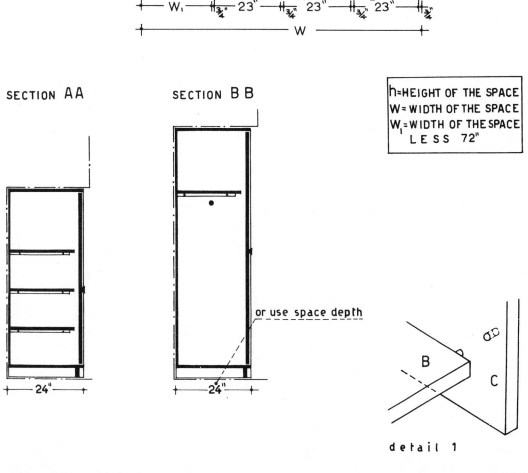

SECTION AA

SECTION BB

h=HEIGHT OF THE SPACE
W= WIDTH OF THE SPACE
W₁=WIDTH OF THE SPACE
LESS 72"

24"

24"

or use space depth

B
C

detail 1

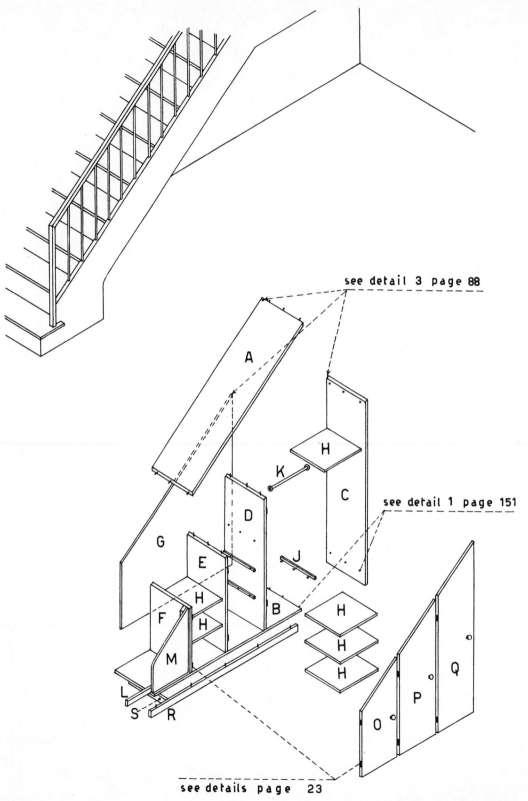

see detail 3 page 88

see detail 1 page 151

see details page 23

Closet Under Stairs

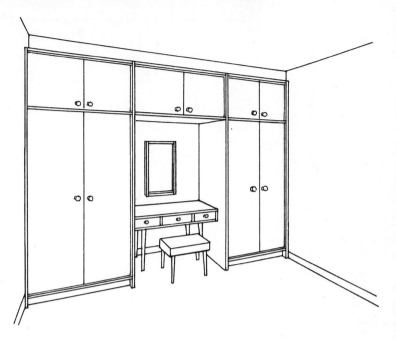

Here is a suggestion for treatment of a bedroom wall, with two closets flanking a vanity dresser and additional storage cabinets provided overhead.

List of Materials

PART	NO.	FUNCTION	DIMENSIONS IN INCHES thickness × width × length		
A	6	top, bottom	¾	24	$w_1 - 1\frac{1}{2}$
B	4	side	¾	24	92
C	2	back	¾	87½	$w_1 - \frac{1}{2}$
D	4	door	¾	to fit	19¼
E	4	door	¾	to fit	66½
F	5	shelf	¾	22	$w_1 - 1\frac{1}{2}$
G	10	cleat	½	½	21
H	2	toeplate	1	4	$w_1 - 1\frac{1}{2}$
J	2	side	¾	24	19¼
K	2	top, bottom	¾	24	to fit
L	2	door	¾	19¼	to fit
M	1	back	¼	20¼	to fit
O	1	cornice	¾	w	h_1

Instructions for Assembly

1. Join top, bottom, and shelf (A) to sides (B).
2. Install back (C).
3. Attach toeplate (H) to bottom (A).
4. Attach brackets (G) to sides (B).
5. Join top and bottom of center cabinet (K) to sides (J) and back (M).
6. Install doors (D), (E), and (L).
7. Apply finish and set closets in position.
8. Insert shelves (F), put vanity in place, and install cornice (O).

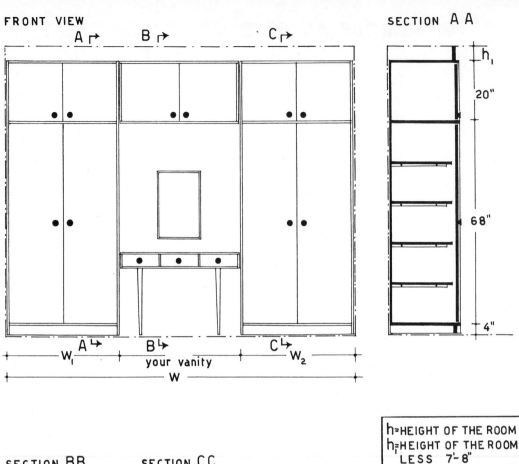

FRONT VIEW

A→ B→ C→

A↳ A→ B↳ B→ C↳ C→
W₁   your vanity   W₂
W

SECTION A A

h₁
20"
68"
4"

SECTION BB

20¾"
h

SECTION CC

h₁
20"
metal pipe
7'-8"
72"
24"

h = HEIGHT OF THE ROOM
h₁ = HEIGHT OF THE ROOM
     LESS 7'-8"
W = WIDTH OF THE ROOM
W₁ + W₂ = WIDTH OF ROOM
LESS YOUR VANITY OR CHEST

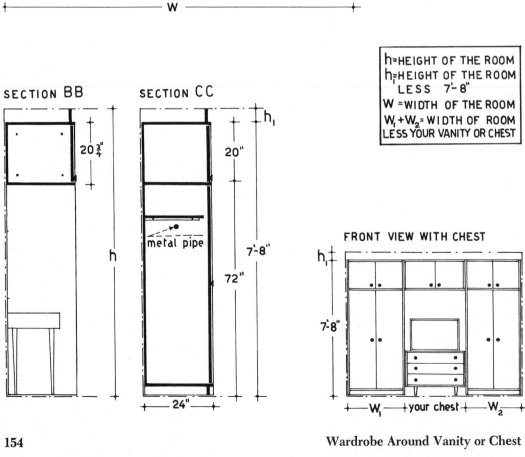

FRONT VIEW WITH CHEST

h₁
7'-8"
W₁ your chest W₂

Wardrobe Around Vanity or Chest

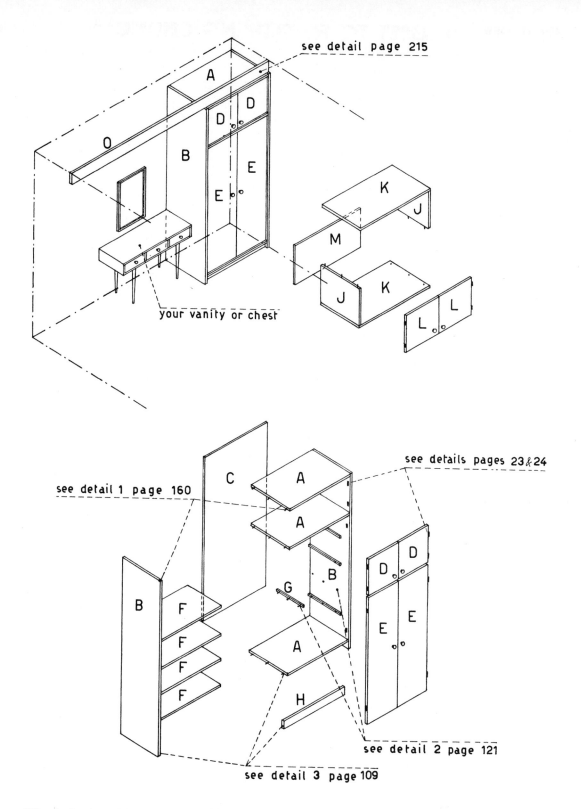

see detail page 215

A

D D

D

O

B

E

E

your vanity or chest

K

J

M

J K

L L

see details pages 23 & 24

see detail 1 page 160

C

A

A

B

B

F

G

F

A

F

F

D D

D

E E

H

see detail 2 page 121

see detail 3 page 109

Wardrobe Around Vanity or Chest

155

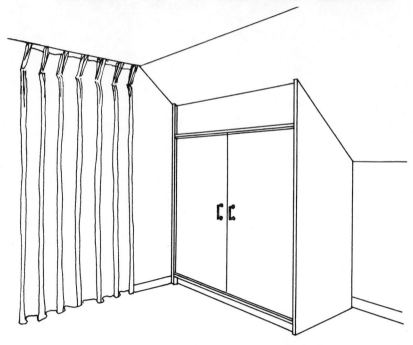

Here is another closet for an attic room, or any room with a sloping ceiling. Because it is taller than the units shown on page 142, this closet is built entirely inside the room rather than extended into the unfinished attic space. It may be fitted either with shelves for linen or with a rod for clothing.

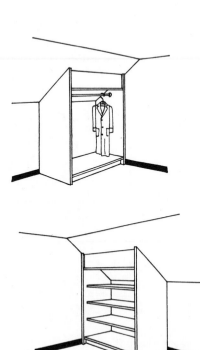

List of Materials

PART	NO.	FUNCTION	DIMENSIONS IN INCHES		
			thickness ×	width ×	length
A	2	side	¾	24	h_1
B	1	closet floor	¾	24	58½
C	1	brace	¾	4	58½
D	1	back	¾	$h_1 - h_2$	58½
E	1	cornice	¾	11	58½
F	2	door	¾	29¼	$h_2 - 4½$
G	1	toeplate	1	3	58½
H	1	hanger bar	1 (round)		58½
J*	3	shelf	¾	22	58½
K*	6	cleat	½	½	21

* Extra materials for linen closet.

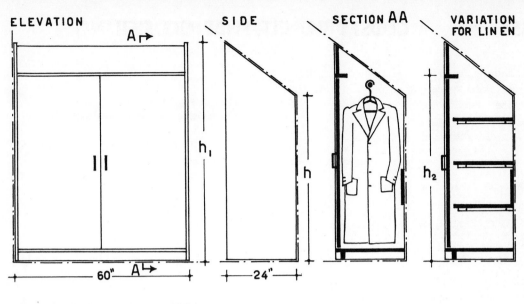

ELEVATION   SIDE   SECTION AA   VARIATION FOR LINEN

h_1

h

h_2

60"

24"

PLAN SECTION

h = HEIGHT FROM FLOOR TO SLOPING CORNER
h_1 = HEIGHT OF FRONT OF THE FURNITURE
h_2 = HEIGHT OF LOWER PART OF FRONT

Instructions for Assembly

1. Attach toeplate (G) to floor of closet (B).
2. Join sides (A) to floor (B), brace (C), back (D), and cornice (E).
3. Attach hanger bar (H) to sides (A).
4. Install doors (F).
5. Apply finish and set closet in place.

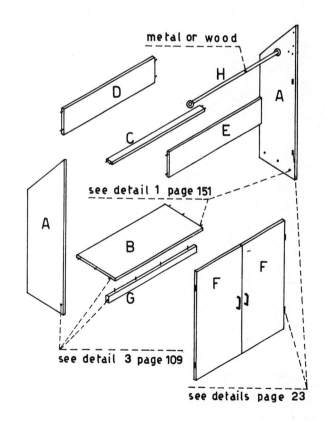

metal or wood

see detail 1 page 151

see detail 3 page 109

see details page 23

Closet to Fit Sloping Ceiling

157

This design offers a good method of building generous closet space into an old house. It can be installed in any room for seasonal storage use.

List of Materials

PART	NO.	FUNCTION	DIMENSIONS IN INCHES thickness × width × length		
A	2	shelf	¾	14	$w_2 - ⅜$
B	1	partition	¾	26½	h
C	2	hanger bar	1-in. pipe		$w_2 - ⅜$
D	6	upright	1¼	2½	h
E	2	rail	1¼	2½	w
F	1	toeplate	1¼	2½	w_1
G	1	toeplate	1¼	2½	17
H	1	filler piece	½	1¾	78½
J	1	panel	½	$w_1 - ½$	78½
K	1	panel	½	17¾	78½
L	1	panel	½	w	$h_1 - ½$
M	2	door	1¼	24	78
O	2	strip	½	1¾	h
P	2	strip	½	1¾	w

Instructions for Assembly

1. Install partition (B), hanger bar (C) and shelf (A).
2. Join uprights (D) with rails (E) and toeplates (F) and (G).
3. Set framework in place.
4. Face upright (D) with filler piece (H).
5. Attach panels (J), (K), and (L) to framework (D-E-F-G).
6. Install doors (M).
7. Attach strips (O) and (P).
8. Apply finish.

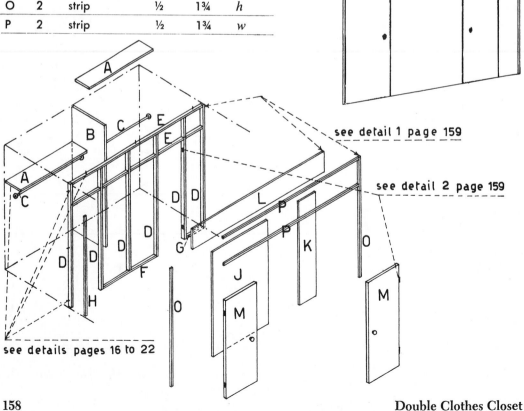

see detail 1 page 159

see detail 2 page 159

see details pages 16 to 22

FRONT VIEW

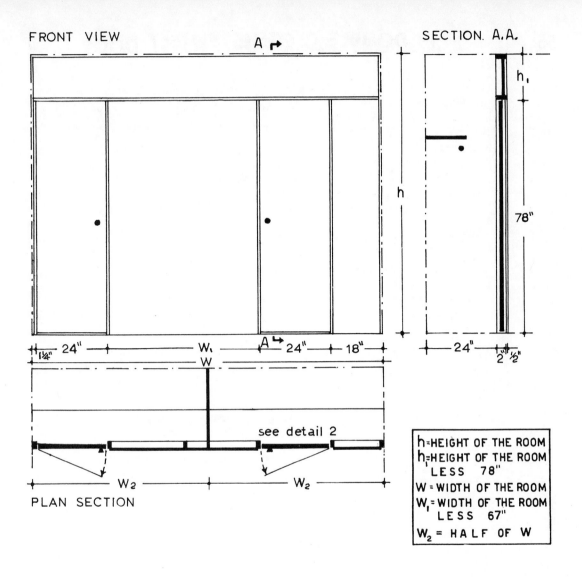

SECTION. A.A.

h_1

78"

A → 24" + 18"

A →

1¼" 24" W₁ 24"

W

PLAN SECTION

W₂ W₂

see detail 2

24" 2" ½"

h = HEIGHT OF THE ROOM
h_1 = HEIGHT OF THE ROOM
    LESS 78"
W = WIDTH OF THE ROOM
W_1 = WIDTH OF THE ROOM
    LESS 67"
W_2 = HALF OF W

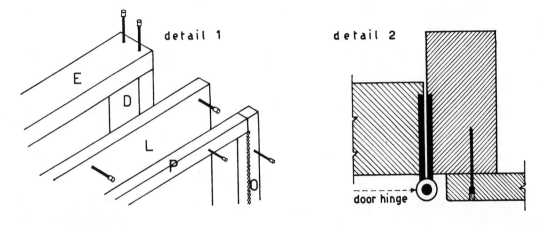

detail 1

E
D
L
P
O

detail 2

door hinge

Double Clothes Closet

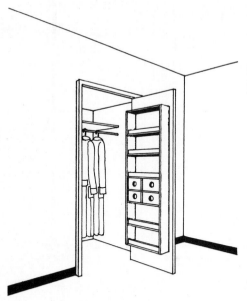

Shelves and drawers inside a closet door are a great convenience for storing accessories, particularly if either closet space or space in the bedroom is limited.

List of Materials

PART	NO.	FUNCTION	DIMENSIONS IN INCHES thickness × width × length		
A	8	shelf	¾	5	18½
B	2	side	¾	5	66
C	5	strip	⅜	2	18½
D	1	partition	¾	5	11¾
E	4	drawer front	½	5½	8⅞
F	4	drawer back	¼	5	8⅜
G	8	drawer side	¼	5½	4¾
H	4	drawer bottom	¼	8⅝	4¾

Instructions for Assembly

1. Attach shelves (A) to sides (B).
2. Join partition (D) and strips (C) to shelves (A).
3. Fasten framework to door.
4. Attach sides of drawer (G) to front (E) and back (F).
5. Attach bottom of drawer (H) to sides (G) and front (E).
6. Apply finish and insert drawers.

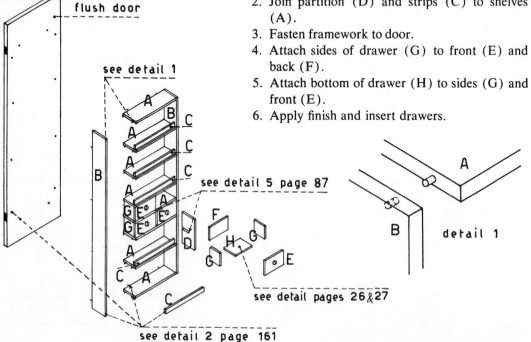

flush door

see detail 1

see detail 5 page 87

see detail pages 26 & 27

detail 1

see detail 2 page 161

FRONT VIEW WITH OPEN DOOR

SECTION AA

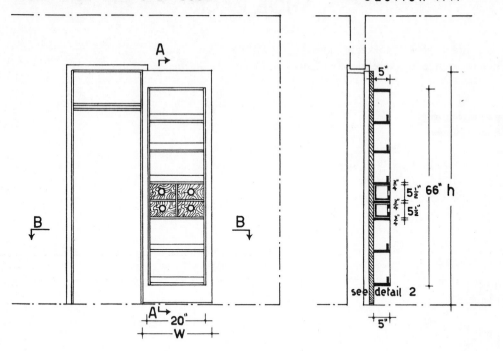

A

B   B

A   20"
           W

5"

5½"
5½"

66" h

see detail 2

5"

SECTION BB

CLOSET

h=HEIGHT OF THE DOOR
W= WIDTH OF THE DOOR

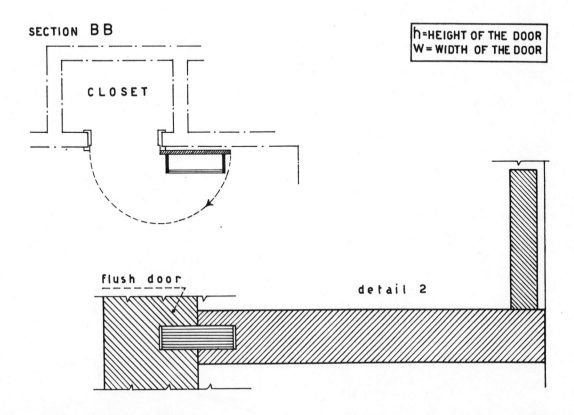

flush door

detail 2

Accessory Rack for Closet Door

SHOE RACK

Here is a practical way to keep shoes neatly off the floor. The rack should be carefully placed in relation to the closet door so that it can be easily reached.

List of Materials

PART	NO.	FUNCTION	DIMENSIONS IN INCHES		
			thickness ×	width ×	length
A	16	dowel	¾ (round)		w
B	2	side	¾	12	h

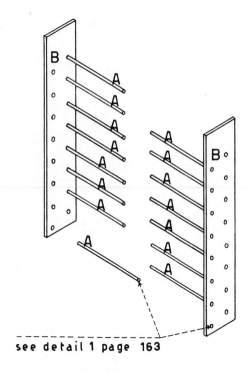

see detail 1 page 163

Instructions for Assembly

1. Attach dowels (A) to sides (B).
2. Apply finish and set rack in place.

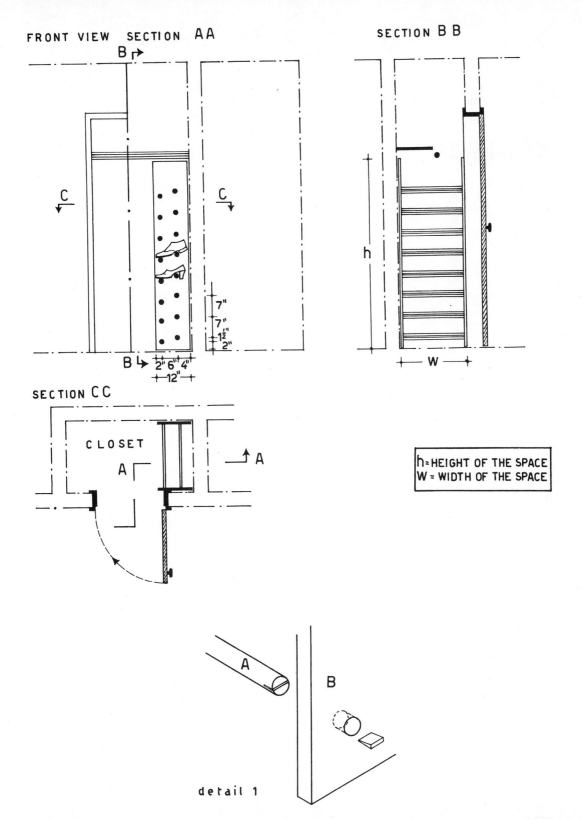

FRONT VIEW   SECTION AA

B →

C ←   C ↓

7"
7"
1½"
2"

B ↓   2" 6" 4"
      12"

SECTION BB

h

W

SECTION CC

CLOSET

A   ↑ A

h = HEIGHT OF THE SPACE
W = WIDTH OF THE SPACE

A

B

detail 1

Shoe Rack   163

These attic storage units are designed to be built under a sloping ceiling. Materials are listed for three closets and two chest units.

List of Materials

PART	NO.	FUNCTION	DIMENSIONS IN INCHES				
			thickness	×	width	×	length
A	1	top	¾		16¼		w
B	1	bottom	¾		23½		w
C	1	back	¾		12		w
D	6	side	¾		23½		54½
E	3	door	¾		22¼		54½
F	2	door	¾		22¼		28¼
G	2	back	½		46		48
H	1	back	½		23⅜		48
W	3	hanger bar	1(round)				22¼
J	2	floor	¾		22¼		23½
K	2	shelf	¾		22¼		22
L	4	cleat	½		½		21
M	8	drawer frame	¾		¾		21½
O	4	drawer frame	¾		2		22¼
P	6	drawer bottom	¼		21¾		23
Q	6	drawer front	¾		8		22¼
R	12	drawer side	⅜		8		23⅛
S	6	drawer back	⅜		7½		21⅜
T	1	toeplate	1		4		w
U	4	base support	1		4		21
V	1	panel	¾		w		h_1

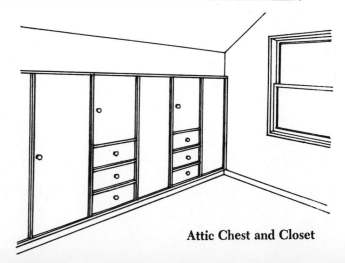

FRONT VIEW

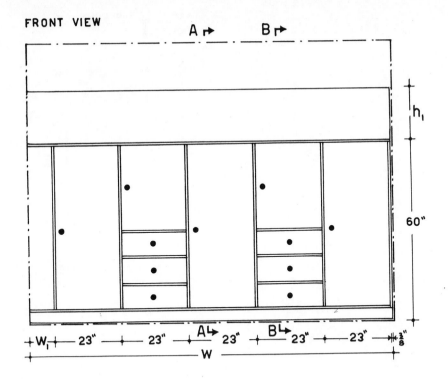

A →   B →

h_1

60"

| W₁ | 23" | 23" | A→ 23" | B→ 23" | 23" | 2⅜" |

W

h_1 = HEIGHT OF FRONT
OF FURNITURE LESS 60"
W = WIDTH OF THE ROOM
W₁ = WIDTH OF THE ROOM
       LESS   9'-7⅜"

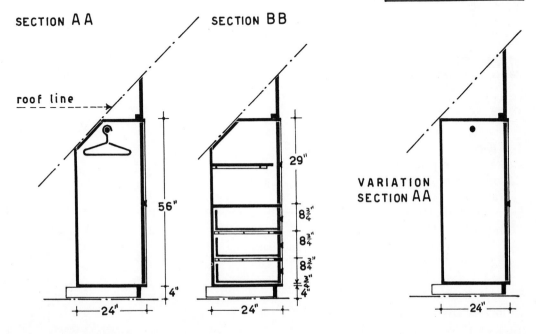

SECTION AA   SECTION BB

roof line

56"

4"

24"

29"

8¾"

8¾"

8¾"

24"

VARIATION
SECTION AA

24"

Attic Chest and Closet

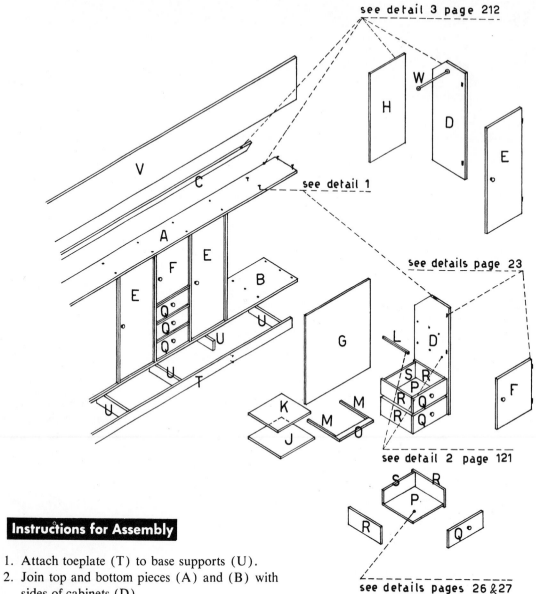

see detail 3 page 212

see detail 1

see details page 23

see detail 2 page 121

see details pages 26 &27

Instructions for Assembly

1. Attach toeplate (T) to base supports (U).
2. Join top and bottom pieces (A) and (B) with sides of cabinets (D).
3. Attach back pieces (C) and (G), (H).
4. Set closet in place and install hanger bar (W), floor of door compartment (J), cleat (L), and frame pieces (M) and (O).
5. Insert panel (V).
6. Install doors (E) and (F).
7. Join sides of drawer (R) with front and back (Q) and (S), and bottom of drawer (P) with (R-Q).
8. Apply finish.
9. Insert shelves (K) and drawers.

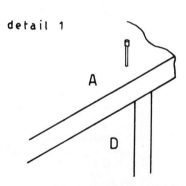

detail 1

166

Attic Chest and Closet

59

CORNER DRESSING TABLE

The wall cabinet of this vanity dresser opens into a three-way mirror; three drawers provide storage space for cosmetics and accessories.

List of Materials

PART	NO.	FUNCTION	thickness	DIMENSIONS IN INCHES width	length
A	1	shelf	¾	48	44
B	2	top, bottom	¾	15	15
C	2	side	¾	15	16½
D	1	back	¼	16	16
E	3	drawer front	¾	5	15
F	6	drawer side	⅜	5	14⅜
G	3	drawer back	⅜	4½	14⅛
H	3	drawer bottom	¼	14½	14⅜
J	2	door	¾	7½	18
K	1	back	¾	14	17
L	2	frame	½	1½	14
M	2	frame	½	1½	18
O	6	drawer glide	¼	½	14⅜
P	1	mirror		14	17
Q	2	mirror		6¾	16½

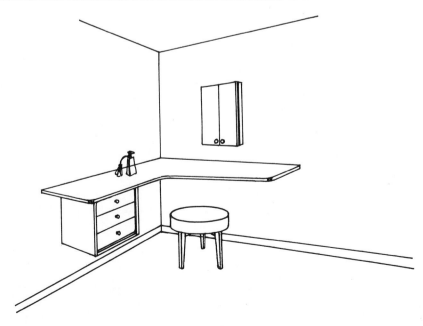

FRONT VIEW

SECTION A.A.

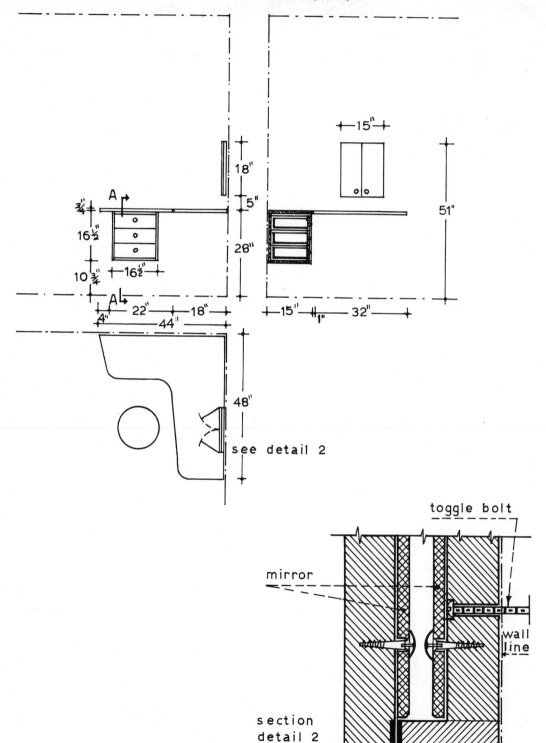

18"

5"

28"

48"

see detail 2

$\frac{3}{4}$"

$16\frac{1}{2}$"

$10\frac{3}{4}$"

A

$16\frac{1}{2}$"

A

22"

18"

4"

44"

15"

15"

51"

1"

32"

toggle bolt

mirror

wall
line

section
detail 2

Corner Dressing Table

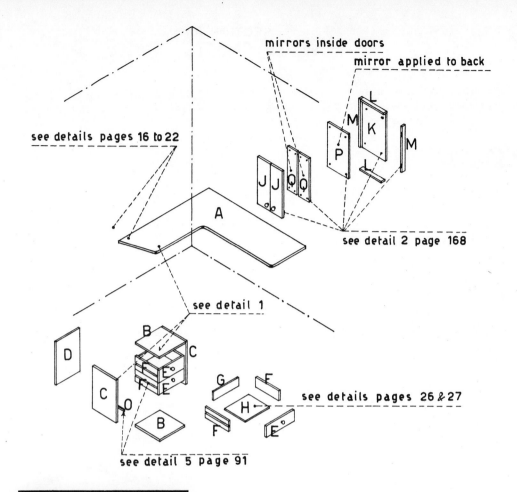

mirrors inside doors

mirror applied to back

see details pages 16 to 22

see detail 2 page 168

see detail 1

see details pages 26 & 27

see detail 5 page 91

Instructions for Assembly

1. Join top and bottom of drawer section (B) to sides (C) and back (D).
2. Attach drawer glides (O) to sides (C).
3. Join sides of drawer (F) with front (E), back (G) and bottom (H).
4. Attach back of cabinet (K) to top and bottom of frame (L) and sides (M).
5. Attach doors (J) to frame (M).
6. Apply finish and attach shelf (A) and cabinet to wall.
7. Install mirrors and attach top of drawer section (B) to shelf (A).
8. Retouch finish and insert drawers.

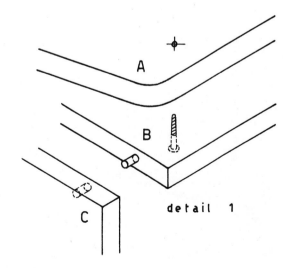

detail 1

Corner Dressing Table

60

WALL CHESTS

These chests, intended for a room with sloping ceiling, are designed with all drawers of one size. As many elements may be used as the width of the room will permit. Materials are listed for one chest and cabinet unit.

List of Materials

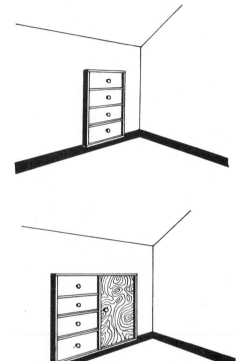

PART	NO.	FUNCTION	DIMENSIONS IN INCHES thickness × width × length		
A	2	top, bottom	¾	35¼	21
B	3	side	¾	21	26¼
C	1	back	¼	35¼	27¾
D	1	door	¾	16½	26¼
E	1	shelf	¾	16½	19
F	2	cleat	½	½	18
G	6	drawer frame	¾	¾	19
H	3	drawer frame	¾	2	16½
J	8	drawer side	⅜	6	20⅝
K	4	drawer back	⅜	5½	15⅝
L	4	drawer bottom	¼	16	20⅝
M	4	drawer front	¾	6	16½
O	2	base	1	4	20

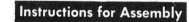

Instructions for Assembly

1. Join top and bottom of chest (A) with sides (B).
2. Attach back (C) to combined (A-B).
3. Attach cleat (F), and frame pieces (G) and (H).
4. Set chest in position on base (O).
5. Install door (D).
6. Join sides of drawer (J) to front and back (M) and (K).
7. Attach bottom of drawer (L) to sides (J) and front (M).
8. Apply finish and insert shelf (E) and drawers.

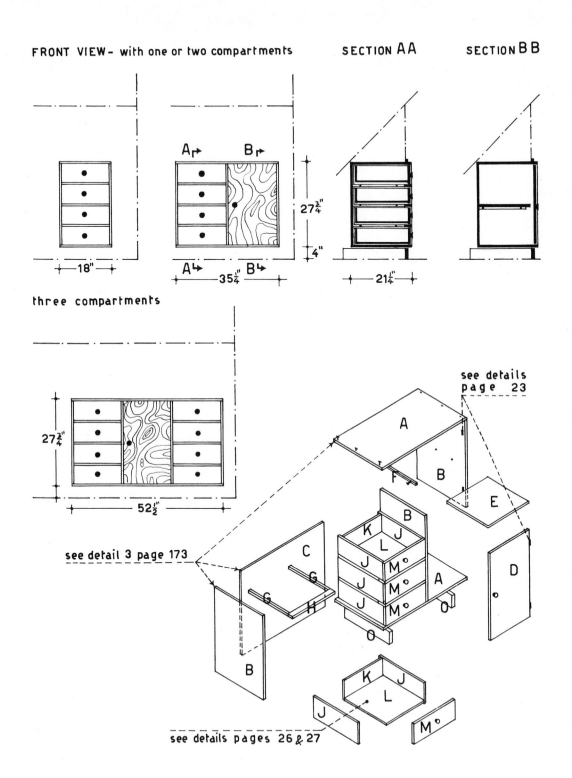

FRONT VIEW- with one or two compartments   SECTION AA   SECTION BB

three compartments

$27\frac{3}{4}''$ $4''$ $35\frac{1}{4}''$ $21\frac{1}{4}''$ $18''$

$27\frac{3}{4}''$ $52\frac{1}{2}''$

A   B

see details page 23

see detail 3 page 173

see details pages 26 & 27

61

FIVE-DRAWER WALL CHEST

This chest is identical with the previous design except for the addition of one drawer. Materials are listed for one chest and cabinet unit.

FRONT VIEW – with one or two compartments

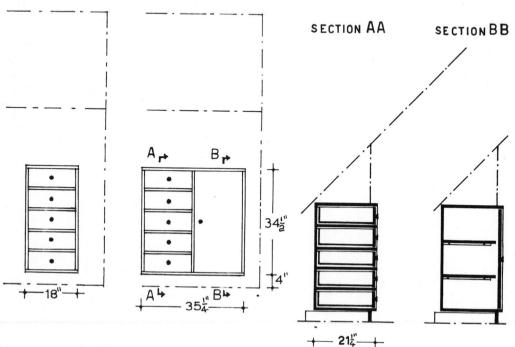

SECTION AA

SECTION BB

three compartments

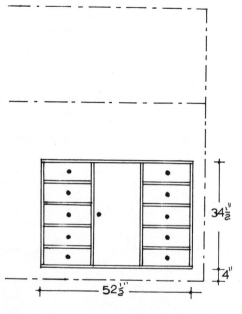

List of Materials

PART	NO.	FUNCTION	DIMENSIONS IN INCHES		
			thickness × width × length		
A	2	top, bottom	¾	35¼	21
B	3	side	¾	21	33
C	1	back	¼	35¼	34½
D	1	door	¾	16½	33
E	2	shelf	¾	16½	19
F	4	cleat	½	½	18
G	8	drawer frame	¾	¾	19
H	4	drawer frame	¾	2	16½
J	10	drawer side	⅜	6	20⅝
K	5	drawer back	⅜	5½	15⅝
L	5	drawer bottom	¼	16	20⅝
M	5	drawer front	¾	6	16½
O	2	base	1	4	20

Five-Drawer Wall Chest

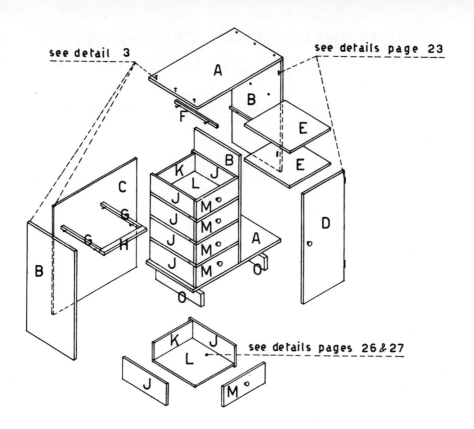

see detail 3

see details page 23

see details pages 26 & 27

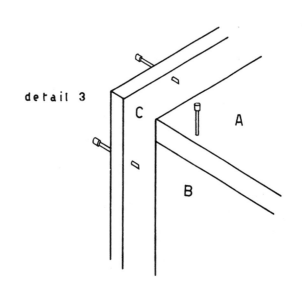

detail 3

Instructions for Assembly

1. Join top and bottom of chest (A) with sides (B).
2. Attach back (C) to combined (A-B).
3. Attach cleat (F) and frame pieces (G) and (H).
4. Set chest in place on base (O).
5. Install door (D).
6. Join sides of drawer (J) with front and back (M) and (K).
7. Attach bottom of drawer (L) to sides (J) and front (M).
8. Apply finish, and insert shelf (E) and drawers.

Five-Drawer Wall Chest

Where there is no space for a night table beside the bed, an overhead cabinet like the one illustrated offers a practical solution. A tubular light can be attached to the bottom of the cabinet.

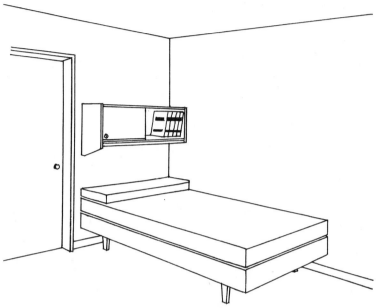

List of Materials

PART	NO.	FUNCTION	DIMENSIONS IN INCHES thickness × width × length		
A	2	top, bottom	¾	12	40½
B	1	end	¾	12	23
C	1	end	¾	12	17½
D	1	partition	¾	10⅞	13½
E	1	back	¼	14½	41½
F	1	rail	½	1¾	40½
G	1	door	¾	13¼	20⅝

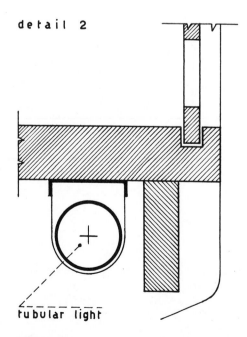

detail 2

tubular light

Instructions for Assembly

1. Join top and bottom of cabinet (A) with partition (D) and ends (B) and (C).
2. Attach back (E).
3. Attach rail (F) to under surface of (A).
4. Apply finish and attach cabinet to wall.
5. Install lamp and door (G).

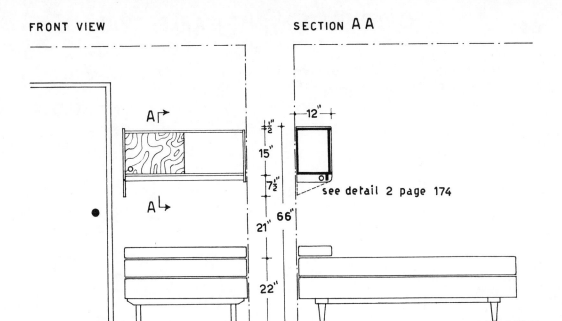

A ⌐►

A └►

$\frac{1}{2}$"

15"

$7\frac{1}{2}$"

21"

22"

66"

42"

12"

see detail 2 page 174

76"

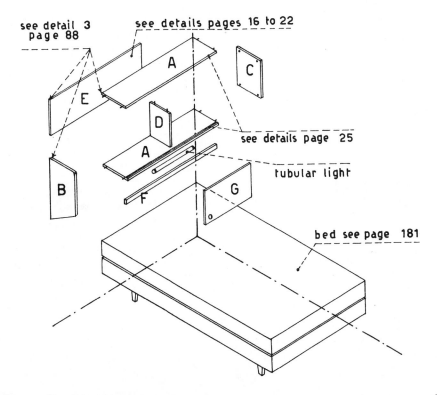

see detail 3
page 88

see details pages 16 to 22

A

C

E

D

A

B

F

see details page 25

tubular light

G

bed see page 181

Overhead Night Table: Two Compartments

VALET CHAIR

A practical example for a bachelor's bedroom. Like all chairs, it requires some cabinet-making ability to build, if results are to be good.

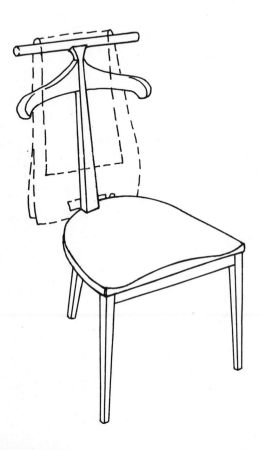

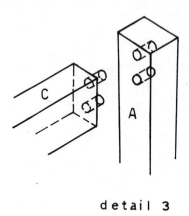

detail 3

List of Materials

PART	NO.	FUNCTION	DIMENSION IN INCHES		
			thickness ×	width ×	length
A	2	legs	1¼	1¼	16¼
B	1	leg	1⅜	4½	39
C	1	rail	1	1½	14
D	1	rail	1	1¾	15
E	2	supports	1¼	4	8
F	1	dowel	1 (diam.)		17
G	1	seat	¾	17	17

Instructions for Assembly

1. Join legs (A, B) with rails (C, D).
2. Attach supports (E), dowel (F), to leg (B) and fasten seat (G) to rails (C, D).
3. Apply finish.

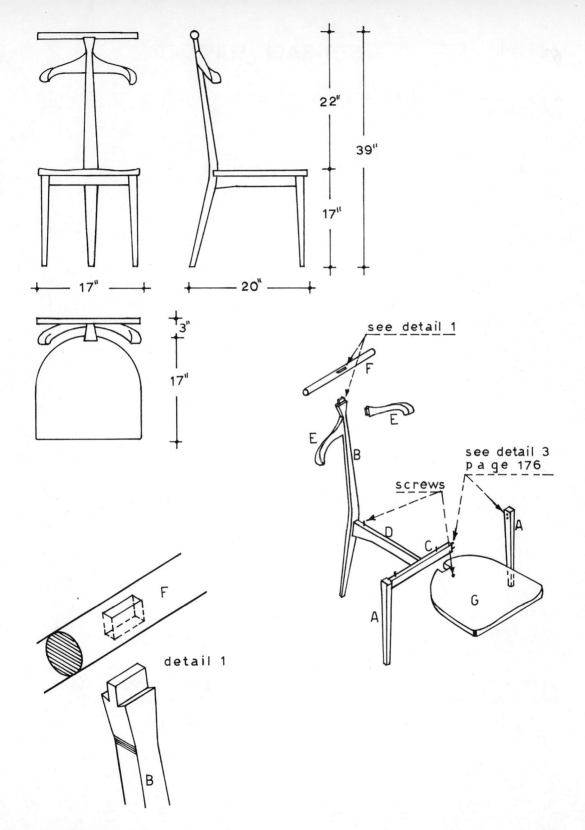

22"

39"

17"

17"

20"

3"

17"

see detail 1

F

E

E

B

see detail 3
page 176

screws

D

C

A

A

G

F

detail 1

B

Valet Chair

Reading in bed without any back support can be very wearisome. This back support is an excellent way of solving the problem.

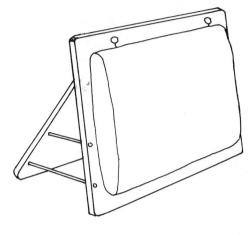

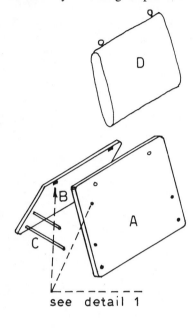

see detail 1

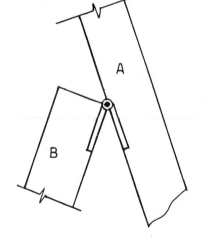

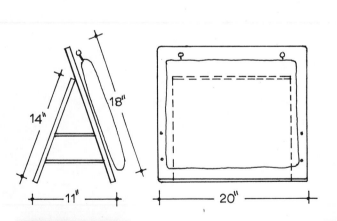

14" 18"

11" 20"

List of Materials

PART	NO.	FUNCTION	DIMENSION IN INCHES thickness × width × length		
A	1	panel	½	18	20
B	1	support	½	14	15
C		nylon string	1 yd.		
D	1	rubber cushion	13	16	

Instructions for Assembly

1. Join panel (A) to support (B) with hinges.
2. Attach string (C).
3. Apply finish and install cushion (D).

This is another piece that is ideal for any bedroom, and it is not hard to build.

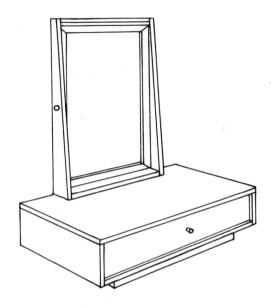

List of Materials

PART	NO.	FUNCTION	DIMENSION IN INCHES		
			thickness ×	width ×	length
A	1	top	3/8	8	14
B	1	bottom	3/8	8	13¼
C	2	sides	3/8	3⅛	8
D	1	back	¼	3¼	13¾
E	1	base	1	7	11
F	1	drawer front	3/8	2¾	13¼
G	1	drawer back	3/8	2¼	12½
H	2	drawer sides	3/8	2¾	7⅝
J	1	drawer bottom	3/16	7½	12⅞
K	2	supports	3/8	2	12

Instructions for Assembly

1. Join top (A) to bottom, sides, back (B, C, D), and attach base (E).
2. Join drawer sides (H) with front (F), back (G), and bottom (J).
3. Attach (K) with (L, M) and fasten to top (A).

(Continued on next page)

L	1	base	3/8	2	8¼
M	1	top	3/8	¾	8¼
O	2	rails	½	¾	10½
P	2	rails	½	¾	8
Q	2	strips	¼	¼	10
R	2	strips	¼	¼	7½
S	1	panel	1/8	7½	10
T	1	mirror		7½	10

4. Join (O) with (P), install mirror (T), panel (S), and strips (Q, R).
5. Apply finish and attach (O) to (K).

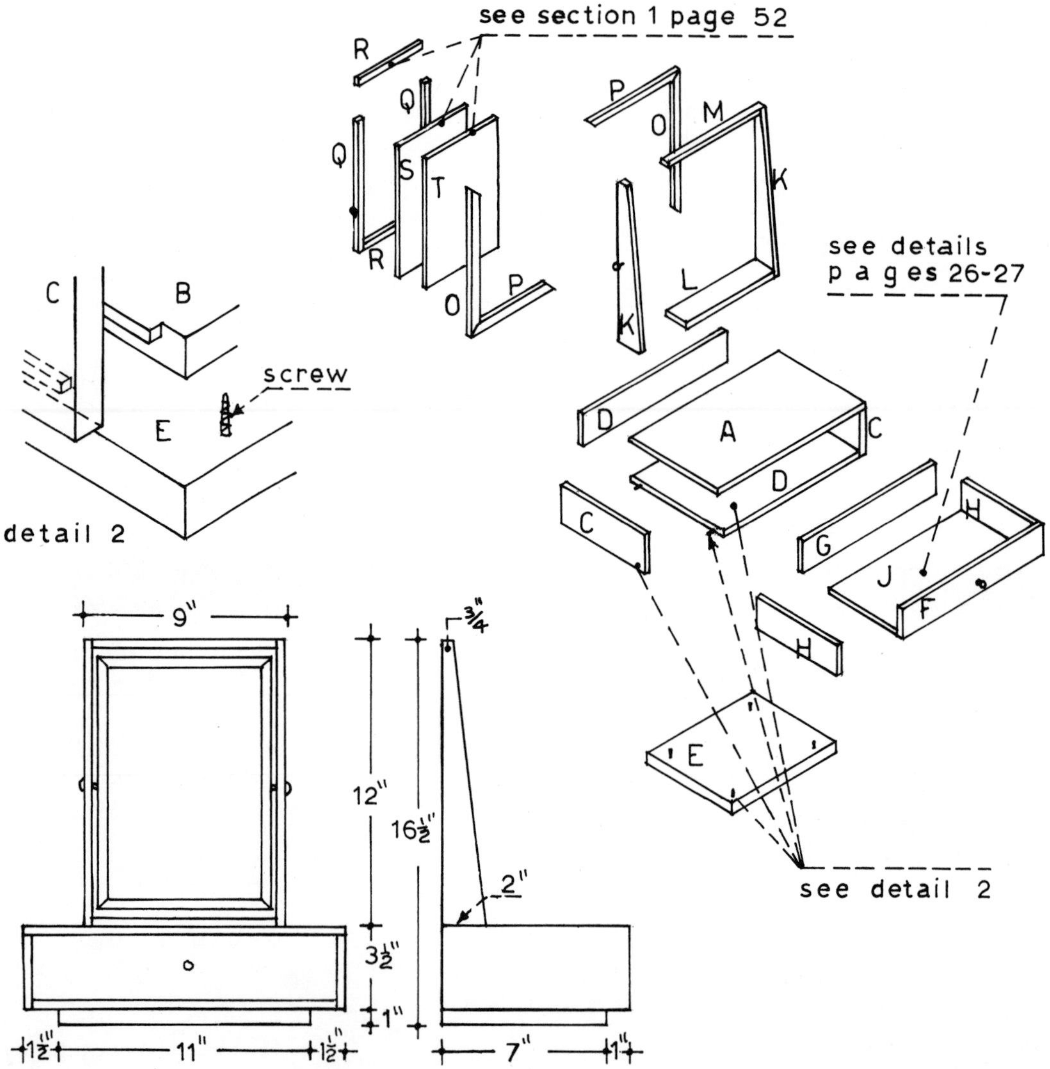

see section 1 page 52
R
Q
Q
S
T
R
O
P
P
O
M
K
K
L
see details pages 26-27
C
B
screw
E
detail 2
D
A
C
D
C
G
H
J
F
H
E
see detail 2
9"
¾"
12"
16½"
2"
3½"
1"
1½"
11"
1½"
7"
1"

BASE FOR BOX SPRING

This base, built to fit a standard single or double box spring and mattress, can be combined with a simple head-board or with the wall units shown in the two designs that follow (pages 182 and 185).

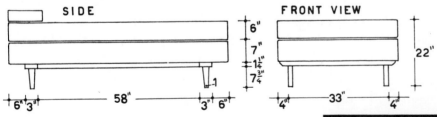

SIDE

FRONT VIEW

6"
7"
1¼"
7¾"

22"

58"
6" 3"
3" 6"

4"
33"
4"

PLAN

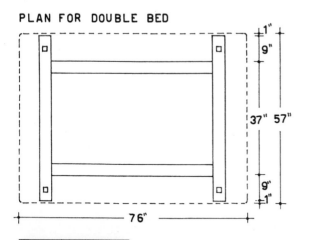

1"
7"

25" 41"

7"
1"

76"

PLAN FOR DOUBLE BED

1"
9"

37" 57"

9"
1"

76"

Instructions for Assembly

1. Join end rails (A) to side rails (B).
2. Attach legs (C).
3. Apply finish.

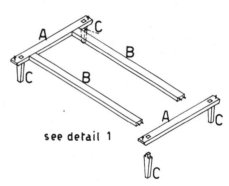

see detail 1

use bolts or screws fixed to base and box spring

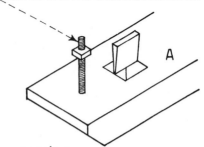

detail 1

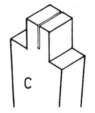

List of Materials

PART	NO.	FUNCTION	DIMENSIONS IN INCHES thickness × width × length		
A	2	end rail	1¼	3	39*
B	2	side rail	1¼	3	58
C	4	leg	1¼	2½	9

* Single bed size; for double bed use 55 in.

This design for a single bed and two wall cabinets provides night table, book shelves, and closed compartments in a compact arrangement. Instructions for building the bed are given on page 181.

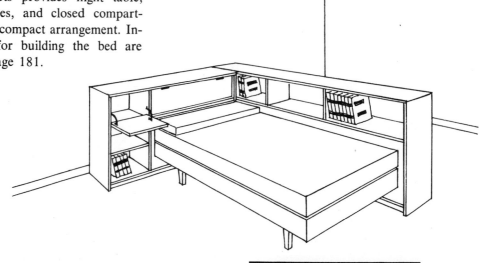

List of Materials

PART	NO.	FUNCTION	thickness	width	length
A	1	top	¾	12	60
B	1	bottom	¾	12	58½
C	4	end	¾	12	38¼
D	1	back	¼	35½	59½
E	1	partition	¾	11¾	34½
F	2	shelf	¾	11¾	15½
G	1	shelf	¾	11¾	42¼
H	1	shelf	¾	10	42¼
J	1	toeplate	¾	3	58½
K	1	door	¾	12¼	15½
L	1	door	¾	12¼	42¼
M	1	door	¾	21½	42¼
O	1	top	¾	12	90
P	2	bottom	¾	12	88½
Q	2	partition	¾	11⅜	21½
R	2	partition	¾	11⅜	12¼
S	1	back	½	12¼	88½
T	1	back	½	21½	88½
U	3	shelf	¾	11⅜	29
V	2	toeplate	¾	3	88½

DIMENSIONS IN INCHES

Instructions for Assembly

Cabinet at Head of Bed:

1. Join top and bottom of cabinet (A) and (B) with ends (C), partition (E), and shelves (F) and (G).
2. Install back (D).
3. Attach toeplate (J) to bottom (B).
4. Install doors (K), (L), and (M).
5. Insert shelves (F) and (H).

Side Cabinet:

6. Join top and bottom of cabinet (O) and (P) with sides (C), partitions (Q) and (R), and backs (S) and (T).
7. Attach toeplates (V).
8. Install shelves (U).
9. Apply finish and set cabinets and bed in place.

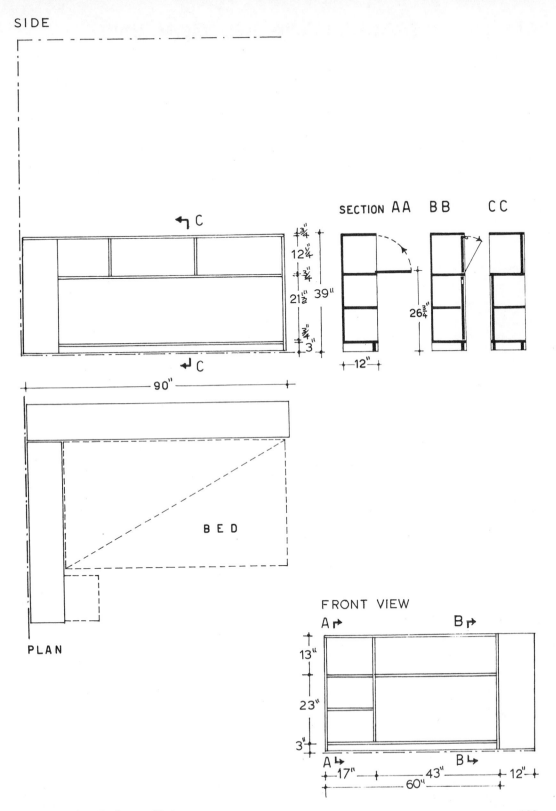

SIDE

C

‖¾"
12¼"
‖¾"
21½"   39"
‖¾"
3"

C

SECTION AA   BB   CC

26¾"

12"

90"

BED

PLAN

FRONT VIEW

A

B

13"

23"

3"

A

B

17"   43"   12"

60"

Space-Saving Bedroom Unit

183

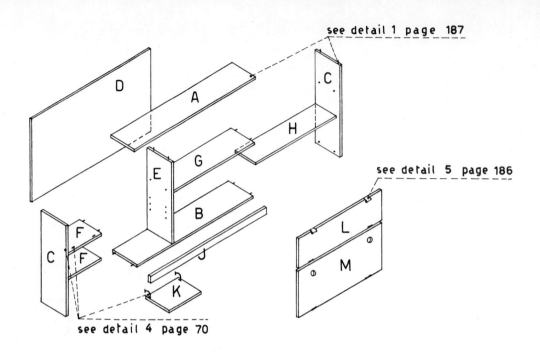

see detail 1 page 187

see detail 5 page 186

see detail 4 page 70

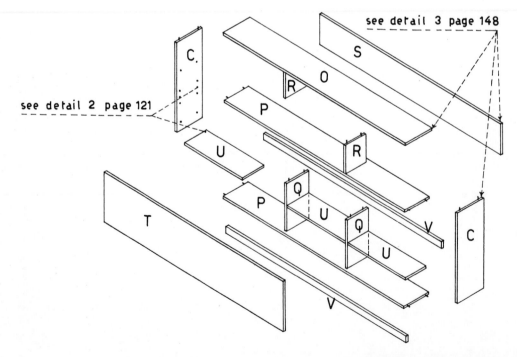

see detail 3 page 148

see detail 2 page 121

Space-Saving Bedroom Unit

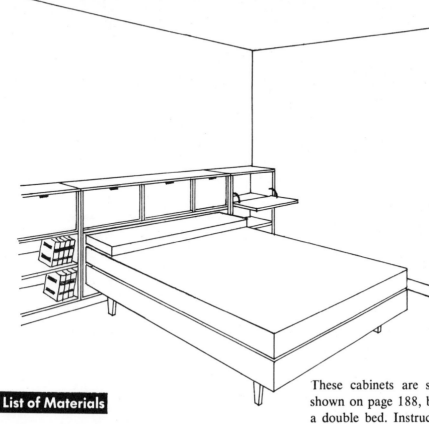

List of Materials

These cabinets are similar to those shown on page 188, but designed for a double bed. Instructions for building the bed itself are given on page 181.

PART	NO.	FUNCTION	DIMENSIONS IN INCHES thickness × width × length		
			thickness	width	length
A	2	top, bottom	¾	12	60
B	1	shelf	¾	11¾	58½
C	6	end	¾	12	34½
D	2	partition	¾	11¾	12¼
E	1	partition	¾	11¾	21½
F	1	back	¼	35½	59½
G	2	shelf	¾	10½	28⅞
H	3	door	¾	12¼	19
J	2	door	¾	21½	28⅞
K	4	top, bottom	¾	12	$w_1 - 1$
L	4	shelf	¾	11¾	$w_1 - 2½$
M	2	door	¾	12¼	$w_1 - 2½$
O	2	back	¼	$w_1 - 1½$	35½
P	1	toeplate	1	3	w
Q	6	base	1	3	10

Instructions for Assembly

Center Cabinet:
1. Join top and bottom (A) and shelf (B) with ends (C) and partitions (D) and (E).
2. Attach back (F).
3. Install doors (H) and (J).
4. Insert shelves (G).
5. Join sides (C) with top and bottom (K), shelf (L), and back (O).
6. Install door (M).
7. Apply finish.
8. Set cabinet on base (P-Q).

FRONT VIEW

SIDE VIEW

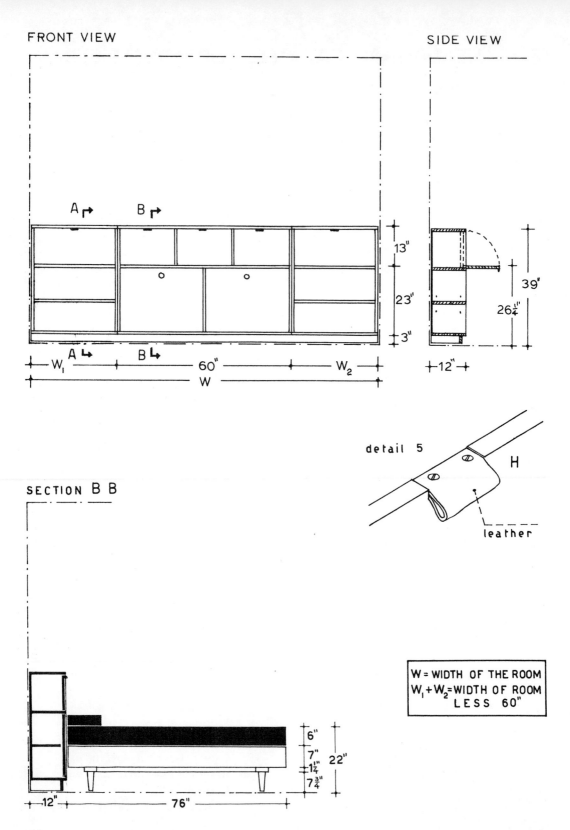

A

B

13"

23"

3"

39"

26¼"

W₁

A

B

60"

W₂

W

12"

W

detail 5

H

leather

SECTION B B

W = WIDTH OF THE ROOM
W₁ + W₂ = WIDTH OF ROOM
LESS 60"

6"

7"

1¼"

22"

7¾"

12"

76"

Headboard Cabinets for Double Bed

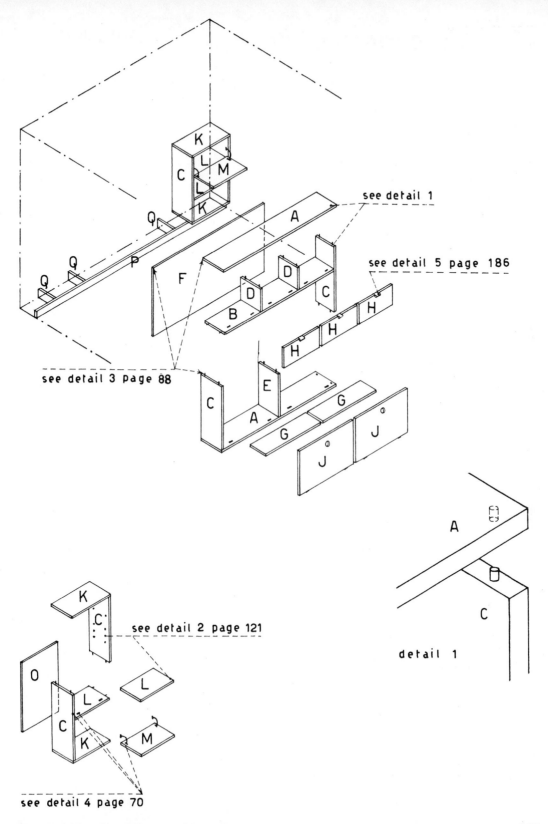

see detail 1

see detail 5 page 186

see detail 3 page 88

see detail 2 page 121

detail 1

see detail 4 page 70

Headboard Cabinets for Double Bed

187

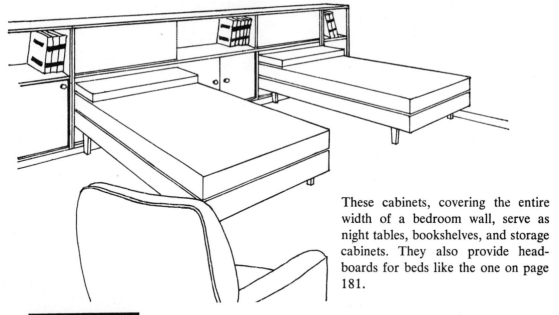

These cabinets, covering the entire width of a bedroom wall, serve as night tables, bookshelves, and storage cabinets. They also provide headboards for beds like the one on page 181.

List of Materials

PART	NO.	FUNCTION	thickness	width	length
			DIMENSIONS IN INCHES		
A	2	top	¾	12	$w_1 - 1$
B	4	shelf, bottom	¾	12	$w_1 - 2\frac{1}{2}$
C	6	side	¾	12	35¼
D	2	back	¼	$w_1 - 1\frac{1}{2}$	35½
E	2	shelf	¾	10½	$w_1 - 2\frac{1}{2}$
F	2	door	¾	$w_1 - 2\frac{1}{2}$	21½
G	2	toeplate	¾	3	$w_1 - 1$
H	8	cross piece	¾	3	10
J	1	toeplate	¾	3	126
K	1	top	¾	12	126
L	2	shelf, bottom	¾	12	124½
M	2	partition	¾	11¾	21½
O	2	partition	¾	10⅞	12¼
P	1	back	¼	35½	42¾
Q	2	back	¼	35½	41⅜
R	2	door	¾	12	41¼
S	2	door	¾	21	21½
T	2	door	¾	21½	40½
U	1	shelf	¾	10½	42

Instructions for Assembly

Side Cabinet
1. Join top of cabinet (A) and shelf and bottom (B) with sides (C) and back (D).
2. Install door (F).
3. Attach base (G-H) to bottom (B).
4. Install shelf (E).

Center Cabinet
5. Join top (K) and shelf and bottom (L) to sides (C) and partitions (M) and (O).
6. Install backs (P) and (Q).
7. Attach base (H-J) to bottom (L).
8. Install doors (S) and (T).
9. Apply finish and set cabinets in position.
10. Insert shelf (U).
11. Install doors (R) and place beds at headboards.

Headboard Cabinets for Twin Beds

FRONT VIEW

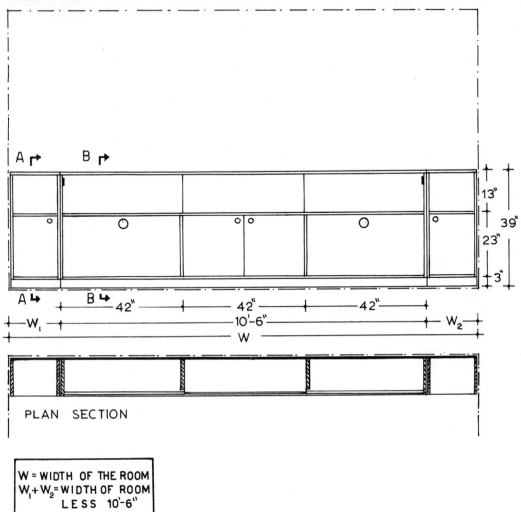

A →   B →

13"
39"
23"
3"

A ↳   B ↳   42"   42"   42"

W₁   10'-6"   W₂

W

PLAN SECTION

W = WIDTH OF THE ROOM
W₁+ W₂= WIDTH OF ROOM
LESS 10'-6"

SECTION AA

6"
7"
1¼"
7¾"

SECTION BB

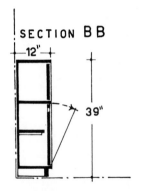

12"

39"

Headboard Cabinets for Twin Beds

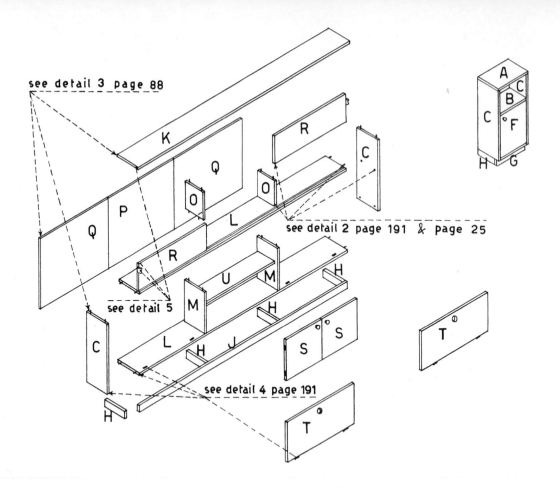

see detail 3 page 88

see detail 2 page 191 & page 25

see detail 5

see detail 4 page 191

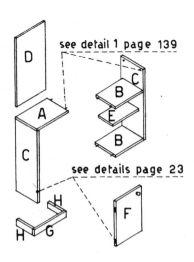

see detail 1 page 139

see details page 23

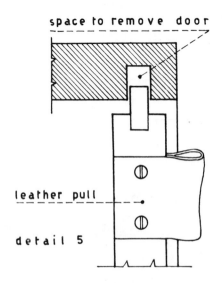

space to remove door

leather pull

detail 5

Headboard Cabinets for Twin Beds

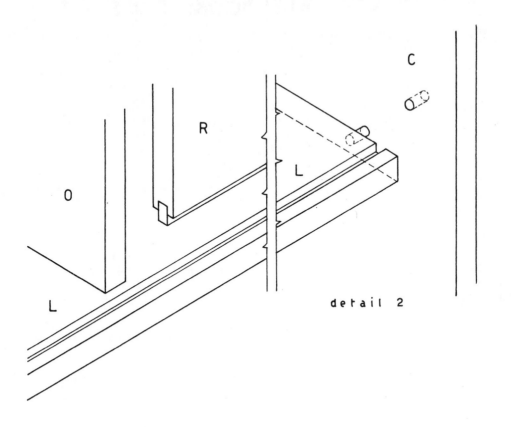

C

R

L

O

L

detail 2

detail 4

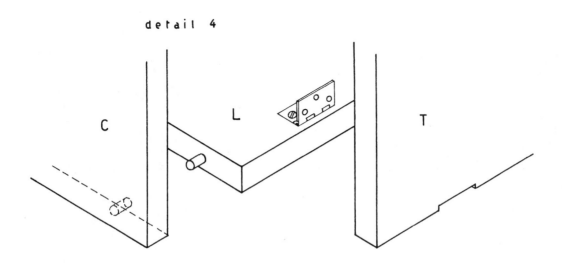

C

L

T

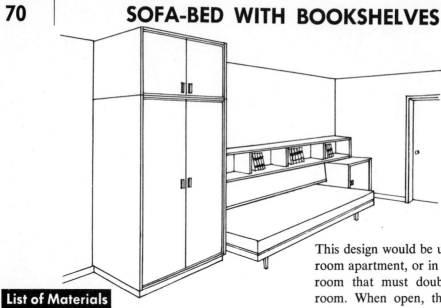

List of Materials

PART	NO.	FUNCTION	DIMENSIONS IN INCHES thickness × width × length		
A	2	top, bottom	¾	11	90
B	3	end	¾	10¼	12½
C	2	partition	¾	9	12½
D	1	back	¼	13½	89½
E	1	door	¾	12½	77
F	1	padding back	¼	10½	75
G	2	back support	¾	1½	9
H	2	side	¾	24	29½
J	1	bottom	¾	11½	24
K	1	top	¾	13	24
L	2	door, back	¾	11½	25½
M	1	toeplate	1	3	11½
O	2	side rail	1	4	76
P	2	end rail	1	4	34
Q	2	leg brace	1	3	34
R	3	cleat	¾	¾	74
S	4	leg	1¼	2½	8
T	4	corner brace	1	3	3
U	1	mattress support	½	34	74
V	1	shelf	¾	11½	20
	1	foam rubber pad	¾	10½	75
	1	foam mattress	5	36	76
		fabric	to cover pad and mattress		

This design would be useful in a one-room apartment, or in a den or living room that must double as a guest room. When open, the door of the bookshelf becomes a backrest, making the bed into a sofa. Instructions and materials for building the closet are given on page 146.

Instructions for Assembly

1. Join top and bottom (A) with ends (B), partitions (C), and back (D).
2. Install door (E).

Cabinet

3. Join top of cabinet (K) and shelves (J) and (V) with sides (H), back (L) and toeplate (M).
4. Install door (L).
5. Attach legs (S) to brace (Q).
6. Join side rails (O) to end rails (P), leg brace (Q), corner brace (T), and cleat (R).
7. Apply finish and set furniture in position.
8. Fasten upholstery on piece (F) and fit (F) to door (E).
9. Fasten back supports (G) to side (H) and side of closet.
10. Place mattress on surface (U) or on springs.

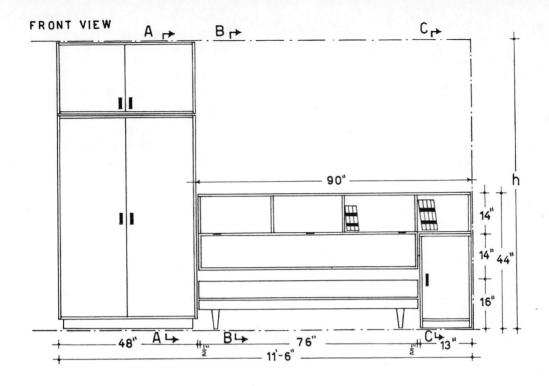

FRONT VIEW

A → B → C →

90"

14"

14" 44"

16"

48" A → B → 76" C → 13"

1/2" 1/2"

11'-6"

h

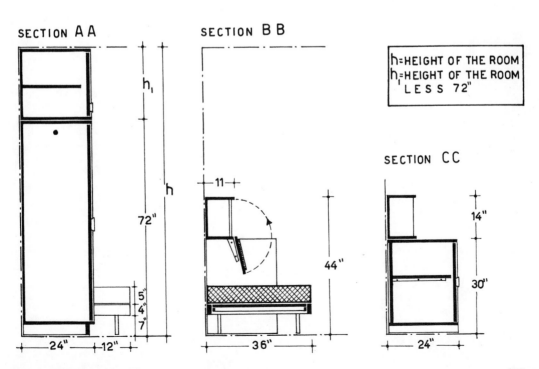

SECTION AA

h₁

h

72"

5"
4"
7"

24" 12"

SECTION BB

11

44"

36"

h = HEIGHT OF THE ROOM
h₁ = HEIGHT OF THE ROOM
LESS 72"

SECTION CC

14"

30"

24"

Sofa Bed with Bookshelves

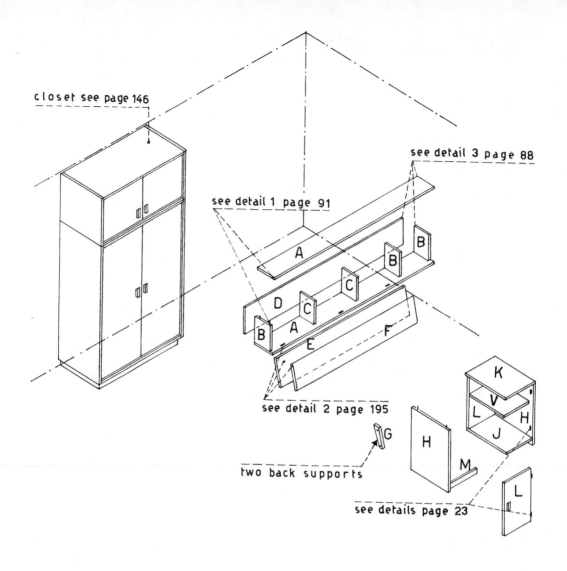

closet see page 146

see detail 3 page 88

see detail 1 page 91

A

B

B

B

C

C

D

C

B

A

E

F

see detail 2 page 195

G

two back supports

K

V

L

H

H

J

H

M

L

see details page 23

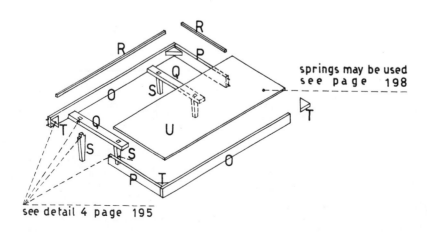

R

R

P

Q

O

S

springs may be used
see page 198

T

T

Q

S

S

U

O

P

T

see detail 4 page 195

Sofa Bed with Bookshelves

detail 2

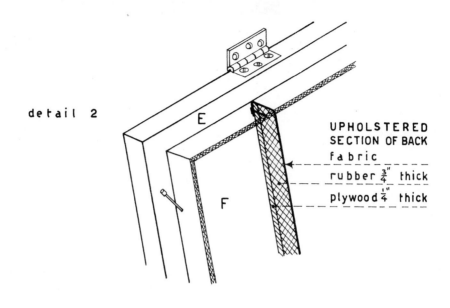

E

F

UPHOLSTERED
SECTION OF BACK
fabric
rubber $\frac{3}{4}''$ thick
plywood $\frac{1}{4}''$ thick

detail 4

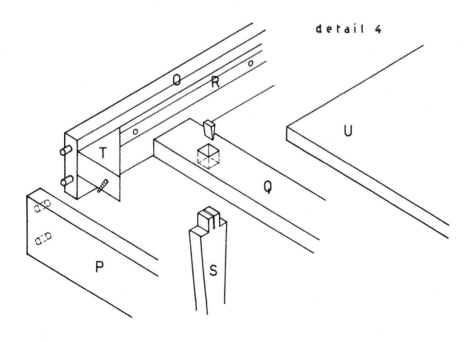

O R

T

U

Q

P

S

Sofa Bed with Bookshelves

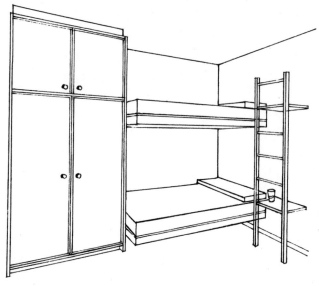

The double-decker arrangement of beds is especially popular for boys' rooms, where it provides more space for play and a touch of adventure. In any small bedroom, however, this arrangement permits placing of two beds in the floor space normally occupied by one. The closet is arranged for use by two persons, with two compartments for hanging clothes and two shelf compartments above.

List of Materials

PART	NO.	FUNCTION	DIMENSIONS IN INCHES thickness	× width	× length
A	2	side	¾	24	92
B	1	partition	¾	23¾	86½
C	3	shelf	¾	24	w_1 − 2½
D	1	back	¼	w_1 − 1½	87½
E	2	shelf	¾	20	to fit
F	1	hanger bar	1-in. (round)		to fit
G	2	door	¾	to fit	27¼
H	2	door	¾	to fit	58½
J	1	toeplate	1	4	w_1 − 2½
K	2	ladder side	1	1¾	81
L	5	rung	¾ (round)		12
M	2	shelf	¾	12	12
O	4	side rail	1	4	76
P	4	end rail	1	4	34
Q	4	cross brace	1	3	34
R	8	corner brace	1	3	3
	2	foam mattress	5	36	76
	1	No-Sag spring			50 ft.

Instructions for Assembly

1. Join sides (A) and partition (B) with top, bottom, and shelf (C).
2. Attach back (D), bar (F), and toeplate (J).
3. Install doors (G) and (H) and shelves (E).

Beds

4. Join side rails (O) with end rails (P), cross braces (Q), and corner braces (R).
5. Install No-Sag spring (to be covered with muslin or canvas after bed is painted, to protect mattress).
6. Join rungs of ladder (L) and shelf (M) to sides (K).
7. Apply finish and install furniture in position.

FRONT VIEW

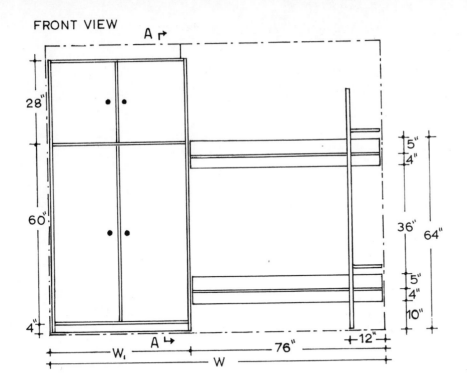

A

28"

60"

4"

5"
4"

36" 64"

5"
4"

10"

W₁

A

76"

12"

W

h=HEIGHT OF THE ROOM
h₁=HEIGHT OF THE ROOM
    LESS 7'-8"
W= WIDTH OF THE ROOM
W₁= WIDTH OF THE ROOM
    LESS 76"

SECTION A A

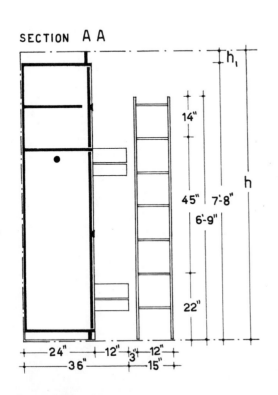

h₁

14"

45" 7'-8"

6'-9"

h

22"

24"   12"   12"
36"   3" 15"

FRONT VIEW VARIATION

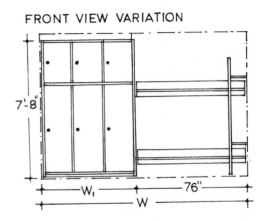

7'-8"

W₁

76"

W

Bunks and Closet

197

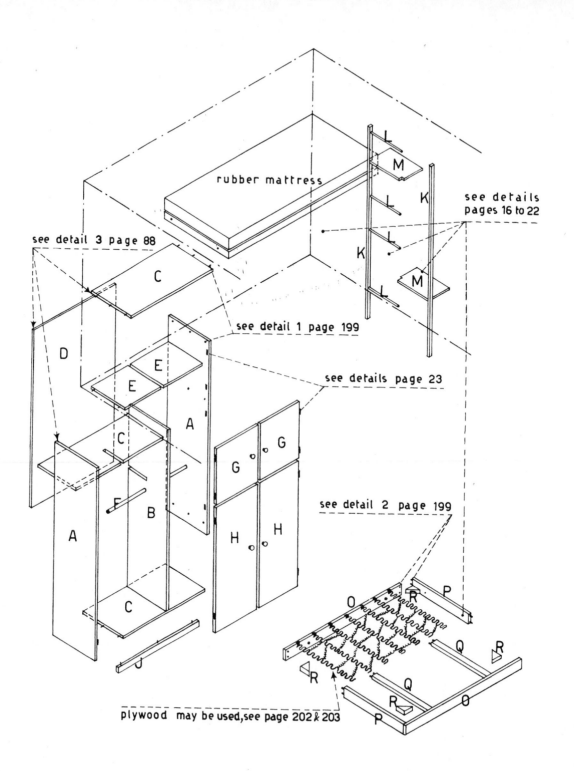

rubber mattress

see details
pages 16 to 22

see detail 3 page 88

see detail 1 page 199

see details page 23

see detail 2 page 199

plywood may be used, see page 202 & 203

Bunks and Closet

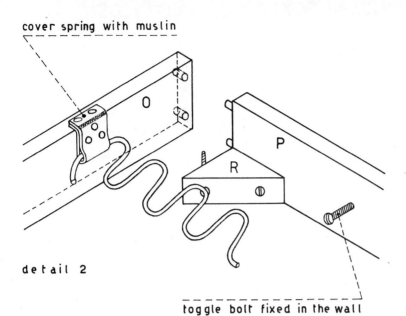

cover spring with muslin

O

P

R

detail 2

toggle bolt fixed in the wall

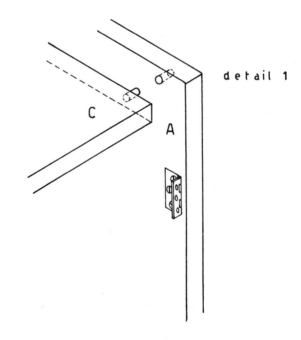

detail 1

C

A

This arrangement of double-decker beds is even better as a space-saver than the previous design, because these beds can be folded against the wall when not in use. Instructions for building the stepladder are given on page 204.

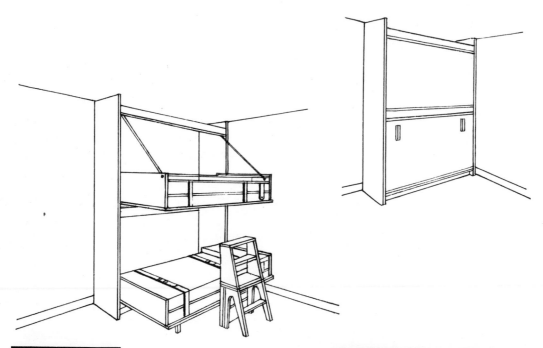

List of Materials

PART	NO.	FUNCTION	DIMENSIONS IN INCHES thickness × width × length		
			thickness	width	length
A	2	side	1	15	h
B	1	bottom	¾	14½	78
C	1	bottom	1	15	78
D	5	rail	1	4	78
E	2	door	¾	36	78
F	4	headboard	¾	13¼	35½
G	4	rail	1	4¼	76⅜
H	4	cleat	¾	¾	33½
J	2	legs	1¼	1¼	6¼
K	2	mattress support	½	34½	76⅜
L	1	guard rail	1	1½	78

Instructions for Assembly

1. Join sides (A) with bottoms (B) and (C) and rails (D).
2. Join rails (G) to head- and footboards (F), and cleats (H) to (F).
3. Attach legs (J) to lower door (E).
4. Apply finish and set frame in position.
5. Attach head- and footboards (F) to sides (A).
6. Attach mattress support (K) to rails (G) and cleats (H).
7. Install guard rail (L).
8. Retouch finish and install mattresses.

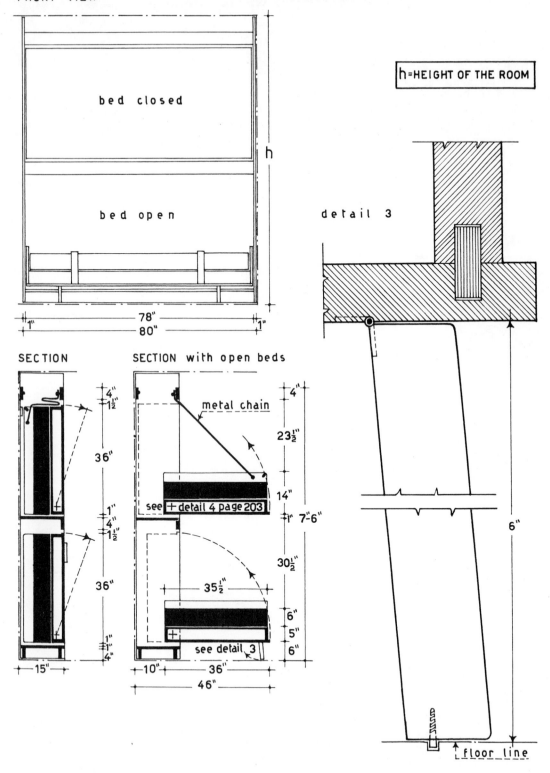

FRONT VIEW

bed closed

bed open

h

78"
80"
1"
1"

h=HEIGHT OF THE ROOM

detail 3

SECTION

4"
1½"
36"
1"
4"
1½"
36"
1"
1"
4"
15"

SECTION with open beds

metal chain

see + detail 4 page 203

see detail 3

4"
23½"
14"
1" 7'-6"
30½"
35½"
6"
5"
6"
10" 36"
46"

6"

floor line

Double-Decker Folding Beds

201

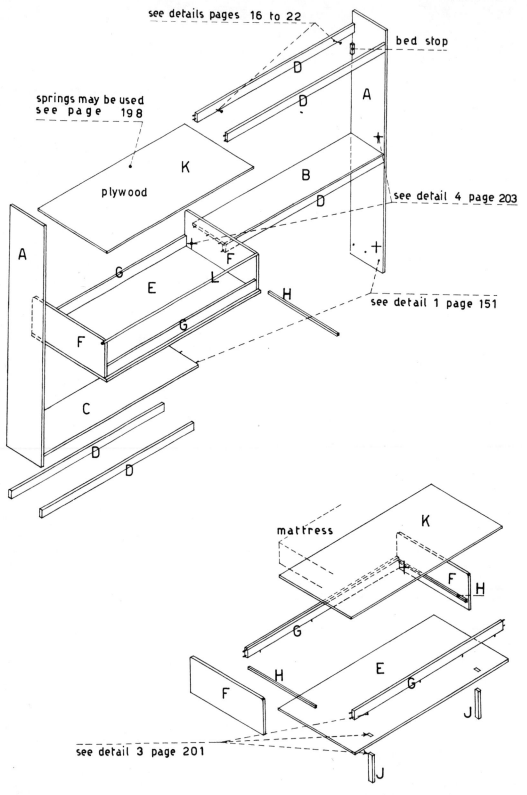

see details pages 16 to 22

bed stop

springs may be used
see page 198

D

D

A

K

plywood

B

D

see detail 4 page 203

A

F

G

L

E

H

F

G

see detail 1 page 151

C

D

D

mattress

K

F

H

G

H

E

G

F

J

J

see detail 3 page 201

Double-Decker Folding Beds

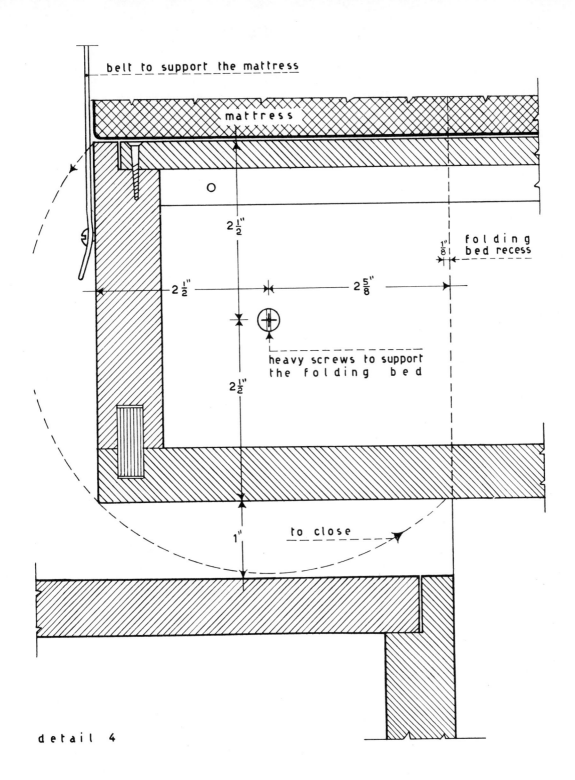

belt to support the mattress

mattress

$2\frac{1}{2}"$

$2\frac{1}{2}"$

$2\frac{5}{8}"$

$\frac{1}{8}"$

folding
bed recess

heavy screws to support
the folding bed

$2\frac{1}{2}"$

$1"$

to close

detail 4

Double-Decker Folding Beds

This convertible stepladder is designed for use with the folding beds shown on page 200, but it has many other household uses. Because it can be folded into the shape of a chair it is more easily stored than the conventional stepladder.

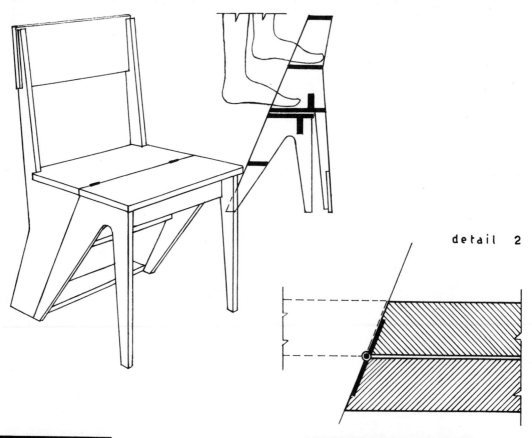

detail 2

PART	NO.	FUNCTION	DIMENSIONS IN INCHES thickness × width × length		
A	2	side	¾	11	32½
B	1	back	½	17½	7
C	2	leg	¾	15	15¾
D	1	seat	¾	10	17½
E	1	seat	¾	8¼	17½
F	2	rail	1	2½	15½
G	1	step	¾	5	15½
H	1	step	¾	6¼	15½
J	1	step	¾	4	15½

Instructions for Assembly

1. Join sides (A) to rails (F) and steps (H) and (G).
2. Attach back (B) to sides (A).
3. Join legs (C) with rails (F) step (J), and seat (E).
4. Join parts of chair seat (D) with sides (A) and rails (F).
5. Join chair seat (D) with hinges to chair seat (E).
6. Apply finish.

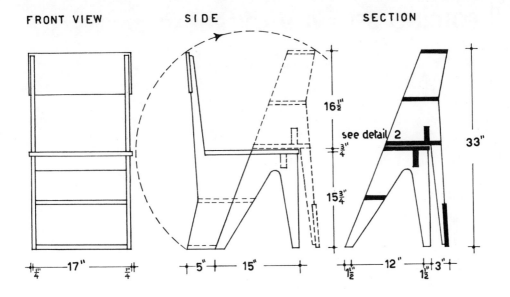

FRONT VIEW   SIDE   SECTION

$16\frac{1}{2}"$

see detail 2

$\frac{3}{4}"$

$15\frac{3}{4}"$

33"

$\frac{1}{4}"$ 17" $\frac{1}{4}"$

5"   15"

$1\frac{1}{2}"$ 12" $1\frac{1}{2}"$ 3"

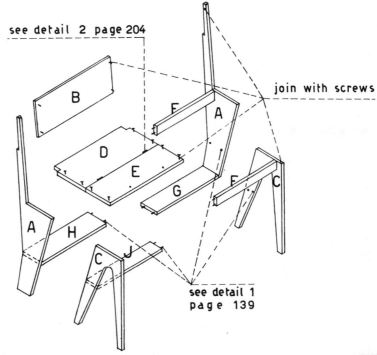

see detail 2 page 204

join with screws

B

F   A

D

E

G

F

C

A   H

C   J

see detail 1
page 139

Stepladder Chair

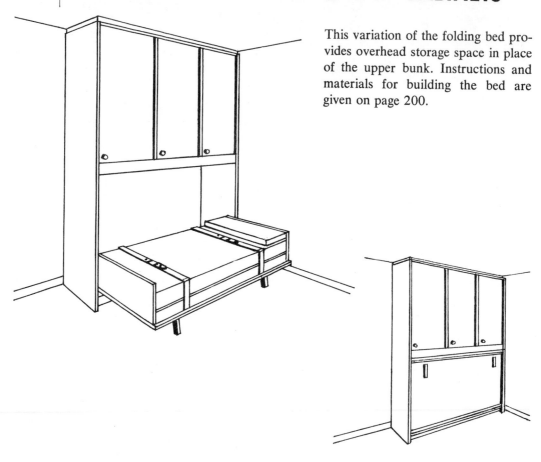

This variation of the folding bed provides overhead storage space in place of the upper bunk. Instructions and materials for building the bed are given on page 200.

1. Join partitions (O) to top and bottom of upper cabinet (B) and (C).
2. Attach rails (D) to bottom of lower cabinet (C).
3. Attach (B) and (C) and (D) to ends (A).
4. Install back (M).
5. Attach cleats (Q) to sides (A) and partitions (O), and install door (R).
6. Assemble bed as shown on page 200.
7. Apply finish and set cabinet in position.
8. Install bed and shelves (P).

List of Materials

PART	NO.	FUNCTION	thickness	× width	× length
			DIMENSIONS IN INCHES		
A	2	side	1	15	h
B	1	shelf	¾	14½	78
C	2	top	1	15	78
D	3	rail	1	4	78
M	1	back	¼	79	$h_1 - 1\frac{1}{2}$
O	2	partition	1	14¾	$h_1 - 2$
P	2	shelf	¾	13½	25⅜
Q	4	cleat	½	½	13
R	3	door	¾	25⅜	$h_1 - 2$

Folding Bed with Overhead Cabinets

see detail 3 page 88

see details page 23

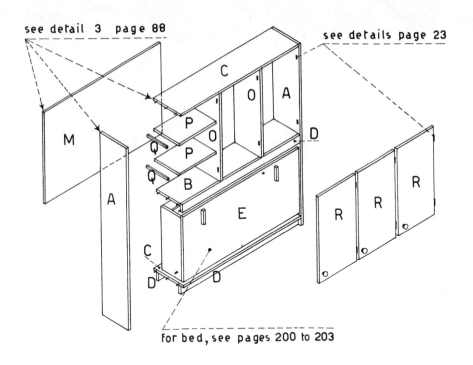

for bed, see pages 200 to 203

h = HEIGHT OF THE ROOM
h₁ = HEIGHT OF THE ROOM
LESS 47½"

FRONT VIEW

SIDE SECTION

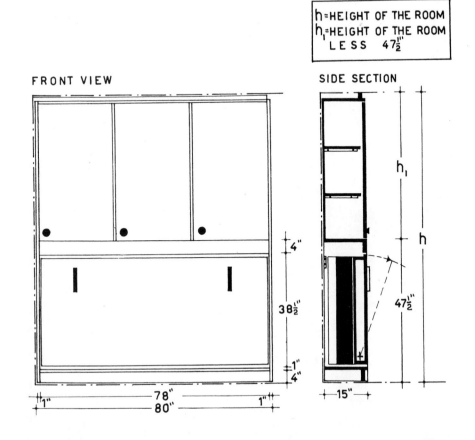

Folding Bed with Overhead Cabinets

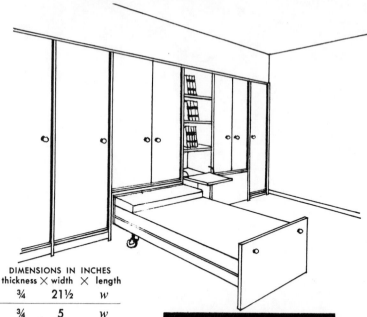

List of Materials

PART	NO.	FUNCTION	DIMENSIONS IN INCHES thickness × width × length		
A	1	top	¾	21½	*w*
B	1	rail	¾	5	*w*
C	1	cornice	¾	h_1	*w*
D	6	side	¾	24	76¼
E	2	door	¾	22½	71½
F	4	door	¾	21	54½
G	3	back	½	23½	70
H	2	back	½	42¾	53
J	3	toeplate	1	4	22½
K	2	shelf	¾	22½	22
L	7	shelf	¾	22½	24
M	2	cabinet floor	¾	42	24
N	2	hangar bar	1(round)		22½
O	6	shelf	¾	42	22
P	16	cleat	½	½	22
Q	1	drop door	¾	22½	15
R	2	door	¾	11¼	16¼
S	2	headboard	¾	40	13½
T	2	footboard	¾	42	21
U	4	rail	1	4	76½
V	2	corner block	1	3	3
W	2	caster block	1½	1½	5½
X	2	bar	1¼	3	38
		No-Sag spring			50 ft.

Instructions for Assembly

1. Join sides (D) with top (A), shelves (L), and cabinet floor (M).
2. Attach toeplate (J) to bottom shelf (L).
3. Join rail (B) with top (A) and sides (D).
4. Install backs (G) and (H).
5. Set framework in place.
6. Attach cleats (P) to sides (D).
7. Install doors (E), (F), (R), (Q), and bar (N).

Bed

8. Attach casters (W) to bar (X).
9. Join rails (U) to head and footboards (S) and (T), and bar (X).
10. Install corner blocks (V).
11. Install No-Sag spring; cover with muslin or canvas after bed is painted.
12. Apply finish and install shelves (L), (O), and (K) and beds.

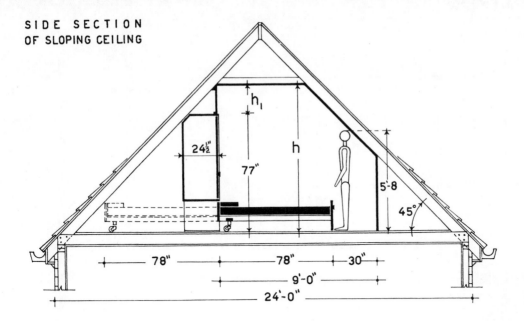

SIDE SECTION
OF SLOPING CEILING

Utilizing the space under a sloping roof provides a compact arrangement of children's furniture. The beds roll into the wall when not in use, leaving most of the floor space free for play.

h = HEIGHT OF THE ROOM
h₁ = HEIGHT OF THE ROOM LESS 77"
W = WIDTH OF THE ROOM
W₁ = WIDTH OF THE ROOM LESS 13'-0"

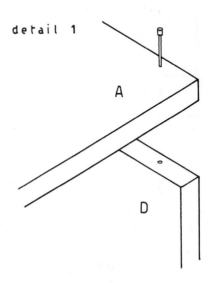

detail 1

FRONT VIEW

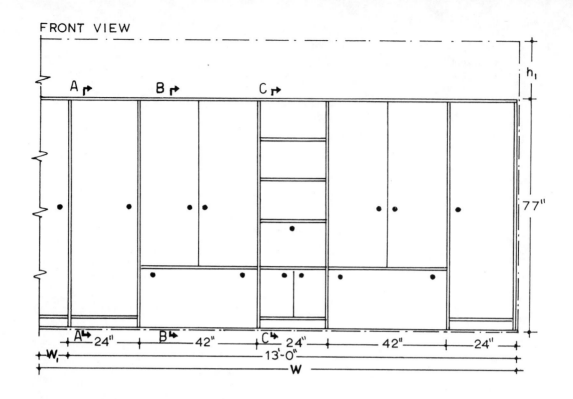

SECTION A A   SECTION B B   SECTION CC

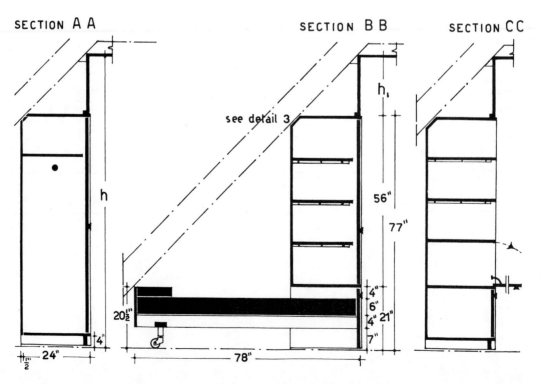

Storage Wall and Roll-away Beds for Children's Room

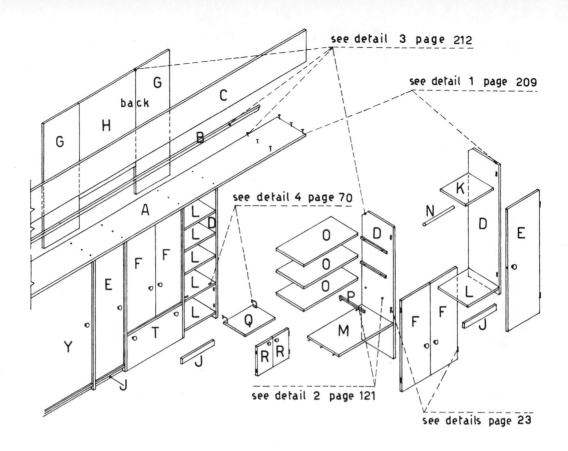

see detail 3 page 212

see detail 1 page 209

back

see detail 4 page 70

see detail 2 page 121

see details page 23

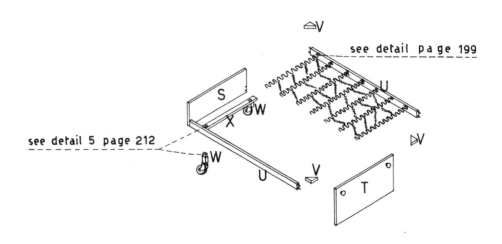

see detail page 199

see detail 5 page 212

Storage Wall and Roll-away Beds for Children's Room

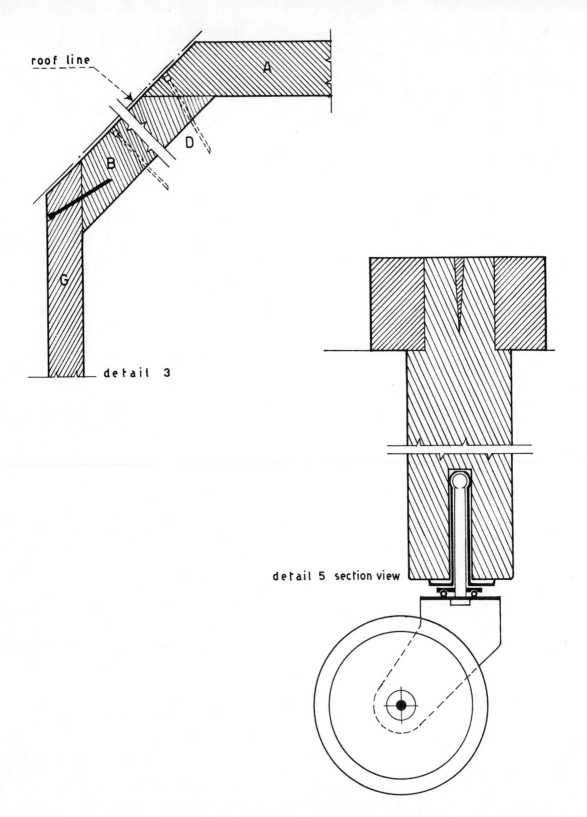

roof line

A

B

D

B

G

detail 3

detail 5 section view

Storage Wall and Roll-away Beds for Children's Room

The following pages show several styles of cabinets which may be selected and arranged to provide efficient work and storage space for the kitchen. One possible arrangement, with cabinets covering one wall beneath a dropped ceiling, is shown above. The diagram at the left shows a method of covering joints between cabinets.

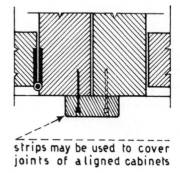

strips may be used to cover joints of aligned cabinets

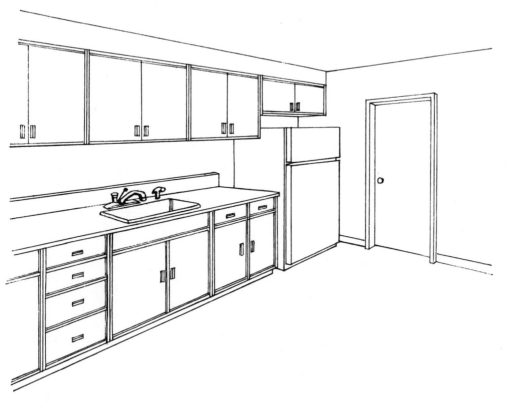

Corner Grouping of Kitchen Cabinets

Another way of arranging kitchen built-ins is to have a corner grouping. Many other arrangements are possible, utilizing the basic cabinet designs shown on the following pages.

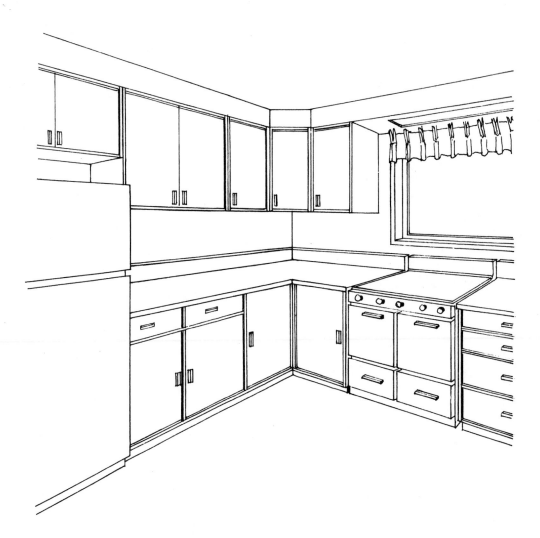

CABINETS SIDE VIEW
dropped ceiling

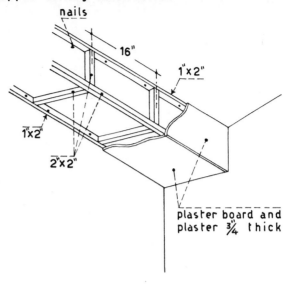

30"

18"

84"

h

36"

dropped ceiling construction

nails

16"

1"x2"

1"x2"

2"x2"

plaster board and
plaster ¾ thick

CABINET SIDE SECTION VIEW

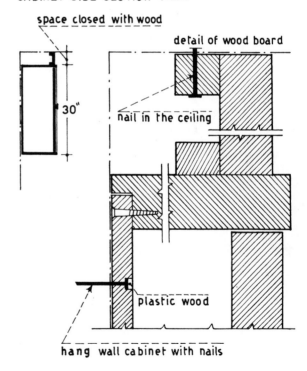

space closed with wood

detail of wood board

30"

nail in the ceiling

plastic wood

hang wall cabinet with nails

Dropped Ceiling

When kitchen cabinets of standard size are placed at the standard height of 18 in. above the counters, there is usually a gap between the top of the cabinets and the ceiling. The diagram at the top of this page shows how a dropped ceiling may be constructed to fill this gap. In the drawing at the right a board is used to fill the space, but this method is practical only when the space to be filled is no more than 6 in. high.

This cabinet can be built with door to open either right or left.

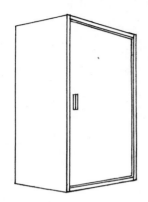

List of Materials

PART	NO.	FUNCTION	DIMENSIONS IN INCHES thickness × width × length		
A	2	top, bottom	¾	12	16½
B	2	side	¾	12	30
C	1	back	¼	17½	29½
D	1	door	¾	16½	28½
E	2	shelf	¾	10½	16½
F	4	cleat	½	½	10

Instructions for Assembly

1. Join top and bottom (A) with sides (B) and back (C).
2. Attach cleats (F) to sides (B).
3. Install door (D).
4. Apply finish and install shelves (E).

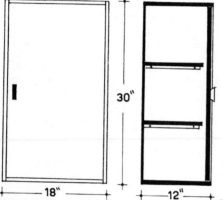

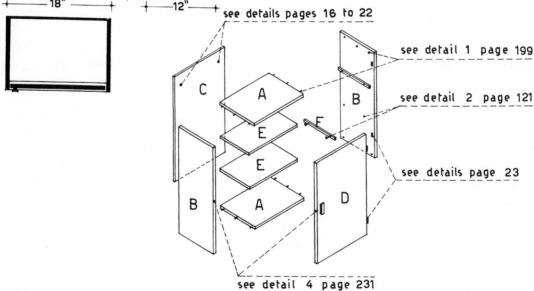

see details pages 16 to 22

see detail 1 page 199

see detail 2 page 121

see details page 23

see detail 4 page 231

When more than one cabinet of the type shown on page 216 is wanted, this double design offers economies in material and labor.

List of Materials

PART	NO.	FUNCTION	thickness	×	DIMENSIONS IN INCHES width	×	length
A	2	top, bottom	¾		12		34½
B	2	side	¾		12		30
C	1	back	¼		35½		29½
D	2	door	¾		17¼		28½
E	2	shelf	¾		10½		34½
F	4	cleat	½		½		10

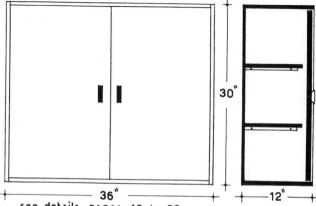

30"

36"

see details pages 16 to 22

12"

Instructions for Assembly

1. Join top and bottom (A) with sides (B) and back (C).
2. Attach cleats (F) to sides (B).
3. Install doors (D).
4. Apply finish and install shelves (E).

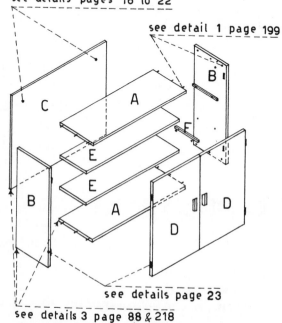

see detail 1 page 199

see details page 23

see details 3 page 88 & 218

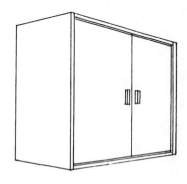

for cupboard catch
see detail 4 page 231

Double Wall Cabinet: Three Shelves

| # DOUBLE WALL CABINET: TWO SHELVES

This design can be used over a refrigerator (see p. 213), or, with a sheet of asbestos attached to the bottom, over a stove.

detail 3

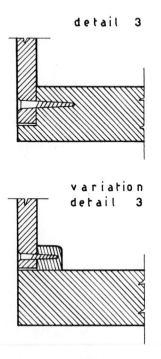

variation
detail 3

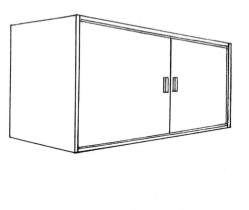

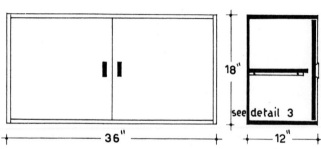

18"

36" 12"

see detail 3

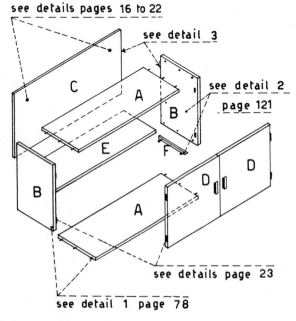

see details pages 16 to 22

see detail 3

see detail 2
page 121

see details page 23

see detail 1 page 78

List of Materials

PART	NO.	FUNCTION	DIMENSIONS IN INCHES thickness × width × length		
A	2	top, bottom	¾	12	34½
B	2	side	¾	12	18
C	1	back	¼	17½	35½
D	2	door	¾	17¼	16½
E	1	shelf	¾	10½	34½
F	2	cleat	½	½	10

Instructions for Assembly

1. Join top and bottom (A) to sides (B) and back (C).
2. Attach cleats (F) to sides (B).
3. Install doors (D).
4. Apply paint and install shelf (E).

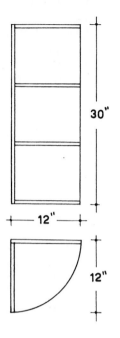

30"

|← 12" →|

12"

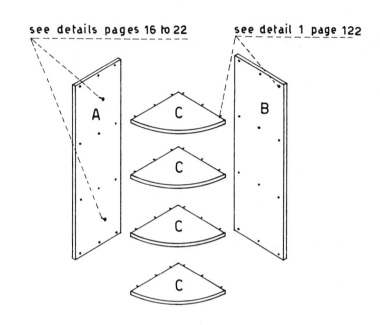

see details pages 16 to 22   see detail 1 page 122

A   C   B

C

C

C

A row of cabinets can be ended very neatly with this design, which also provides display space for plants or ornamental objects. A pair of these shelves flanking a window will prevent the closed-in appearance that standard cabinets would give.

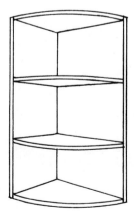

Instructions for Assembly

1. Round shelves (C) and attach to (A) and (B).
2. Apply finish.

List of Materials

PART	NO.	FUNCTION	thickness	width	length
			DIMENSIONS IN INCHES		
A	1	side	¾	11¼	30
B	1	side	¾	12	30
C	4	shelf	¾	11¼	11¼

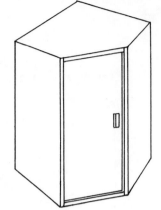

see details pages 16 to 22

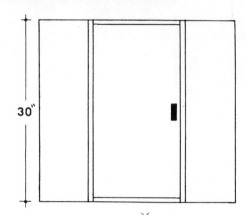

30"

see detail 1 page 122

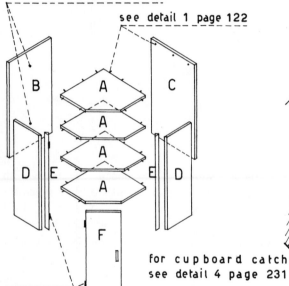

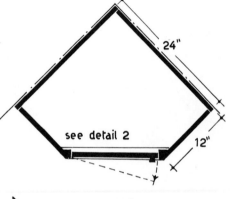

24"

see detail 2

12"

detail 2

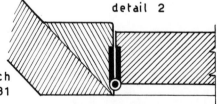

see detail 2

for cupboard catch
see detail 4 page 231

This cabinet makes use of otherwise "dead" space in a corner where two rows of wall cabinets meet.

List of Materials

PART	NO.	FUNCTION	DIMENSIONS IN INCHES thickness × width × length		
A	4	shelf	¾	22½	22½
B	1	side	¾	24	30
C	1	side	¾	23¼	30
D	2	side	¾	12	30
E	1*	jamb	1¼	1¼	28½
F	1	door	¾	15	28½

* Cut diagonally to make two.

Instructions for Assembly

1. Attach shelves (A) to sides (B) and (C).
2. Attach sides (D) to (A-B-C).
3. Attach jambs (E) to sides (D).
4. Install door (F).
5. Apply finish.

Wall-hung Corner Cabinet

KITCHEN STORAGE CABINET

Instructions for Assembly

1. Join top and bottom (A) with sides (B) and back (C).
2. Attach cleats (F) to sides (B).
3. Attach toeplate (G).
4. Install shelves (E) and door (P) and apply finish.

Plentiful storage for canned foods, groceries, and other supplies is provided by the compartments of this cabinet. Ready-made spice shelves may be attached to the inside of the door.

List of Materials

PART	NO.	FUNCTION	DIMENSIONS IN INCHES thickness × width × length		
A	2	top, bottom	¾	16½	12
B	2	side	¾	12	60
C	1	back	¼	17½	55½
D	1	door	¾	16½	54½
E	4	shelf	¾	16½	10½
F	8	cleat	½	½	10
G	1	toeplate	¾	4	16½

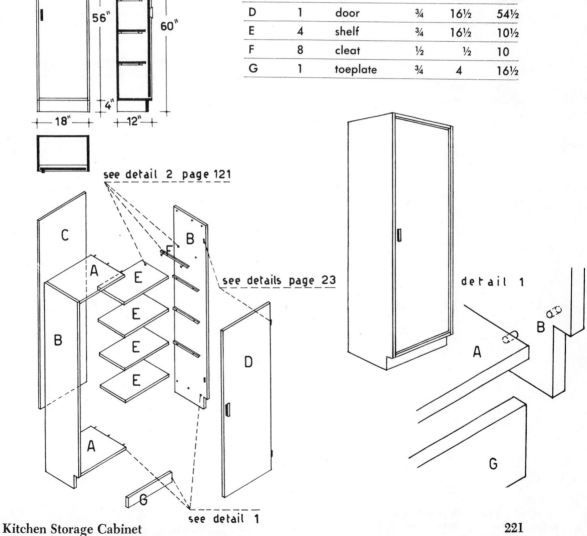

see detail 2 page 121

see details page 23

detail 1

see detail 1

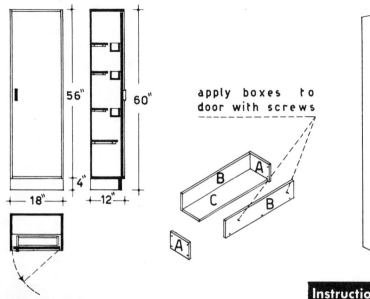

apply boxes to
door with screws

List of Materials

Use list given on page 221, cutting three of the four shelves 16½ x 6½ rather than 16½ by 10½, to allow space for boxes attached to door. For boxes, add these pieces:

PART	NO.	FUNCTION	DIMENSIONS IN INCHES thickness × width × length		
			thickness	width	length
A	6	side	⅜	3	4
B	6	back, front	⅜	3	15
C	3	bottom	⅜	3¼	15

Instructions for Assembly

This cabinet may be built either with shelves, as shown above, or with broom closet fixtures, as shown below. Shallow boxes attached to the door offer additional shelf space.

Follow instructions on page 221, adding door boxes for design above, and omitting shelves and adding metal fixtures for broom closet below.

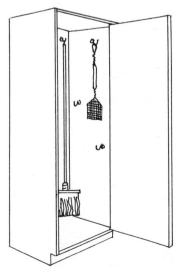

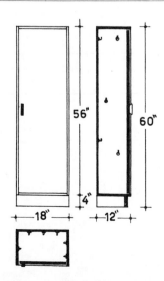

Kitchen Storage Cabinet or Broom Closet

COUNTER TOP

SIDE SECTION

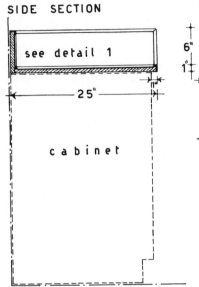

FRONT VIEW

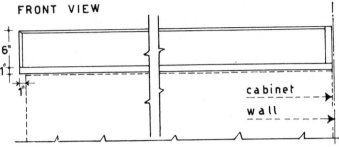

A variety of waterproof surfacing materials is available for covering kitchen work surfaces. These range from battleship linoleum to rubber tile and synthetic mica-type materials. They can be purchased alone in sheets, or ready-bonded to plywood. Some require professional installation, so it would be wise for the home craftsman to consult his dealer before making a selection. Metal molding is customarily used to protect and finish the counter edges, but the same surfacing material can also be used.

Details on this page and page 224 show how to measure and install surface material and molding. Instructions for bonding the synthetic surfacing material to the plywood are given on page 225.

Standard depth measurement is 25 in.; the splashback against the wall should be 6 in. high.

detail 1

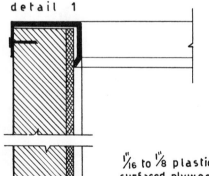

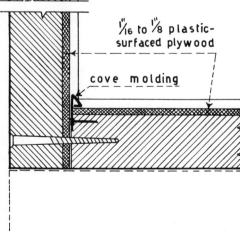

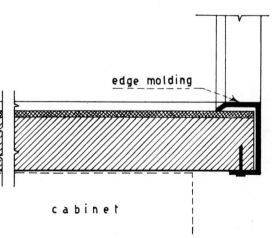

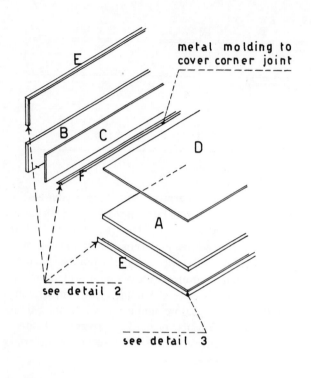

E

metal molding to
cover corner joint

B C

D

F

A

E

see detail 2

see detail 3

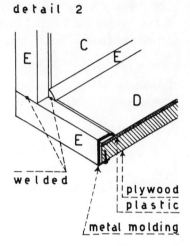

detail 2

E   C   E

D

E

welded

plywood
plastic

metal molding

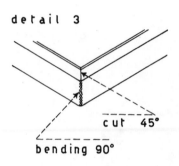

detail 3

cut 45°

bending 90°

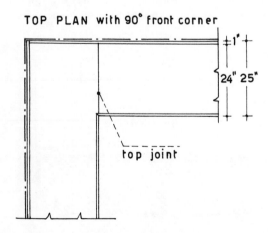

TOP PLAN with 90° front corner

1"

24" 25"

top joint

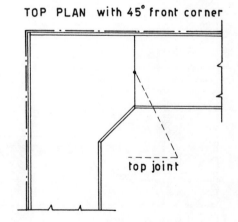

TOP PLAN with 45° front corner

top joint

Bonding Counter Surfacing Material to Plywood

The sketches below show the steps to be followed in attaching surface material to plywood. If the panel to be laminated is securely fastened to the frame of the cabinet, only the outer surface is covered, but if the panel is simply to rest on the frame, a balance sheet must be applied to the under surface to prevent warpage.

1. Smooth the plywood with sand paper.
2. Cut the surfacing material carefully to size with a saw. For a clean cut use clamps and keep the saw as horizontal as possible.
3. Place the surfacing material on the plywood to check the fit; shave off any excess.
4. A plastic adhesive and pressure give the best contact bonding. Manufacturer's instructions should be observed.
5. Roll the surface to insure a tight bond. An ordinary rolling pin may be used.
6. When the surfacing is firmly bonded to the plywood, edges may be beveled with a file and metal molding applied or the strips of the surfacing material can be applied to the edges of the plywood.

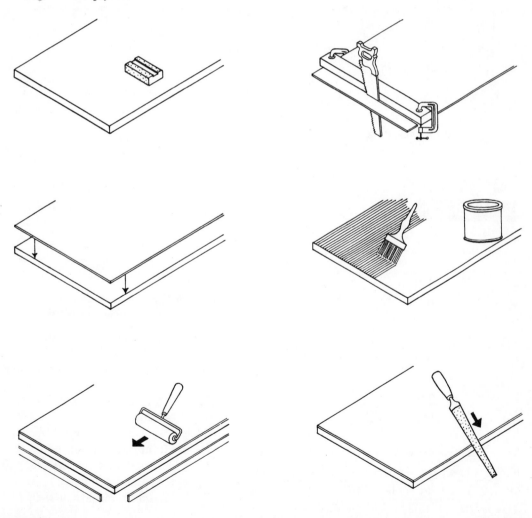

These units provide kitchen storage and a base for the counter top (see pages 223-225).

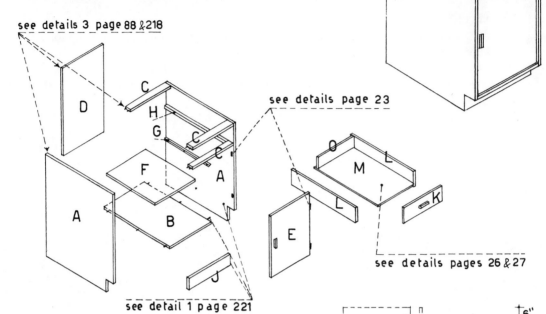

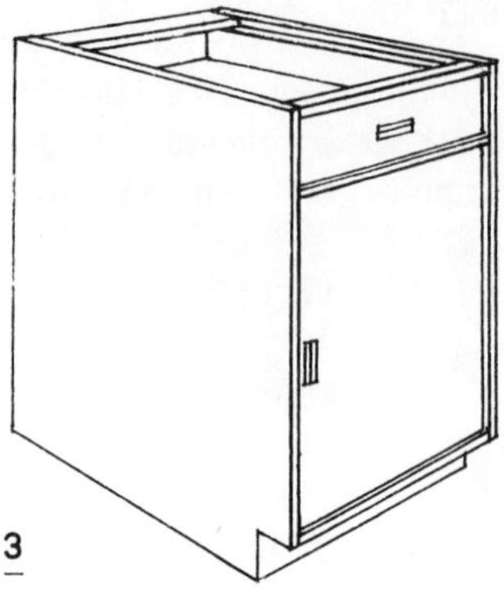

see details 3 page 88 & 218

see details page 23

see details pages 26 & 27

see detail 1 page 221

for cupboard catch
see detail 4 page 231

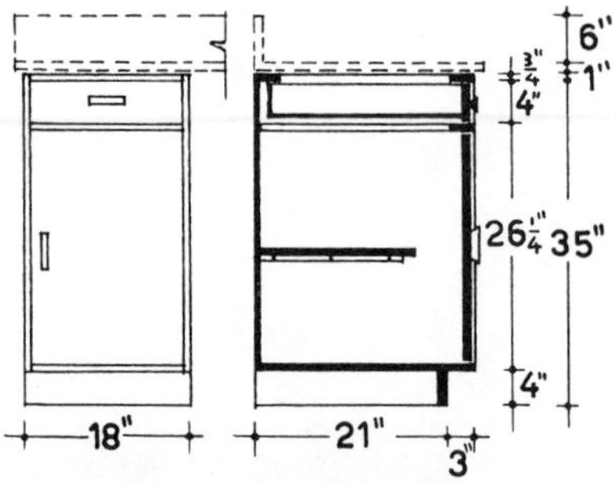

List of Materials

PART	NO.	FUNCTION	thickness ×	width ×	length
			DIMENSIONS IN INCHES		
A	2	side	¾	24	35
B	1	bottom	¾	16½	24
C	3	rail	¾	2½	16½
D	1	back	¼	17½	30½
E	1	door	¾	16½	24¾
F	1	shelf	¾	16½	18
G	2	cleat	½	½	17
H	2	drawer glide	¾	¾	21¼
J	1	toeplate	1	4	16½
K	1	drawer front	¾	4	16½
L	2	drawer side	⅜	4	23⅜
M	1	drawer bottom	¼	16	23¼
O	1	drawer back	⅜	3½	15⅝

Instructions for Assembly

1. Join sides (A) with bottom (B), rails (C), and back (D).
2. Attach cleats (G) and drawer glides (H) to sides (A).
3. Attach toeplate (J) to (A-B).
4. Install door (E).
5. Join sides of drawer (L) to back and front (O) and (K).
6. Attach bottom of drawer (M) to sides (L) and front (K).
7. Apply finish and install shelf (F).

No kitchen can have enough drawer space. This design provides two deep and two shallow drawers for a variety of uses.

List of Materials

PART	NO.	FUNCTION	thickness ×	width ×	length
			DIMENSIONS IN INCHES		
A	2	side	¾	24	35
B	1	bottom	¾	16½	24
C	5	rail	¾	2½	16½
D	1	back	¼	17½	30½
E	6	drawer glide	¾	¾	21¼
F	1	toeplate	1	4	16½
G	2	drawer front	¾	4	16½
H	4	drawer bottom	¼	16	23¼
J	4	drawer side	⅜	4	23⅜
K	2	drawer back	⅜	3½	15⅝
L	2	drawer front	¾	9⅝	16½
M	4	drawer side	⅜	9⅝	23⅜
O	2	drawer back	⅜	9⅛	15⅝

Instructions for Assembly

1. Join sides (A) with bottom (B), rails (C), and back (D).
2. Attach drawer glides (E) and toeplate (F) to sides (A).
3. Join sides of drawer (J) with front and back (G) and (K).
4. Attach bottom of drawer (H) to sides and front (J) and (G).
5. Join sides of larger drawer (M) with front and back (L) and (O) and attach bottom of drawer (H) to front and sides (L-M).
6. Apply finish and insert drawers.

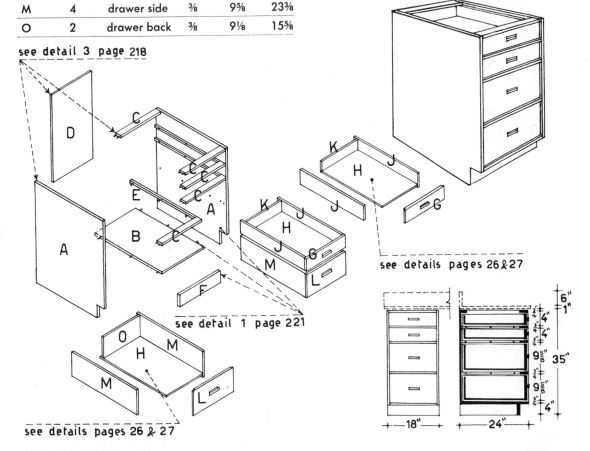

see detail 3 page 218

see details pages 26 & 27

see detail 1 page 221

see details pages 26 & 27

This base cabinet serves the same purpose as the wall-hung corner cabinet on page 220. The inside shelves rotate to provide maximum accessibility.

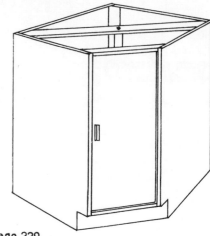

FRONT VIEW

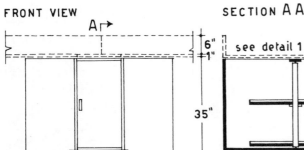

6"
1"
35"

SECTION A A

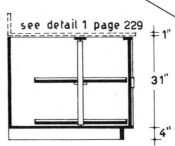

see detail 1 page 229

1"
31"
4"

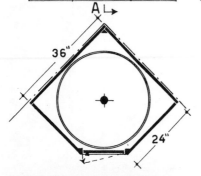

36"
24"

Instructions for Assembly

1. Join backs (B) and (C) with bottom (O), brace (G), and rail (D).
2. Join sides (A) with back (B-C), bottom (O), and rail (E).
3. Attach door jambs (F) to sides (A).
4. Attach base (L) to toeplate (M) and bottom (O).
5. Join shelves (J) with spindle (K).
6. Attach spindle (K) to bottom (O) and rail (D).
7. Install door (F) and apply finish.

List of Materials

PART	NO.	FUNCTION	DIMENSIONS IN INCHES		
			thickness	width	length
A	2	side	¾	24	35
B	1	back	¾	36	31
C	1	back	¾	35¼	31
D	1	rail	¾	3	49
E	1	rail	¾	2½	20
F	1*	jamb	1¼	1¼	29½
G	1*	brace	2	2	30¼
H	1	door	¾	15¼	29½
J	2	shelf	¾	30	30
K	1	spindle	1½ (round)		29¼
L	1	base	1	4	38
M	1	toeplate	1	4	23
O	1	bottom	¾	34½	34½

* Cut diagonally to make two.

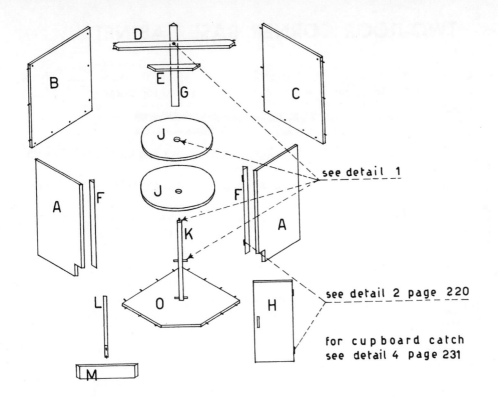

see detail 1

see detail 2 page 220

for cupboard catch
see detail 4 page 231

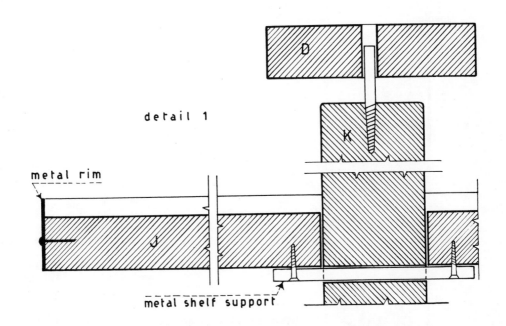

detail 1

metal rim

metal shelf support

This alternative to the corner base cabinet on page 228 does not offer the convenience of rotating shelves, but instead utilizes much more of the enclosed area for storage.

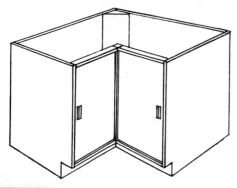

List of Materials

PART	NO.	FUNCTION	DIMENSIONS IN INCHES thickness × width × length		
A	2	side	¾	24	35
B	1	back	¾	35¼	31
C	1	back	¾	34½	31
D	2	rail	¾	1¾	11¼
E	1	door jamb	1¾	1¾	30¼
F	1	false back	¾	10	30¼
G	4	cleat	¾	¾	27
H	2	door	¾	11¼	29½
J	2	toeplate	1	4	15
K	2	shelf	¾	34½	34½

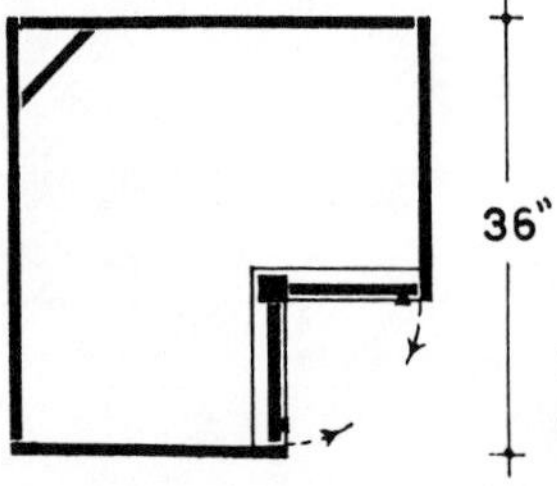

Instructions for Assembly

1. Join bottom shelf (K) and false back (F) with backs (B) and (C).
2. Attach door jamb (E) to shelves (K) and rails (D).
3. Attach sides (A) to backs (B) and (C), bottom shelf (K), and rails (D).
4. Attach toeplate (J) to sides (A) and bottom shelf (K).
5. Attach cleats (G) to backs (B).
6. Install door (H).
7. Apply finish and insert top shelf (K).

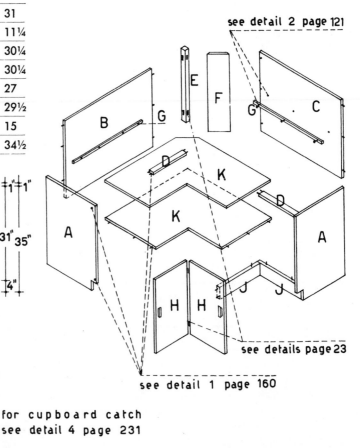

see detail 2 page 121

see details page 23

see detail 1 page 160

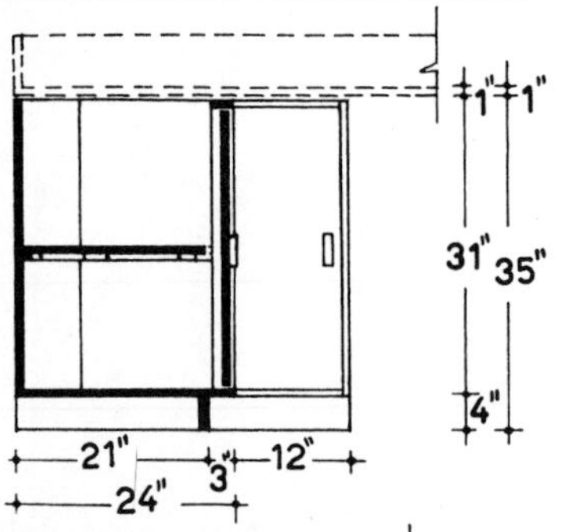

for cupboard catch
see detail 4 page 231

This simple cabinet may be built to fill the odd space between a row of standard cabinets and a wall. It is designed with standard height and depth, but variable width.

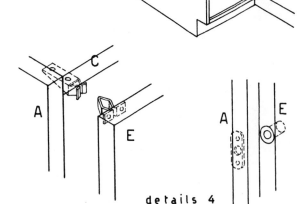

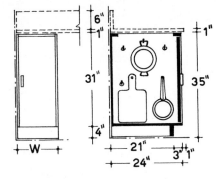

```
W = SPACE BETWEEN WALL
AND STANDARD CABINET
```

see detail 3 page 218

see details 4

details 4

see details 4

List of Materials

PART	NO.	FUNCTION	thickness ×	width ×	length
			DIMENSIONS IN INCHES		
A	2	side	¾	24	35
B	1	back	¼	30½	w − 1½
C	2	rail	¾	2½	w − 2½
D	1	bottom	¾	24	w − 2½
E	1	door	¾	29½	w − 2½
F	1	toeplate	1	4	w − 2½

see detail 1 page 221

see details page 23

Instructions for Assembly

1. Join sides (A) with rails (C) and bottom (D).
2. Install back (B).
3. Attach toeplate (F) to sides (A) and bottom (D).
4. Install door (E).
5. Apply finish.

This design can be used for either wall or base cabinets at the end of a row, especially if near a passageway where the opening of a cabinet door would be inconvenient.

see detail 1 page 187

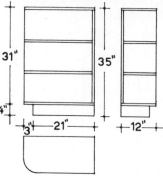

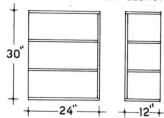

variation
make 30" h. when used as a wall cabinet

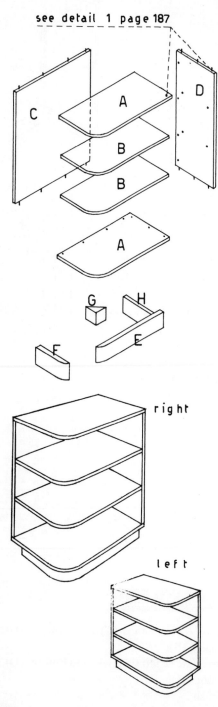

right

left

List of Materials

PART	NO.	FUNCTION	DIMENSIONS IN INCHES thickness × width × length		
			thickness	width	length
A	2	top, bottom	¾	12	24
B	2	shelf	¾	11¼	23¼
C	1	back	¾	23¼	29½
D	1	side	¾	12	29½
E	1	toeplate	1	4	21
F	1	toeplate	1	4	8
G	1	corner brace	4	2	2
H	1	base	1	4	8

Instructions for Assembly

1. Join top and bottom (A) and shelves (B) with back (C) and side (D).
2. Attach toeplates (E) and (F) to base (H) and corner brace (G).
3. Attach base (E-F-G-H) to bottom (A).
4. Apply finish.

This double unit may be substituted for two separate cabinets of the type shown on page 226, with consequent saving in materials and labor.

List of Materials

PART	NO.	FUNCTION	thickness	width	length
A	2	side	¾	24	35
B	1	bottom	¾	34½	24
C	3	rail	¾	2½	34½
D	1	back	¼	35½	30½
E	2	door	¾	17¼	24¾
F	1	shelf	¾	18	34½
G	2	cleat	½	½	17
H	2	drawer glide	¾	¾	21¼
J	1	partition	¾	4	23¾
K	1	drawer glide	¾	3	21¼
L	1	toeplate	¾	4	34½
M	2	drawer front	¾	4	16⅞
O	2	drawer bottom	¼	16⅜	23¼
P	4	drawer side	⅜	4	23⅜
Q	2	drawer back	⅜	3½	16

DIMENSIONS IN INCHES: thickness × width × length

for cupboard catch see detail 4 page 231

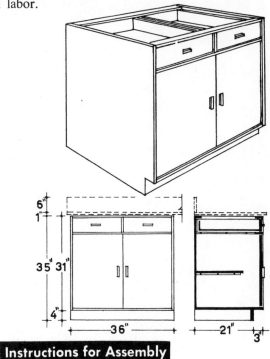

Instructions for Assembly

1. Attach sides (A) to bottom (B) and rails (C).
2. Join partition (J) with center drawer glide (K).
3. Attach (J-K) to rails (C).
4. Install back (D).
5. Attach cleats (G) and drawer glides (H) to sides (A).
6. Attach toeplate (L) to sides (A) and bottom (B).
7. Install doors (E).
8. Join sides of drawer (P) to front and back (M) and (Q).
9. Attach bottom of drawer (O) to sides (P) and front (M).
10. Apply finish and install shelf (F) and drawers.

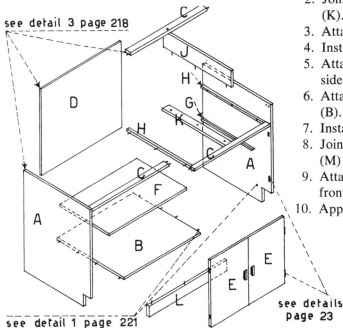

see detail 3 page 218

see detail 1 page 221

see details page 23

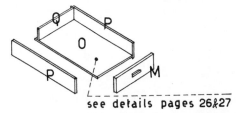

see details pages 26&27

Two-Door Base Cabinet

This plan is intended for a standard single-basin kitchen sink. It may be adapted to accommodate a two-basin model.

List of Materials

PART	NO.	FUNCTION	DIMENSIONS IN INCHES thickness × width × length		
A	2	side	¾	24	35
B	1	bottom	¾	34½	24
C	1	ventilator	¾	34½	5½
D	1	rail	1	1	34½
E	1	rail	1	3	34½
F	2	door	¾	17¼	24¾
G	1	stop	⅜	¾	24¾
H	1	toeplate	1	4	34½

Instructions for Assembly

1. Attach rail (D) to front panel (C).
2. Join sides (A) with bottom (B), front panel (C), and rail (E).
3. Attach toeplate (H) to sides (A) and bottom (B).
4. Install doors (F) and attach stop (G).
5. Apply finish.

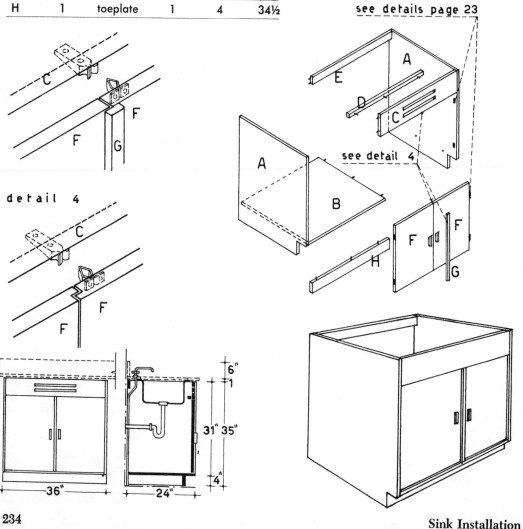

detail 4

see details page 23

see detail 4

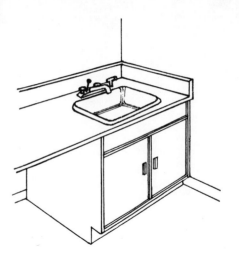

SIDE SECTION
see detail 1

sink

25

PLAN VIEW

top

sink line

opening line

cut opening to
conform to shape
of sink less 1"

hole for water pipe

cabinet line

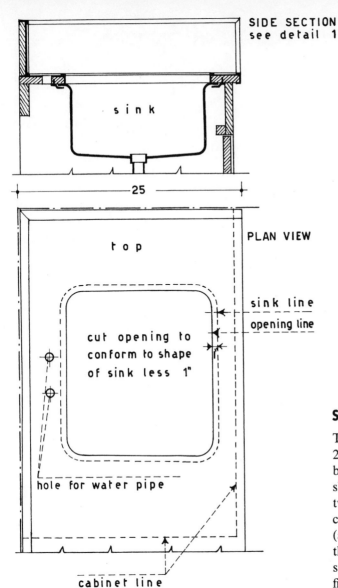

Sink Installation

The drawings show how cabinet (page 234) and counter top (page 223) can be fitted to a sink. Waterproof cement should be used to caulk the space between the top and the metal or porcelain sink surface, and metal clamps (as shown below) will hold the top to the sink. A plumber should be consulted on the installation of pipes and fixtures.

detail 1

water proof cement

$\frac{1}{16}$" laminate plastic

stainless sink

clamp

cabinet front

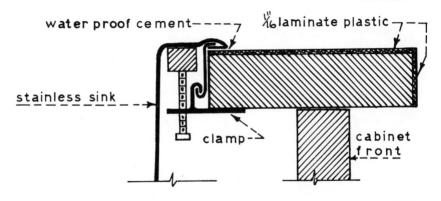

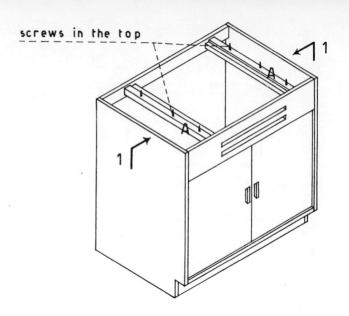

This method of sink installation substitutes rabbeted wooden rails for the metal clamps. The upper drawing shows the position of these rails. The sink is sealed between the rails with waterproof cement, and the rails are fastened to the counter top by means of wood screws. A separately applied sink rim, also sealed with waterproof cement, protects the edge of the wooden counter top.

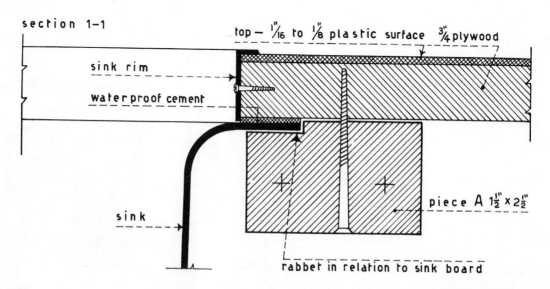

section 1–1

top — 1/16" to 1/8" plastic surface   3/4" plywood

sink rim

waterproof cement

sink

piece A 1 1/2" x 2 1/2"

rabbet in relation to sink board

Sink Installation

SPICE CABINET, NAPKIN CONTAINER, AND KNIFE HOLDER

To utilize the bare part of the wall and for decorative purposes, it is a good idea to hang in the kitchen a small cabinet like the one shown on this page. This and the other two accessories are practical and easy to make.

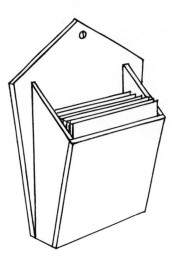

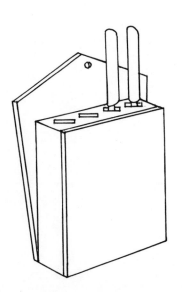

PART	NO.	FUNCTION	DIMENSION IN INCHES		
			thickness ×	width ×	length
A	1	shelf	½	4	14
B	2	shelves	½	2¾	14
C	2	fronts	½	1½	14
D	2	sides	½	4	10½
E	1	back	¼	10	14½

1. Attach fronts (C) to shelves (B); and join sides (D) with shelves (A, B).
2. Install back (E).
3. Apply finish.

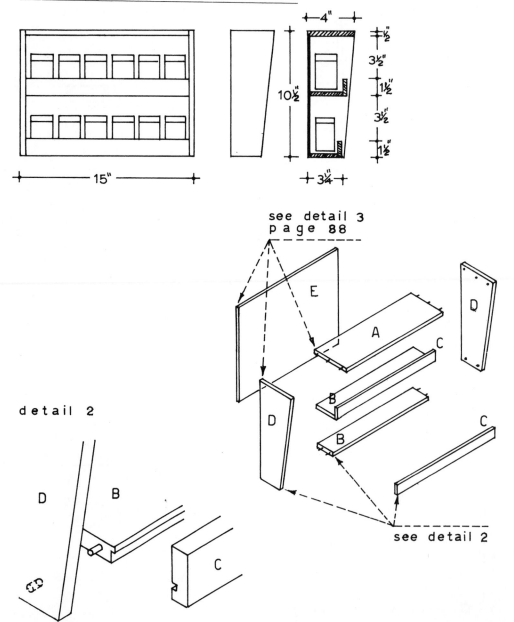

see detail 3
page 88

detail 2

see detail 2

238   Spice Cabinet, Napkin Container, and Knife Holder

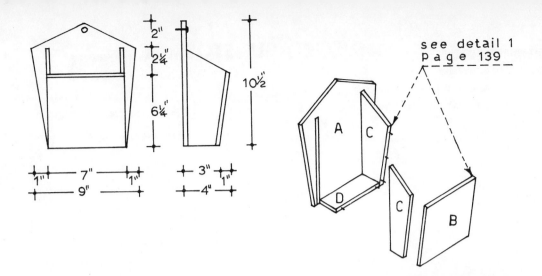

see detail 1
page 139

List of Materials

PART	NO.	FUNCTION	thickness	× width	× length
A	1	back	³⁄₈	9	10½
B	1	front	³⁄₈	7	6½
C	2	sides	³⁄₈	3	8½
D	1	bottom	³⁄₈	6¼	2¼

DIMENSION IN INCHES

Instructions for Assembly

1. Join back (A) with sides (C), bottom (D), and attach front (B).
2. Apply finish.

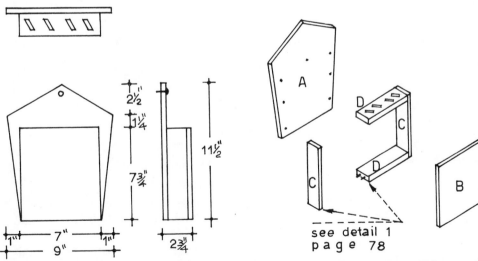

see detail 1
page 78

1. Join (C) to (D), attach front (B) and back (A).
2. Apply finish.

PART	NO.	FUNCTION	thickness	× width	× length
A	1	back	³⁄₈	9	11½
B	1	front	³⁄₈	7	7¾
C	2	sides	³⁄₈	2	7¾
D	2	top and bottom	¾	2	6¼

DIMENSION IN INCHES

Spice Cabinet, Napkin Container, and Knife Holder

It is more practical to keep potatoes, onions, apples, etc., in a clean-looking storage bin like the example shown than in store bags.

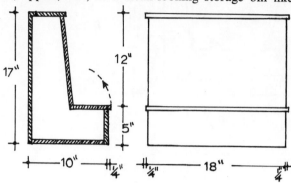

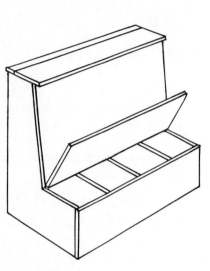

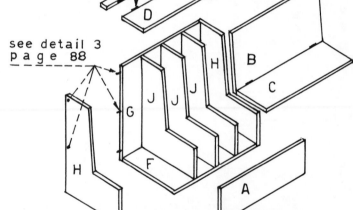

see details page 23

see detail 3 page 88

List of Materials

PART	NO.	FUNCTION	DIMENSION IN INCHES thickness × width × length		
			thickness	width	length
A	1	front	½	4½	18
B	1	front	½	12¼	18
C	1	top	½	5	18½
D	1	top	½	4	18½
E	1	top	½	1	18½
F	1	bottom	½	9	17
G	1	back	½	16½	17
H	2	sides	½	9½	16½
J	3	partitions	½	9	16

Instructions for Assembly

1. Join bottom (F) to back (G), sides (H) and partitions (J).
2. Attach fronts (A, B) to (H) and (J).
3. Fasten top (E) to (G, H) and join top (C) to (B) and top (D) to (E) with hinges.
4. Apply finish.

95

BREAKFAST BAR

Here is a good space-saving arrangement for a small kitchen. The cabinets are described on page 217.

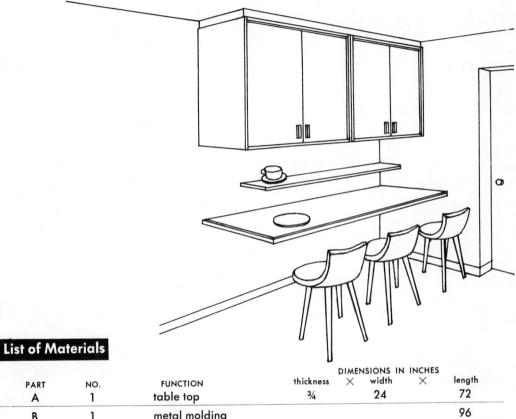

List of Materials

PART	NO.	FUNCTION	DIMENSIONS IN INCHES		
			thickness ×	width ×	length
A	1	table top	¾	24	72
B	1	metal molding			96
C	1	bench rail	1	2	71
D	1	bench rail	1	2	22
E	1	shelf	¾	6	60

Instructions for Assembly

1. Apply linoleum or other counter top material to top (A), following instructions on page 225. (Synthetic mica-type materials should be bonded to both sides.)
2. Attach metal molding to edges of (A).
3. Attach rails (C) and (D) to wall.
4. Install top (A) and shelf (E).
5. Install cabinets and apply finish.

SECTION A A

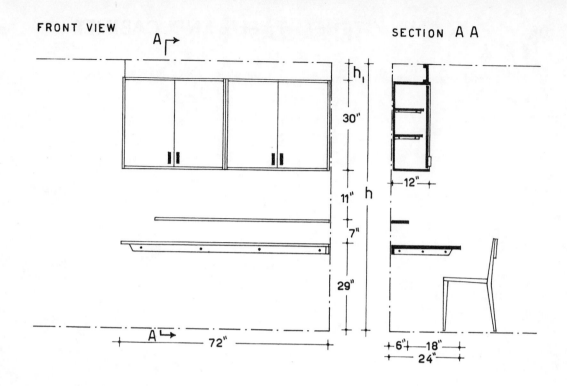

A

h_1

30"

h

11"

7"

29"

A 72"

12"

6" 18"

24"

```
h = HEIGHT OF THE ROOM
h₁= HEIGHT OF THE ROOM
      LESS 77"
```

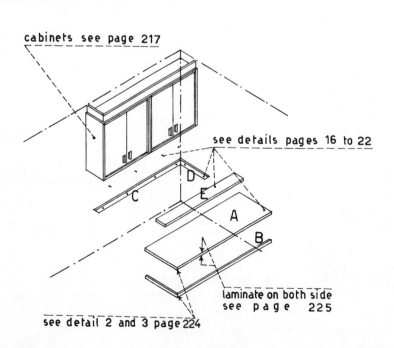

cabinets see page 217

see details pages 16 to 22

D

C

E

A

B

laminate on both side
see page 225

see detail 2 and 3 page 224

Breakfast Bar

96

ISLAND KITCHEN TABLE AND CABINET

This arrangement of table and cabinet helps to utilize all available space in a kitchen.

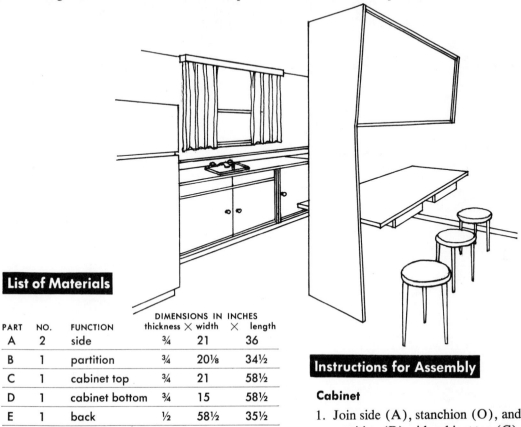

List of Materials

PART	NO.	FUNCTION	thickness	width	length
			DIMENSIONS IN INCHES		
A	2	side	¾	21	36
B	1	partition	¾	20⅛	34½
C	1	cabinet top	¾	21	58½
D	1	cabinet bottom	¾	15	58½
E	1	back	½	58½	35½
F	2	shelf	¾	17	28⅞
G	2	shelf	¾	15	28⅞
H	4	door	¾	14½	34½
J	1	table top*	¾	60	30
K	1	metal molding			15 ft.
L	2	cross rail	1	2½	26
M	1	center rail	1¼	3	59
O	1	stanchion	¾	21	*h*
P	4	drawer back	⅜	3½	17⅛
Q	4	drawer front	¾	4	18⅝
R	8	drawer side	⅜	4	13
S	4	drawer bottom	¼	17½	13
T	8	drawer guide	⅜	½	13
U	8	drawer slide	1	1	13

* Including surfacing material.

Instructions for Assembly

Cabinet

1. Join side (A), stanchion (O), and partition (B) with cabinet top (C), bottom (D), back (E), and shelves (F) and (G).
2. Install doors (H).

Table

3. Attach center rail (M) to cross rails (L).
4. Attach rail (M) to vertical support (O).
5. Join sides of drawer (R) with back (P) and front (Q).
6. Attach bottom of drawer (S) to sides (R) and front (Q).
7. Fasten surfacing materials to top (J) and add metal molding (K).
8. Set furniture in place, insert drawers, and apply finish.

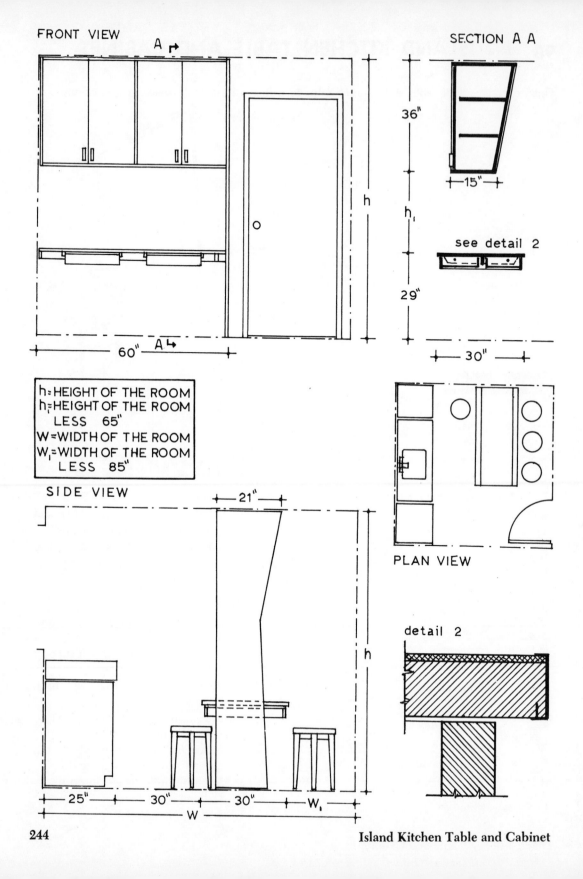

FRONT VIEW

A

SECTION A A

36"

15"

h

h₁

see detail 2

29"

60"

A

30"

h = HEIGHT OF THE ROOM
h₁ = HEIGHT OF THE ROOM
     LESS 65"
W = WIDTH OF THE ROOM
W₁ = WIDTH OF THE ROOM
     LESS 85"

SIDE VIEW

21"

PLAN VIEW

h

detail 2

25"   30"   30"   W₁

W

244   **Island Kitchen Table and Cabinet**

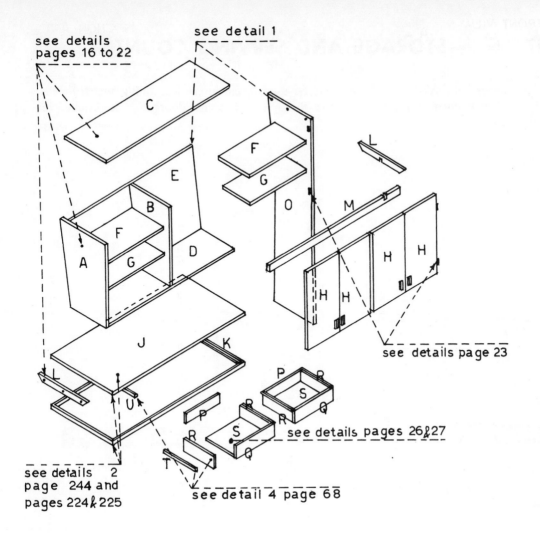

see details
pages 16 to 22

see detail 1

C

F
G

E

B
F
A
G
D

O
M
L

H H
H
H

see details page 23

J
K
L
U

P
R
S
R
Q

P
R
S
Q

see details pages 26&27

R
S
Q
P
T

see detail 4 page 68

see details   2
page   244 and
pages 224 & 225

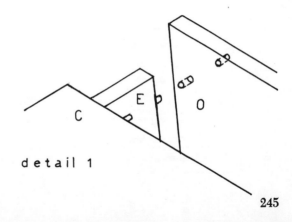

C
E
O

detail 1

Island Kitchen Table and Cabinet

This counter with overhead cabinets may be used to partition off a dining area from the kitchen. The counter itself serves as a pass-through, and cabinet doors may be installed on both sides.

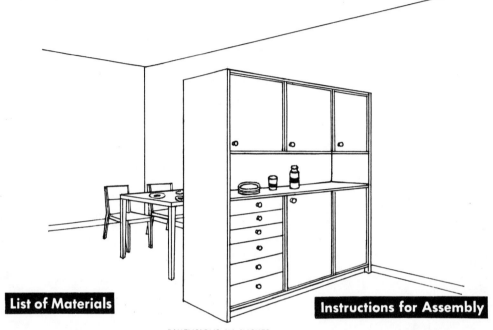

List of Materials

PART	NO.	FUNCTION	DIMENSIONS IN INCHES thickness × width × length		
A	4	top, bottom	¾	18	70½
B	2	side	¾	18	72
C	6	panel, door	¾	23	22½
D	5	panel, door	¾	23	30
E	2	partition	¾	18	22½
F	2	partition	¾	18	30
G	7	shelf	¾	23	15
H	14	cleat	½	½	14
J	2	toeplate	1	4	70½
K	6	drawer side	⅜	4	16¾
L	3	drawer front	¾	4	23
M	3	drawer back	⅜	3½	22⅛
O	6	drawer bottom	¼	22½	16¾
P	6	drawer side	⅜	6	16¾
Q	3	drawer front	¾	6	23
R	3	drawer back	⅜	5½	22⅛
S	12	drawer slide	¼	½	16¾

Instructions for Assembly

1. Join tops and bottoms of cabinets (A) with sides (B), partitions (E) and (F), and panels (C) and (D).
2. Attach toeplates (J) to bottom (A).
3. Attach cleats (H) to side supports (B) and partitions (E) and (F).
4. Attach cleats (H) to partitions (E) and (F).
5. Install doors (C) and (D).
6. Join sides of drawer (K) with front and back (L) and (M), and attach bottom of drawer (O) to sides (K) and front (L).
7. Join sides of drawer (P) to front and back (Q) and (R), and attach bottom of drawer (O) to sides (P) and front (Q).
8. Attach drawer slide (S) to sides (B) and partition (F).
9. Apply finish, and insert shelves (G) and drawers.

FRONT VIEW   SECTION AA   SECTION BB

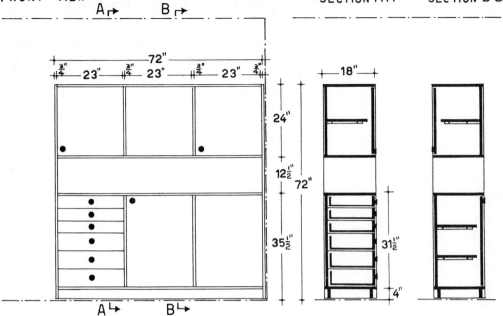

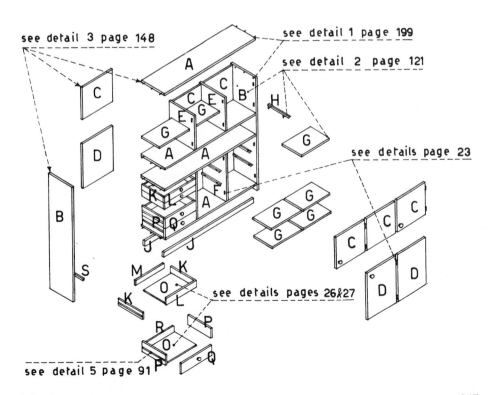

see detail 3 page 148
see detail 1 page 199
see detail 2 page 121
see details page 23
see details pages 26 & 27
see detail 5 page 91

Storage and Serving Counter   247

98

KITCHEN STORAGE WALL

This large cabinet for kitchen storage runs from floor to ceiling. Other units may be easily added to this basic design, or substituted for the units shown.

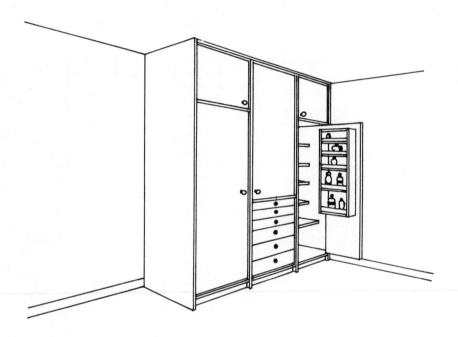

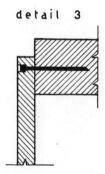

detail 3

Kitchen Storage Wall

List of Materials

PART	NO.	FUNCTION	thickness	×	width	×	length
A	9	top, bottom	¾		18		23
B	4	side	¾		18		$h-1$
C	1	back	¼		47¾		$h-5$
D	1	back	¼		23¾		$h-5$
E	2	door	¾		23		66½
F	1	door	¾		23		$h-37¼$
G	9	shelf	¾		16		23
H	6	shelf	¾		11		23
J	28	cleat	½		¾		15
K	2	side	½		5		45
L	6	shelf	½		5		19
M	5	edge	⅜		2		19
O	3	toeplate	1		4		23
P	3	drawer back	⅜		3½		22⅛
Q	6	drawer side	⅜		4		17⅝
R	3	drawer front	¾		4		23
S	6	drawer bottom	¼		17½		22½
T	3	drawer back	⅜		5½		22⅛
U	6	drawer side	⅜		6		17⅝
V	3	drawer front	¾		6		23
W	12	drawer slide	¼		½		17⅝
X	2	door	¾		23		$h-73¾$

detail 4

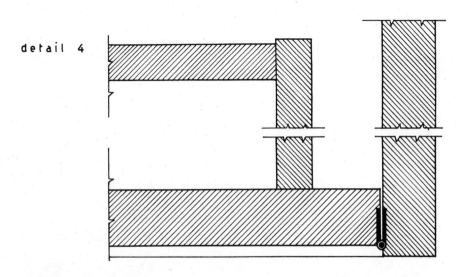

Kitchen Storage Wall

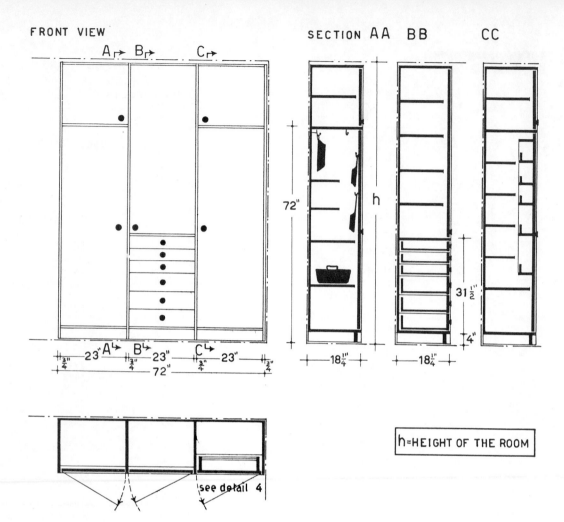

FRONT VIEW

SECTION AA BB CC

72"

h

31½"

4"

23" 23" 23"

¾ ¾ ¾ ¾

72"

18¼" 18¼"

see detail 4

h=HEIGHT OF THE ROOM

Instructions for Assembly

1. Join tops and bottoms of cabinets (A) with side supports (B).
2. Install backs (C) and (D).
3. Attach cleats (J) to side supports (B).
4. Attach toeplates (O) to (A) and (B).
5. Attach edges (M) to shelves (L) and join (L-M) to sides (K).
6. Attach (K) and (L) to door (E).
7. Install doors (E), (F), and (X).
8. Set cabinets in position.
9. Join sides of drawer (Q) with front and back (R) and (P), and attach bottom of drawer (S) to (Q) and (R).
10. Join sides of drawer (U) with front and back (V) and (T), and attach bottom of drawer (S) to (U) and (V).
11. Attach brace (W) to sides (B).
12. Apply finish.
13. Insert shelves (G) and (H) and install drawers.

250

Kitchen Storage Wall

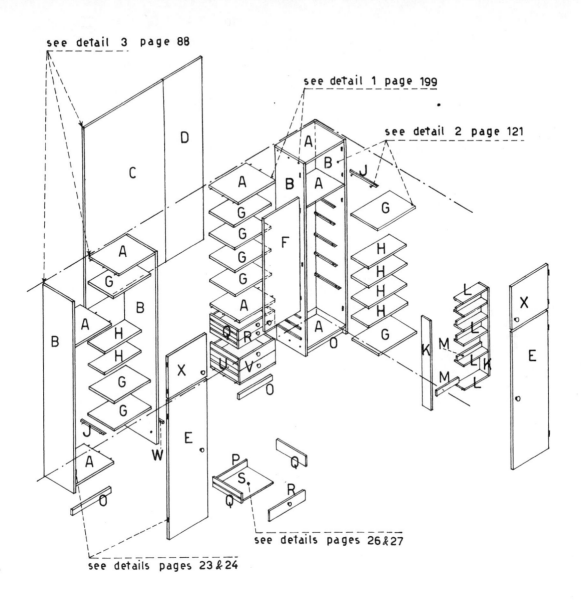

see detail 3 page 88

see detail 1 page 199

see detail 2 page 121

see details pages 26 & 27

see details pages 23 & 24

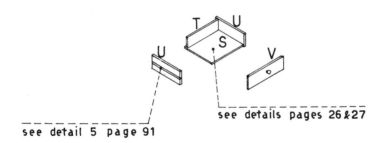

see details pages 26 & 27

see detail 5 page 91

Kitchen Storage Wall

99

BATHROOM CABINET

This bathroom built-in includes linen and medicine closets above a laundry bin.

Instructions for Assembly

1. Join side supports (A) with top and bottom (B) and partitions (C).
2. Install back (D).
3. Attach cleats (F) to sides (A).
4. Attach toeplate (G) to sides (A) and bottom (B).
5. Join bottom of bin (M) with back (K) and sides (L).
6. Attach front (O) to (L-M).
7 Attach (O) by hinges to bottom (B).
8. Apply finish and set cabinet in position.
9. Insert shelves (E) and install doors (H) and (J).

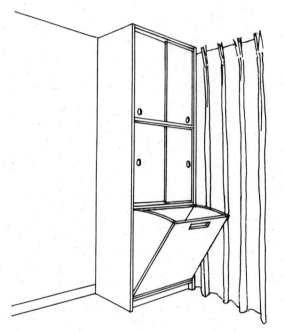

List of Materials

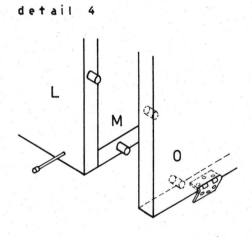

detail 4

PART	NO.	FUNCTION	DIMENSIONS IN INCHES thickness × width × length		
			thickness	width	length
A	2	side	¾	12	h
B	2	top, bottom	¾	12	34½
C	2	partition	¾	11¾	34½
D	1	back	¼	35½	h — 4½
E	4	shelf	¾	9½	34½
F	8	cleat	½	½	9
G	1	toeplate	1	4	34½
H	2	door	¾	18	to fit
J	2	door	¾	17¼	to fit
K	1	back	½	21¼	33⅜
L	2	side	½	10¾	24½
M	1	bottom	½	10¼	33⅜
O	1	front	¾	34½	24½

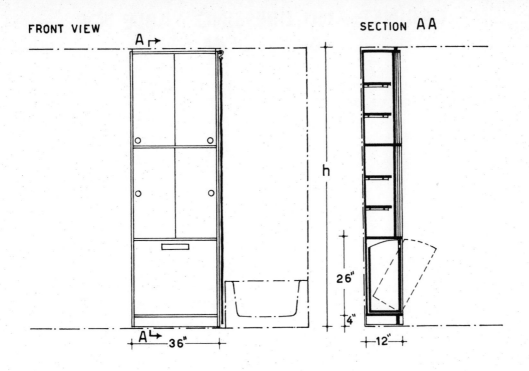

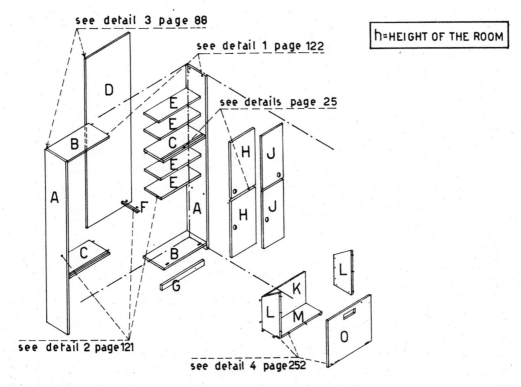

see detail 3 page 88

see detail 1 page 122

see details page 25

h=HEIGHT OF THE ROOM

see detail 2 page 121

see detail 4 page 252

Bathroom Cabinet

100

CABINET AND DRESSING TABLE FOR BATHROOM

Mirrors are used as sliding doors for this cabinet. The top of the dressing table may be covered with linoleum or other counter top material.

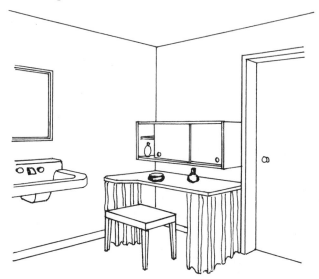

List of Materials

PART	NO.	FUNCTION	thickness	×	width	×	length
					DIMENSIONS IN INCHES		
A	1	top*	¾		24		w
B	2	top, bottom	¾		9		w − 1½
C	2	side	¾		9		18
D	1	back	¼		17½		w − ½
E	1	plate glass shelf			7		w − 1⅝
F	2	mirror door			17		to fit

* Including surfacing material and necessary molding.

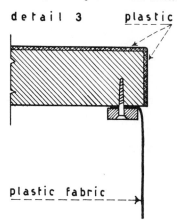

detail 3   plastic

plastic fabric

Instructions for Assembly

1. Apply linoleum or other counter top material to top (A), following instructions on page 225. (Synthetic mica-type materials should be bonded to both sides.)
2. Cover visible edges of top (A) with metal molding or strips of surfacing material.
3. Join top and bottom of cabinet (B) with sides (C) and back (D).
4. Set cabinet and table top in position and apply finish.
5. Insert shelves (E).
6. Install doors (F).

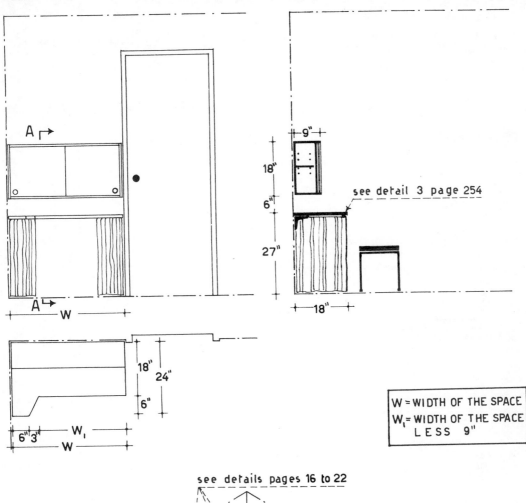

FRONT VIEW

SECTION A A

A →

9"

18"

6"

27"

see detail 3 page 254

A → W

18"

18"
24"
6"

6" 3"
W₁
W

W = WIDTH OF THE SPACE
W₁ = WIDTH OF THE SPACE
LESS 9"

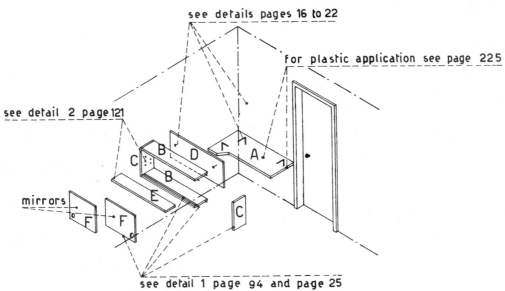

see details pages 16 to 22

for plastic application see page 225

see detail 2 page 121

B D
C B
A
E

mirrors
F → F

C

see detail 1 page 94 and page 25

Cabinet and Dressing Table for Bathroom

To keep your wine and liquor bottles aligned and in view, you can build this stacking type of storage rack.

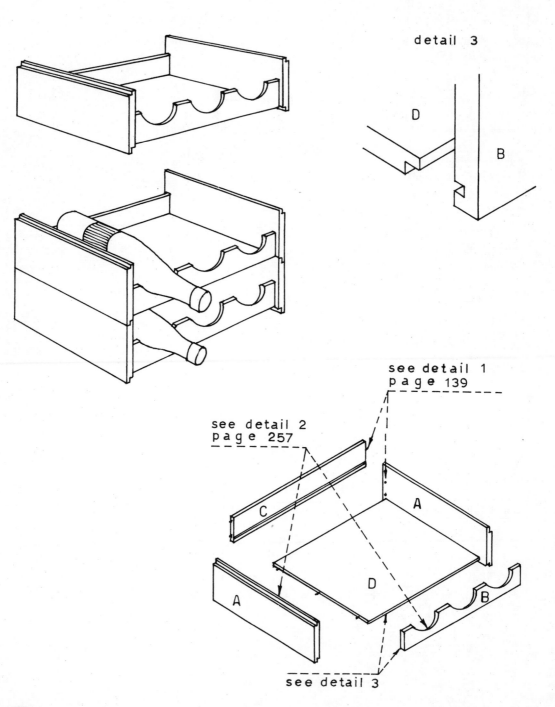

detail 3

see detail 1
page 139

see detail 2
page 257

see detail 3

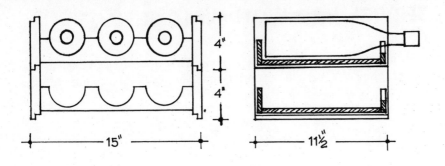

List of Materials

PART	NO.	FUNCTION	DIMENSION IN INCHES thickness × width × length		
A	2	sides	¾	4¼	11½
B	1	front	½	2	13½
C	1	back	½	2	13½
D	1	bottom	½	10½	13½

Instructions for Assembly

1. Join bottom (D) with front (B) and back (C).
2. Fasten sides (A) to front (B), back (C), and bottom (D).
3. Apply finish.

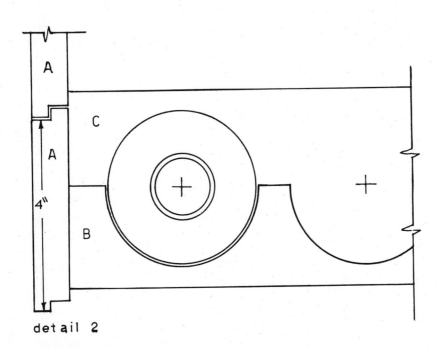

detail 2

Bottle Storage

Here is another style of bar for the family recreation room. This one has wall shelves instead of an under-counter cabinet. A surfacing material can be applied to the counter top, as shown on page 225.

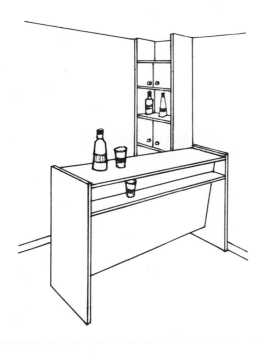

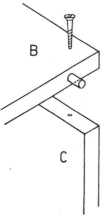

detail 2

List of Materials

PART	NO.	FUNCTION	thickness	× width	× length
			DIMENSIONS IN INCHES		
A	2	side	¾	12	h
B	6	shelf	¾	12	24
C	2	back	½	24	13
D	1	back	½	24	22
E	4	door	¾	13	12
F	2	door	¾	12	22
G	1	toeplate	1	4	24
H	1	counter	¾	70½	20
J	1	shelf	¾	11¾	70½
K	1	shelf	¾	10¾	70½
L	1	shelf	¾	9	70½
M	2	bar side	¾	20	42
O	10	strip	¼	½	48
P	1	bar front	¾	35	70½
Q	1	shelf	¾	7½	70½

Instructions for Assembly

1. Attach shelves (B) to backs (C) and (D).
2. Attach side pieces (A) to combined (B-C-D).
3. Install doors (E) and (F).
4. Attach toeplate (G) to bottom shelf (B).
5. Attach front of bar (P) to shelves (J), (K), (L), and shelf (Q).
6. Attach sides of bar (M) to counter (H), shelves (J), (K), and (L), front of bar (P) and (Q).
7. Install strips (O).
8. Apply finish and set bar in position.

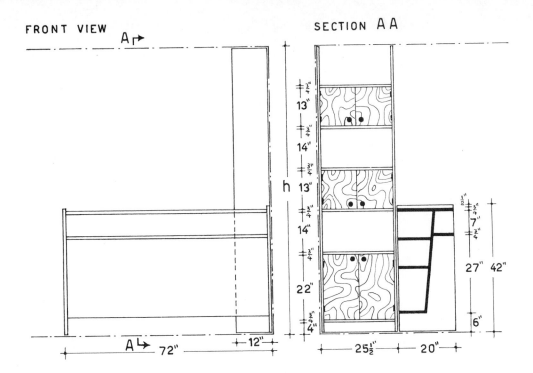

FRONT VIEW   A→

SECTION AA

13"
14"
h 13"
14"
22"

72"   12"

25½"   20"

42"
27"
7"
6"

h = HEIGHT OF THE ROOM

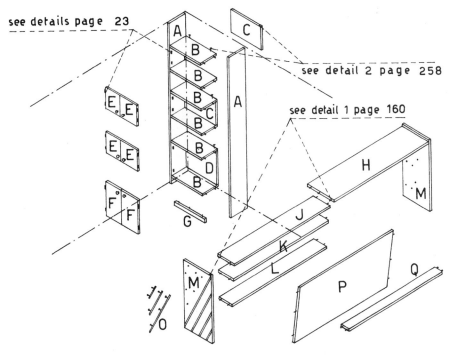

see details page 23

A
B
B
B
C
B
B
D
B

C

see detail 2 page 258

E E

E E

F F

G

A

see detail 1 page 160

H

M

J

K

L

M

P

Q

O

Service Bar with Wall Shelves

INDEX